Praise for *Tumblehome*

"Brenda Missen, a self-described 'keen canoeist,' has been a pilgrim of solitude. She has entered a world in which language has not yet been born and offers us the gift of her memoir, *Tumblehome*."

– **Diana Beresford-Kroeger, author of** *To Speak for the Trees: My Life's Journey from Ancient Celtic Wisdom to a Healing Vision of the Forest*

"Reading *Tumblehome* is like waking to the morning sun shining on your face through the sharp-pointed spruce on a mist-coated morning. It is like paddling along the shining path of a rising full moon. Most stories about solo canoeing are based on being 'alone against the wilderness.' They dwell on the anguish and risk of coping with whatever nature tosses, pushing physical limits to the extreme, and overcoming (most of the time) the dangers of paddling farther or faster or where no one has gone (and perhaps should not have gone) before. Brenda Missen's memoir is not one of those. It is the story of a blossoming love affair with a landscape, the 'near wilderness' of Algonquin Park. Through a series of solo trips, Brenda's journey shows the transformative power that travelling alone (especially a woman travelling alone) through the Canadian Shield can have on one's mind and soul. It is pure joy to follow Brenda as she strays, and finds, her way through the wilderness and through life. And as you stray with Brenda, you will surely also find what she is seeking for on her journeys."

– **Max Finkelstein, author of** *Canoeing a Continent: On the Trail of Alexander Mackenzie*

"*Tumblehome* takes us on an intimate journey into an emotional, spiritual, and physical wilderness where fears are overcome, relationships scrutinized, and enlightenment sought. A canoe trip with many twists and challenges, by the end I truly felt that I had been forest-bathing with Missen."

– **Becky Mason, canoe instructor, filmmaker, writer, and artist**

"*Tumblehome*, Brenda Missen's compelling memoir, is the story of one woman's canoeing adventures in the Canadian wilderness. Yet it is simultaneously a profound meditation on the complexities of human relationships, our common interface with the natural world, and a journey of spiritual transformation. In its pages, it is as if Annie Dillard meets the Taoist sage Lao Tzu. In Brenda, explorer, writer, and spiritual seeker converge in the telling. From the first line – 'My paddle mines for diamonds that sparkle on the wind-riffled lake' – to the last, Missen cups us in the palm of her hands. As Brenda comes to trust her spiritual mentor Asante, to whom the book is dedicated, so readers can trust Brenda to gently open their hearts and minds to their own interior depths where 'joy is [our] birthright' and we are the diamonds we seek."

– **Susan McCaslin, author of** *Into the Open: Poems New and Selected*

TUMBLEHOME

TUMBLEHOME

TUMBLEHOME

One Woman's Canoeing Adventures
in the Divine Near Wilderness

BRENDA MISSEN

INANNA memoir series

www.inanna.ca
Toronto, Ontario, Canada

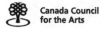   Canadä

We gratefully acknowledge the support of the Canada Council for the Arts and the Ontario Arts Council for our publishing program. We also acknowledge the financial support of the Government of Canada.

Cover design: Val Fullard
Cover art: *Autumn Sojourn*, by Linda Sorensen lindasorensen.com

Library and Archives Canada Cataloguing in Publication
Title: Tumblehome : one woman's canoeing adventures in the divine near wilderness / Brenda Missen.
Names: Missen, Brenda, 1961- author.
Series: Inanna memoir series.
Description: Series statement: Inanna memoir series | Includes bibliographical references.
Identifiers: Canadiana (print) 20220156352 | Canadiana (ebook) 20220163111 | ISBN 9781771338455 (softcover) | ISBN 9781771338462 (HTML) | ISBN 9781771338479 (PDF)
Subjects: LCSH: Missen, Brenda, 1961- | LCSH: Missen, Brenda, 1961-—Travel—Ontario. | LCSH: Canoes and canoeing—Ontario—Anecdotes. | LCSH: Human beings—Effect of environment on—Anecdotes. | CSH:
  Authors, Canadian (English)—Biography. | LCGFT: Autobiographies.
Classification: LCC GV784 .M57 2022 | DDC 797.122092—dc23

Printed and bound in Canada
Inanna Publications and Education Inc.
210 Founders College, York University
4700 Keele Street, Toronto, Ontario, Canada M3J 1P3
Telephone: (416) 736-5356 Fax: (416) 736-5765
Email: inanna.publications@inanna.ca Website: www.inanna.ca

Portions of Chapter 3 were published, in a different and much shorter form, in the five-minute monologue "Meeting the Bear of My Dreams," written and recorded for the First Person Singular feature of the CBC Radio One program *This Morning* (March 2001), as well as in the personal essay "Nightmare Bear?", published in *Canadian Wildlife*, Vol. 10, No. 5, March 2005.

Photos are by the author unless otherwise indicated.

In memory of my soul sister, Asante,
without whose gentle guidance, wisdom, and love
I would not be who I am today.

The natural world is the larger sacred community to which we belong.
– Thomas Berry

CONTENTS

Preface

THE GENESIS OF *Tumblehome* was an email from a friend, who, after hearing me describe my fifth or sixth solo canoe trip, suggested I write a book – a combination of canoe-trip chronicles and "how-to" guide for women or other solo paddlers. I thought this was a great idea except a) my qualifications to dispense canoeing advice were suspect and b), even more crucially, nothing (usually, thankfully) happens on my trips, which would make for decidedly *unscintillating* reading. It came to me to weave my interior journey into the exterior journeys, especially since the canoe trips were leading me into a deeper awareness of our intrinsic, sacred connection with the Earth.

In the interests of full disclosure, I did not spend my canoe trips pondering all of the themes included in each chapter. For the most part I was in the moment, immersed in my travels (chapters four and five being notable exceptions). However, when it came to the writing, I was amazed to discover how seamlessly my chosen themes wove themselves into the canoe-trip narratives. This natural fit caused some minor angst on subsequent trips; suddenly I needed to have a pre-planned theme and at least one major revelation *on* each trip. No pressure! Once those additional chapters were drafted (with ease), it struck me I didn't need to do anything except keep on canoeing and keep on evolving; the two didn't need to happen in tandem, in a tidy *Tumblehome*-chapter-put-together kind of way. This organic threading of canoeing chronicle with personal evolution has continued to astonish me – and prompted my Inanna editor to compare it, movingly, to "dappled sunlight." It has me convinced that a Master Tapestry Weaver is at work in my life and that I need only open my surrendered, willing arms and be the canvas. (Oh that it were that simple and that multiple rewrites and edits were not required…)

Two words author Timothy Findley once said have stayed with me. Responding to a comment that his writing in later years seemed to have a new openness about certain aspects of his life (or something to that effect), he said, simply, "People died." I've been very open about certain aspects of my life in *Tumblehome*, even though the other parties are all still very much alive (except my dear friend Asante, who died in 2017). It has not been my intention to expose people, or to invade their privacy, and for this reason I've changed or obscured identifying details. However, the stories – our interactions and the ways they helped me on my journey, deliberately or inadvertently – are true. This doesn't mean the stories are *complete*. They've been presented from only one perspective, mine, and I've focused on aspects relevant to my interior journey. There was, of course, so much more to these relationships, and no doubt a different story would be recounted by the other parties. Something to bear in mind while reading.

Another thing to keep in mind is that although the canoe-trip narratives are written in present tense (with flashbacks in past tense), nearly twenty years have passed since the final chapter, and my current now is very different, emotionally and spiritually, from the now of the memoir. Few of the people featured in *Tumblehome* are still in my life; we've all moved on. What remains is my gratitude to them.

There are many others who do not appear in the now of the memoir or who receive only passing mention: my parents, my sisters and their families, other friends, loves, and lovers. Their shadow appearance or omission in no way reflects on their importance to me. It means only that they weren't involved in the particular stories and events I've chronicled – and quite possibly they'll be relieved by that. All this to say, those who *are* featured are by no means the only significant influences in my life; I'm grateful to all. (The acknowledgements are filled with even more gratitude, especially for the considerable encouragement, support, and assistance I received during the decade and a half it took to gestate and birth *Tumblehome*.)

The "near wilderness" referred to in the subtitle is Algonquin Provincial Park, a three- or four-hour drive from Ontario's major cities, an hour for me. The presence of cottages, summer camps, several lodges and stores, two outfitters, a visitor centre, and a logging museum (most located on or near the one highway that bisects the park) definitely disqualifies the park from wilderness status. We are not talking about pristine forests and lakes untouched by human development, no matter how much canoe trippers might wish otherwise. "Near" wilderness might also be a stretch, even for the vast interior, with its more than two thousand lakes and miles of snaking rivers. Those rivers and lakes have been dammed, the forests have been logged (though now more selectively than the nineteenth-century free-for-all felling of old-growth white pine), and, thanks to the park rangers, the extensive network of portages and campsites is well maintained. Each campsite has a designated fire pit, a level (or mostly level) clearing for the tent, and, a discreet distance into the woods, a lidded wooden box affectionately known as a thunder box, or biffy. (I should note that on recent printings of the official Algonquin Park Canoe Routes map, the maintained campsites and portages are marked in black and the non-maintained, little-used ones in red. This is a switch from the map in the years chronicled in *Tumblehome*, which is why you'll find references to the red triangles that mark campsites.)

Notwithstanding these undeniable and indelible human marks on the land, once you have paddled and portaged your canoe through the first two or three lakes into the back country, you are in wild animal and wild weather territory, and you're on your own, far from the tap of a cell phone in an emergency. (Since I capitulated to a cell phone only in 2015 I've never wished for cell service in the park, which did arrive around 2004, but only, to my relief, along the Highway 60 corridor, where the towers are disguised as giant white pines – yes, really – and service is spotty.) Once in the park interior, you need to rely on your own smarts for your safety or, in a pinch (or bear encounter), the kindness of fellow trippers. Part of me longs to explore truer wilderness areas, but as a woman with a contemplative bent who travels alone, Algonquin is near enough – and dear enough – wilderness for me.

My editor's suggestion that I add the above note about lack of cell reception led me down a rabbit hole… Should I not then also include a note about park history and geography? That it was created in 1893 as a (still-logged) forest preserve, a wildlife sanctuary, and a "place of health resort" that spurred the building of lodges, inns, cottages, and summer camps? Should I not mention that a railway, built by a lumber baron through the park, transported tourists in and timber out, until it was removed, rail tie by rail tie, in the late 1950s? In my rabbit-hole Internet search, I refreshed my memory that the park is now twice its original size and that most of this 7,630-square-kilometre tract of lake, river, and mixed boreal and deciduous forest is the traditional hunting, fishing, and trapping grounds of the Algonquin First Nations – who, not incidentally, had inhabited the area for 8,000 years before the first Europeans arrived. The park was, most appropriately, named for the Algonquins, and then the authorities barred them from hunting and gathering on these traditional lands for the next sixty years (under threat of fine or imprisonment), until a licensing agreement allowed them to resume hunting and trapping in selected areas. Ninety percent of Algonquin Park is currently included in Ontario's largest land claim (which encompasses most of the eastern part of the province). Under the current agreement-in-principle, no park lands will be transferred to the Algonquins, but they will have a greater role in the care, protection, and sustainable management of the park. Rightfully so.

No question this is all important information about the most major presence in this work, and there is a very short list of online resources at the back if you want to learn more. However, you'll find few cultural or historical references in *Tumblehome*'s chapters, and only a few of my descriptions of the natural world could be considered scientific. Even as I acknowledge and appreciate the human-created (albeit flawed) system that allows me to travel with relative ease in the park interior, the Algonquin of *Tumblehome* is not explored for its cultural, recreational, or natural "values" (to quote park literature) but experienced, and portrayed, as a Presence.

Integral to that Presence are the creatures I meet (or fear to meet) along the way. In the spiritualities of the First Nations, all of the Earth's creatures, from largest mammal to smallest insect, carry "medicine" that, if we attend to it, can bring healing to ourselves and the Earth. The medicine or symbolism of each creature varies according to the particular beliefs of individual Nations. Unfortunately, the two main sources I quote from in *Tumblehome* don't specify which beliefs are from which First Nation. Both books refer in general to "Native Americans" (a term we wouldn't use in Canada), although in their introduction the authors of *Medicine Cards* do explain that they drew their teachings from the Choctaw, Lakota, Seneca, Aztec, Yaqui, Cheyenne, Cherokee, Iroquois, and Mayan traditions. The author of *Animal-Speak*, my second source, describes the lore surrounding birds and animals from cultural perspectives around the world. It just happened that the particular teachings and symbolism that spoke to me whenever I reached for his book were from Indigenous cultures in North America, which is why only those are mentioned in this memoir. As a non-Indigenous person, I did have some concern that in quoting from these sources I might be seen to be encroaching on spiritual territory where I didn't belong (and I would be equally guilty of encroaching on Buddhist and Hindu territory). It was reassuring to read that the *Medicine Cards* authors felt it was time to share the teachings beyond their culture – to "aid the mass consciousness" and open a new doorway of understanding about our connection to the Earth. It is my humble hope that *Tumblehome* might crack open that doorway just a little bit more.

Brenda Missen
January 3, 2022

1
RECONNAISSANCE MISSION
Kioshkokwi Lake: July 31–August 4, 1998

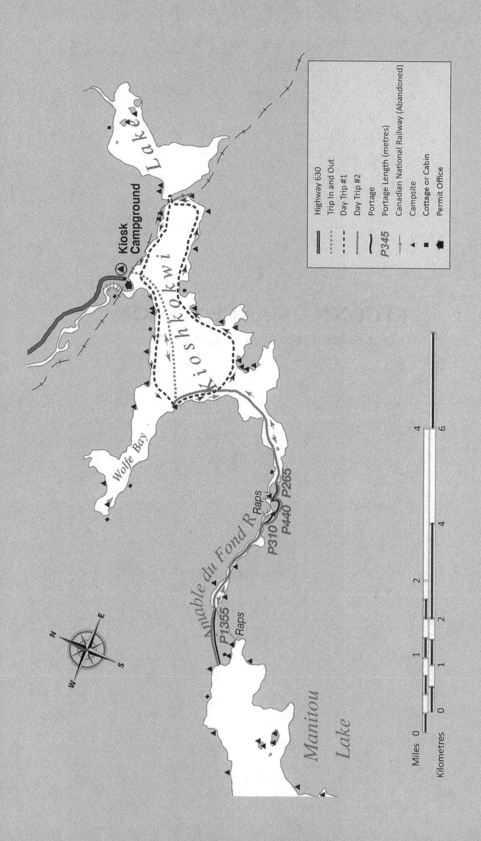

Kiosk Campground

Kiosk

Lake

Kioshkokwi

Wolfe Bay

Amable du Fond R.

Raps

P310

P440

P265

P1355

Raps

Manitou

Lake

N
W E
S

Highway 630
Trip In and Out
Day Trip #1
Day Trip #2
Portage
P345   Portage Length (metres)
Canadian National Railway (Abandoned)
Campsite
Cottage or Cabin
Permit Office

Miles 0   1   2   4

Kilometres 0   1   2   4   6

MY PADDLE MINES for diamonds that sparkle on the wind-riffled lake as I stroke and pry along the north shore. The canoe, a comfortable tub not designed for speed, is loaded down with a big bulky waterproof gear bag, heavy plastic food barrel, and spare paddle I hope I won't need. Progress is slow, even with the breeze at my back. Kioshkokwi is a big lake, and the last time I started a trip here, five years ago with Roz, the headwinds and waves were a challenge even for two. Today, I'm grateful for the tailwind, though not in any hurry. A kind of keyed-up happy calm settles over me in the afternoon sun.

Along the shore, cottages peek out sporadically from the trees — rustic structures with mullioned windows reflecting myriad lakes. From a dock, just up ahead, a hand rises in greeting. The man attached to the hand leans back in a wooden deck chair, a paperback creased open on his lap. He's slim, in brightly coloured Hawaiian shorts, hair curly and grey. "It's nice to see someone who knows how to paddle for a change," he calls out on my approach.

Cottages are allowed on only a handful of lakes in Algonquin Park, located on the lakes accessible by roads (the head lakes), as opposed to the interior lakes, reachable only by portage. Motorboats are permitted only on the head lakes too, up to twenty horsepower.

"They taught me well at Camp Pioneer," I call back, forgetting I skipped my solo classes at summer camp all those years ago, forgetting it was my old friend Max who taught me this stroke.

"Usually they're switching sides every three strokes as the canoe zigzags down the lake." He mimes the erratic motion with his hand. "Usually they're not alone either. Are you camping on your own?"

I nod, reluctant for another male on the lake to know I'm a Woman Camping Alone.

A point of land on the opposite shore comes into view and beyond it a slight narrowing. I peer at the plastic-encased map at my knees. This must be the beginning of Wolfe Bay. On its south shore the map shows a small solid red triangle – symbol for a campsite. The woman at the park office pointed to this triangle when I asked if there were any sites with rock.

I angle the bow toward a large grey mass amid the green across the bay. A flash of orange on a tree confirms the grey mass is my campsite. All Algonquin campsites are indicated by a fluorescent orange sign that bears the black silhouette of a tent.

I nose the boat into a little natural harbour defined by a half-submerged log, and haul my gear up the slope. A quick glance around the site and I'm smiling. The park attendant steered me right. There's an abundance of shoreline rock that will get sun most of the day and a chapel-serene hemlock grove set well back from the water, perfect for the tent.

Perfect writing rocks on the Kioshkokwi campsite, 1998

I lug the pack over to the grove, unbuckle the straps, and pull out tent, sleeping bag, clothes, and inflatable air mattress – all stored in individual waterproof bags. I drag lifeless nylon over to a flat spot carpeted in hemlock needles. The erected tent is so large I barely have to duck to step through the vestibule, and even with the sleeping bag unrolled, there's still plenty of room. For the first time, only one person will be sleeping in this four-person tent. It's a forest-green, darned heavy Diamond Brand A-frame I bought second hand in 1988. It was the closest I could find to the more reasonable two-person size owned by the boyfriend who had just broken up with me. At the time I was feeling sentimental about all things associated with my shy botany PhD-student ex-beau, including his tent – the first I ever slept in, the first I ever had exuberant sweaty sex in. It was a comfort to find one the same brand and colour, if a size larger. I call it Brenda's Palace.

Brenda's Palace looks at home in the hemlock grove, 1998

Bedroom arranged, the kitchen is next. In addition to the usual fire pit, this one boasts a picnic table and a counter someone made from a piece of plywood lashed between two trees. It's too civilized for a canoe trip. But this isn't a real trip. More of a reconnaissance mission. I figure I'm allowed the luxury of a picnic table. And a two-litre bag of wine, which I pull out of the barrel after my one-burner Coleman stove and dishes. Into a blue tin mug, I pour a generous amount of Merlot.

Down at the water's edge, I find a natural throne of rock aglow in the early evening sun. The boxed wine has a thin acidic taste but I don't care; I'm sitting on a Canadian Shield rock by a lake in my favourite provincial park.

I paid twenty-eight dollars to be here – seven dollars times four nights – though I told the park attendant I may not last that long. Nevertheless she advised me to pay the full amount. "Better have a valid permit, because if the park warden shows up and you don't have one, he's going to want to know what you're doing here. You can get a refund if you come out early," she added. "As long as you're out before two."

"Out" is an hour's paddle away, with no portages in between. Only an hour's paddle if I have to abort the mission.

I look around the peaceful bay in the evening sunlight and breathe in deeply, and in some awe. I'm here, on the edge of the wilderness, by myself. I raise the tin mug of Merlot to the sky. A toast. To me. On my first solo camping trip. However long it lasts.

The reason I'm here, on this August long weekend, is that I'm between visits on a month-long cottage-hopping "writing vacation." A writing vacation means I've bought time from freelance editing to work on my novel. Various friends and family members have cottages around Ontario, and they didn't seem to object to the idea that I spend part of my stay writing. My most recent visit was with one of my sisters and her husband's family in Parry Sound, and my next destination happens to be here in Algonquin, where an old friend just bought a cottage on one of the head lakes. The four days in between seemed an ideal opportunity to try camping on my own. Not that this has been a burning desire or goal. It's just become harder to find a tripping partner. Roz and the other friends I used to paddle with are now married with children, and even though I'm thirty-seven, my One True Paddling Partner continues to elude me. Last summer my niece Harriet came with me on her first trip, and we did a second one together only a few weeks ago. Suddenly I was the responsible adult. The *only* adult. That's what made me decide to try solo. If I can be the sole adult responsible for an adolescent girl out in the near wilderness, and the carrier of the canoe and heavy gear, I can be the sole adult responsible for myself.

At least that's the theory. Even more than the practical consideration of whether I can do everything on my own is whether I have the nerve to be out here by myself. There's the little matter of a near-wilderness-inhabiting creature called a bear.

I completed many trips with Roz in blissful ignorance of bears. At some point, though, people seemed to think I should know. They thrust magazine and newspaper clippings at me and recounted harrowing tales of bear encounters, bear maulings, nuisance bears, and killer bears. With these stories branded onto my brain, an unwelcome third party invited itself on our canoe trips: a phantom companion called My Nerves.

I couldn't get on a lake close to my next cottage-hopping destination on Smoke Lake. Everything in that part of the park was booked up for the long weekend. So I'm here in the less popular northwest corner up near North Bay, a three-hour drive away, with my novel and my nerves. Committed to working on neither.

The boil-in-a-bag cabbage rolls have come to a rolling boil on the little stove. I slit open the bag and plop the steaming contents into a bowl. Eschewing the picnic table, I find a west-facing dining rock and lean back in my new Crazy Creek camping chair – a lightweight legless nylon-covered seat with backrest that folds up for easy transportation. The sun heads for the hills, inflaming the clouds on its way.

Into this idyllic scene drifts the putt-putt of a motor. I look out onto the lake and, sure enough, a motorized canoe is coming my way, spot-lit in the evening sun. Dismay. It's the other male on the lake who knows I'm here on my own. Before she pointed to this choice site, the park attendant asked a man hovering at the counter if it was taken. He was a tall, gruff-looking older guy, obviously already settled on the lake. "It's free," he confirmed. "But if it isn't," he added, turning to me, "I'm right across the bay. You can camp on my site. I won't bother you."

It never occurred to me I might have to worry about men out here. They've never been a problem for me, in Algonquin or anywhere else. This one, though, walked by the car as I unloaded the canoe pack from the trunk and shifted some cottage-hopping bedding I wasn't planning to bring.

"Take your pillow," he quipped. "Supper's at five."

Then he departed, in his electric-powered canoe. And I wasn't too happy about him.

Mr. Motorized Canoe, as I've dubbed him, skirts the shore below my campsite. He doesn't seem to be looking for my attention. Just putters by, elbow on knee, chin in hand, apparently on an evening tour of the lake. Perfectly within his rights.

Once he's out of sight I head down to a rock close to the water. How, I wonder, over my wine, will I occupy myself when I'm not paddling? I should work on the novel, but it's the weekend and I had a pretty good few days at the Parry Sound cottage this past week. So if I'm not going to write – or portage and paddle all day like on a real trip – what will I do?

Do? I chastise myself. You don't need to do. You only need to be.

It's a revelation peculiar to canoe trips and always, it seems, forgotten in between. I think that's the real reason I come out here every summer. To remember to be.

———

M Y FIRST CANOE TRIP was with Roz, in 1988. She was my roommate for a year in Toronto while she articled for a law firm and I tried to kick-start a writing career after completing my English degree. It was after she moved back to Ottawa that we planned the trip. Neither of us had done one before but that didn't stop us. We had each canoed, each camped; we just hadn't combined the two. We came here to Algonquin that summer, and many summers after that. What kept us coming back wasn't just our delight in travelling, lightly and intimately, through the back country. It was something we weren't expecting to experience amid the continual physical activity and camping chores and only two lakes away from "civilization": stillness.

On that trip I brought along a book by the American Trappist monk Thomas Merton. I was introduced to his writings, and to the contemplative side of Christianity, in one of the many religion courses I took at university in an attempt to reconcile my faith with my rapidly changing beliefs. In a chapter called "Being and Doing," Merton proclaims that there are times when "in order to keep ourselves in existence at all we simply have to sit back for a while and do nothing." Roz and I were not doing nothing. We were paddling and portaging, setting up camp and packing it up again, collecting firewood and building fires, preparing meals and cleaning up afterward. It wasn't, however, what Merton called "thoughtless and automatic activity," nor were we doing it to get it over with so we could enjoy ourselves. There was an unhurried quality to everything we did, a stillness inside ourselves while we worked, and it struck me that even in our doing we were being.

Just being... on Big Porcupine Lake, 1988

EVERY SUMMER SINCE I first *got* it, on that Big Porcupine Lake campsite with Roz and Merton, I've come back to the park or the Temagami region to the north or northwestern Quebec to get it again, to remind myself how to be. I don't know why it's easier on a canoe trip than in "real" life, except when I'm performing the countless tasks that constitute camping, I don't think too much. I don't analyze myself or my relationships or my life. I don't stew over things that aren't going the way I wish they would. I just am. I'm with the person I'm with, and we work and laugh together and eat together and share a tent.

And when the only person with me is me, and my work on my first evening is done – what do I "do" then? I sit on a shoreline rock and sip wine from a tin mug and watch the undulating pale blue waves that seem to contain loon silhouettes in their black shadows. I listen to five real loons across the bay call out and beat their wings along the water's surface and take off in all directions. I watch the water bugs ricochet off each other in a zigzagging parody of inept paddlers.

The sun slips behind the hills and the no-see-ums nip at me, herding me to the tent. The way is lit by a headlamp – an ingenious flashlight that straps around my head like a miner's lamp, leaving both hands free for camping chores. Those chores are done: canoe turned upside down on shore and tied to a tree root, dishes washed, food put away in the barrel. The barrel, made of thick plastic with a snap-hinged lid, is bear-proof – or so I was told – and doesn't have to be hung in a tree like a regular pack. Still, I always walk it a distance into the woods before bed, to be safe.

The chill arrives with the dark. I burrow into the sleeping bag and aim the headlamp beam at my book. It feels strange to be alone in the tent. Though not quite alone... My phantom companion keeps her ears peeled and interrupts my reading every few minutes to elbow me in the ribs. *Hear that?*

Each time, I jump, listen hard, identify the sound. The wind, a creaking branch. *Not* a bear.

The bears may not be outside (yet...) but they're already stomping around my imagination. Particularly the one that mauled a couple to death right here in Algonquin only a few years ago on Opeongo (a lake far, far from here, I tell myself). When the park rangers arrived at the island site, they found a pound of raw ground beef, the couple's intended dinner, sitting right out in the open, untouched, and the bear standing guard over the bodies. I try to tell my phantom companion there was clearly something wrong with this bear – black bears don't normally attack humans. It's our food they want, and mine is safely stored in a bear-proof barrel. It doesn't help. I lie awake and worry about black bears who prefer humans to hamburger.

What was that? I listen hard. Nothing.

Then I hear it. Rather, I hear it *again*: the faint putt-putt of a small motor.

The sound gets louder. Closer. Then, abrupt silence.

Darn. I switch off the headlamp and sit up. The tent is set far back, camouflaged in the hemlock grove. Surely he can't see it? Will he have the nerve to get out on shore? Which is worse – to get up and risk being seen, or to lie here, unseen but unable to see?

I strain my ears in the dark.

At last, the motor starts up and fades into the distance.

I lie back down and wait for my heart to slow down.

He came over, I decide, to see if there was a campfire. He's not inherently harmful. Merely insensitive to the effect his arrival in the dark would have on a Woman Camping Alone (For the First Time). A nuisance bear of a man.

The motor fades into the safe distance, and my phantom companion and I settle back down. I close my eyes and into my head comes a fragment of prayer I haven't said in decades: *Keep me safe 'til morning light amen.* In the awareness-heightened dark, the whole prayer comes back, the way my three sisters and I droned it at our bedsides, running all the words together in chanted monotone:

Jesustendershepherdhearme
GodblessNancyKathrynBrendaLynnetonight.
Throughthedarknessbenearme
Keepmesafetilmorninglightamen.

I never questioned saying my prayers. It was what you did before you got into bed and read under the covers by flashlight (a headlamp would have been just the thing). Chanting prayers was also what I did every Sunday morning in the family pew and at the Sunday evening youth service with my sisters and, in my most devout later teen years, at the Tuesday morning communion and breakfast I attended before school with a small group of retired older folk. In those devout teen years, I also assisted with the communion vessels at the altar as a server, a role I continued in the church I joined at university. At that downtown church, The Redeemer, I sponsored a candidate in a baptism preparation course and then took over running the course.

All this church involvement was not devoutly doubt free. During university I struggled with the Church's arrogance in insisting that the only way to God is through his son, Jesus, and, not incidentally, my lack of any real experience of that son. I was secretly embarrassed by the whole notion of having a "Saviour." The idea of being a "sinner" who needed to be "saved" by a "Redeemer" and "Lord" made me cringe. Even the word "Christian" embarrassed me. I began to doubt the very divinity of Jesus and the whole concept of a three-personed, male-gendered God in the sky. Lord knows what bog of guilty church-going unbelief I might still be mired in if I hadn't met Asante.

I MET MY SPIRITUAL confidant in, of all places, the Medical Sciences Building at the University of Toronto. It was the spring before the final year of my degree, and I arrived in the main office of the clinical science division to start a part-time typing job. A woman appeared in the doorway, a woman with shoulder-length wavy blond hair, a high forehead, and sparkling Mediterranean-blue eyes. She smiled, and I had that split-second moment of recognition, as if I *knew* her, though I knew we'd never met before.

She turned out to be the typist I was to fill in for while she replaced the administrative assistant on maternity leave. Our offices were located at either end of the main office, and we began each day with a ten-minute chat over tea in her office or mine.

My eczema got us talking about non-work-related matters. Between the pressures of university and my relationship with an older man who was separated but not yet divorced, I was stressed. Asante, who had just got her certification as a registered massage therapist, noticed the raw flaking skin on my neck and eyelids. She brought in a vial of herbal oil that gave me much more relief than the doctor's prescriptions, and suggested I might be deficient in vitamin B. She spoke with a comforting combination of authority and compassion. And the B vitamins helped.

We became close friends. She had eleven years on me, but it made no difference. There was an innate empathy between us. She was a prairie girl raised a Seventh-day Adventist, though no longer a church goer. She was following other spiritual paths. I was still going to church, though more and more wondering why.

"What puts me off," I told her on a lunch break one day on the Queen's Park lawn, "is that the Church claims God is Love but then seems to restrict that love to those who believe in and follow Jesus in a particular way."

"I know," she said, between bites of her sandwich. "I was told that God is All but at the same time that so many things are sinful. But if God is all, then God must be in everything – it's only logical. That's what became the impetus in my search for the truth. I set specific criteria for it. Whatever I explore has to have a connection to Love. That's my safety net."

Asante in my Clinical Science Division office, 1983

Instinctively I knew I could trust Asante. I knew she had wisdom and compassion *and* my best interests at heart. She never pressured or led me in a particular direction. The stimulus to search came from inside me. In simply sharing her own journey, she showed me a possibility I had never considered: the spiritual life without the religious.

O N AN EAST-FACING morning seat of a rock, I crunch dry granola and down two mugs of coffee. Dishes washed and food barrel loaded, I heft the canoe down to the little harbour and go back for the blue food barrel, which will be good ballast in the front – my bowman Blue.

As soon as I'm in the boat, a small stern voice starts in on me: *You should be staying put to write.*

U NTIL I MET ASANTE, I thought this was a normal sort of voice to have in your head, a normal necessary sort of voice whose function is to point out your shortcomings and keep you in line and make you a less selfish person. In the first few years after we met, Asante saw me through my breakup with the man who wasn't yet divorced and then through the tumultuous on-off relationship with my botany PhD-student beau. She listened to me beat myself up for being too needy, for wishing he was more affectionate and verbal about his feelings, for not giving him enough space, for not being perfect... She counselled me to stop being so hard on myself.

"Love yourself just the way you are."

She uttered these gentle, shocking words in the middle of the Baldwin Street Cafe in the middle of a work day in the middle of Toronto, and they brought sudden tears to my eyes. I wiped them away. "I'm not supposed to love myself. I'm supposed to love others."

"It's not an either/or proposition." She was smiling. "Jesus didn't say, 'Love your neighbour and *not* yourself.' He said, 'Love your neighbour *as* yourself.'"

"But he also said I'm supposed to deny myself."

"Denying is not rejecting."

I stared at her. It was the first time I'd ever considered there might be a difference. "What *is* denying then?" I felt like I was five years old, not twenty-seven, asking a question everyone else already knew the answer to.

Certainly Asante did. Denying, she explained, is surrendering the desires of your ego to the Divine.

I told her I already tried to do that.

"But you can do it without beating up on yourself. When you beat yourself up, you're rejecting your *Self* – Self with a capital 's.' Not your ego self but the core of your Divinely created being."

It was hard to take all this in, and so, instead of inundating me with information, Asante gave me a simple exercise to do when I got home – an exercise I couldn't imagine doing. Nevertheless, at home I closed my bedroom door and stood in front of the three-quarter-length mirror that had belonged to my Grandma (the only member of my family who had no trouble saying "I love you"). I ignored the reflection of the hateful bit of flesh that bulged over my waistband and the ugly pimple on my chin and the new one about to come to a head. I looked into my eyes and tried to say out loud the three words Asante wanted me to tell myself (the three words I wanted my beau to say).

All that came were tears.

I made myself stay there in front of the mirror and watch my face get blotchy and red. It felt weird watching myself this way. Even so, I felt stirrings of compassion for the poor little girl sobbing in front of me.

Asante wasn't surprised at the results of my first attempt. It had been the same for her. "Keep trying. You don't have to be harsh with yourself to grow and change," she added. "Criticism doesn't change anything. It just breaks down your spirit." She showed me just how much I beat up on myself, the endless criticism I heaped on my head. She suggested, gently, without criticism, that I stop. That the critical voices might not be necessary, that they might in fact be harmful, that I might be able to stop them and accept myself and find acceptance from others – all that was unfathomable.

THE WIND PUSHES ME into the south bay. I ignore the Critical Chorus, which after a decade of hard work, some of it in the mirror, still provides a running, judgmental commentary on everything I do or say, or don't do or say. On this sun-drenched, perfect paddling day, I'm determined not to let it make me feel bad.

From behind, I hear the now-familiar sound of a small motor. It overtakes me – as a motorized canoe will overtake a non-motorized one – but it's at a discreet distance and the driver doesn't look my way. To my relief it disappears into the marsh that leads to the Amable du Fond River. That's tomorrow's destination. Today's mission is a tour of the lake, to explore my boundaries before I stretch them a little.

I follow the shore until I reach the narrows that separate the most easterly bay from the rest of the lake. Over the narrows is an iron bridge that the map indicates is the crossing for an old railway line. I contemplate a walk on the tracks, but the space seems too open in the hot sun. Lunch is a better option. I land the canoe at a pebbly beach below the bridge.

Absorbed in slicing kielbasa and cheddar, I'm startled to hear a vehicle. A pickup truck appears on the bridge, an aluminum canoe propped in the back. I stare in astonishment – the rails must be gone from the railway line – and then indignation; someone is clearly making a buck driving campers to an interior lake.

The truck disappears down the line, and I finish my lunch.

A stiff west wind puts an end to my plan to circumnavigate that last bay. I head back to camp, sticking close to shore. The trick to gaining distance without being blown into the rocks is, I discover, to paddle on the shore side and angle the canoe so the wind hits on the other side of the bow. Between the two opposing forces, the boat more or less maintains a straight line.

I inch my way, progress painstaking but sure. I measure it not in muscle-straining strokes but in the muscle-straining satisfaction of discovering that I (and my bowman Blue) can handle the winds Kioshkokwi thrusts our way. I measure it in the bolstering of my confidence – confidence that will, I hope, take me through the interior lakes one day.

Back on the campsite I raise a mug to the day's accomplishments. The box wine tastes better. I must be officially in camping mode.

The day's paddle and the evening's wine have nicely tuckered me out. It's that good kind of tired from a day of physical exercise. I've paddled all my usual fidgetiness out of me. On a shoreline seat, I close my eyes and, without consciously summoning it, begin to repeat the word "maranatha."

The automatic repetition of this little word, my mantra, is the result of more than a decade of practising silent meditation.

<hr />

IT WAS MY SCIENCE-WORSHIPPING PhD boyfriend who unwittingly steered me to meditation. He was so busy with his research he could never plan ahead, and I never knew when we were going to get together. The day I finally confessed my frustration, he asked, in equal frustration, and with what sounded like genuine incredulity, "Am I the most dominant thing in your life?"

The question stunned me into silence. Not because I didn't know the answer but because I did. And the answer was *wrong*. The most important thing in my life should definitely not be my botany beau. I was not supposed to spend all my waking hours obsessing about him. I had effectively made God in the image of my man.

And no wonder. My teenage self had consumed a steady diet of romance novels and romantic comedies and pop songs, all drilling into me the idea that I couldn't live without the love of a man, that my happiness and fulfillment depended on finding my soulmate. In short, a man would complete me. These ideas burrowed even deeper into my bones than my church beliefs. And there they sat, fairy-tale beliefs about men and remnants of fundamentalist beliefs about God, in complete and unconscious contradiction.

My botany beau's question woke me up. I spent the next day in distraught prayer, trying to open my heart again to God, and terrified that if I did God would call me to leave my boyfriend because he wasn't a Christian (or because I wanted him too much). I prayed to be able to stop *thinking* about him all the time, to be able to get on with my writing. I prayed for the panicky sick feeling in my stomach to go away. And of course I called Asante for solace and wisdom.

Asante, who wasn't free to get together that evening, invited me to come along to a meditation she planned to attend on the weekend. She thought meditation might bring me to a different, healing perspective. I wanted a different perspective badly, and after some hesitation (it was a night my beau and I *might* get together) I told her I would go.

I WAKE UP IN THE PITCH dark, heart rate elevated. Listening. Hearing nothing. Not even the usual rustling of small creatures that sound like large bears clomping around the tent when your ear is so close to the ground. Nothing except my louder-than-usual heartbeat. Why don't I hear anything?

The strange night silence lulls me to sleep, and wakes me up, through the night. Each time I wake, the prayer sounds in my head like a mantra: *Keep me safe 'til morning light amen.*

EVERYTHING FELT STRANGE and scary, even with Asante beside me. The meditation host smiled at the six of us who sat cross-legged on his white-carpeted living room floor. He was a slight man with pale delicate features, fair hair, and an aura of gentleness that helped to calm me.

"You know that prayer is speaking to God. Well, meditation is listening to God. It's best to concentrate on one thing – your breathing, a peaceful experience, a word. When your mind wanders – and," he smiled, "it will – just keep bringing your attention back to your breathing or your word. We'll meditate for twenty minutes, then I'll lead you through an exercise of imagining the gates of heaven and a gift that will be waiting for you there."

A jolt of panic. Asante had tried visualization exercises with me. I was hopeless. My mind always stayed blank.

The host asked us to close our eyes and relax.

I shut my eyes and felt an unexpected, tangible sense of stillness and peace come into the room. I turned my attention to my breathing.

I was concentrating so hard that the sound of the host's voice some time later startled me.

"Imagine," he said, into the silence, "a rose bud."

Immediately the image of a rose bud came to me – ruby red. The ease with which the image arrived was a relief. Maybe this was going to work after all.

"It's a red rose," he added.

I was delighted – I had already pictured that colour. *Now there's going to be a white light.*

It was Asante who had first spoken to me of White Light, as an image for God that wasn't human or gender-based.

"The rose is opening," came the host's voice.

At his words I chided myself for presuming I could anticipate what he was going to say.

"The rose is now open," he continued in his calm, quiet voice. "Emanating from within is a white light. The light grows brighter and brighter."

I *saw* the white light. Saw it grow brighter. Felt its intensity and warmth.

"Now, imagine you are being carried up to heaven in the white light."

I felt enveloped in an indescribable warmth and gentleness and love. A yearning such as I had never experienced rose inside me. Silent tears streamed down my face.

"You're arriving at the gates of heaven," came the host's voice again. "Visualize the gates. What do they look like?"

My attempt to visualize the gates broke the vision – and feel – of the white light. Nothing. My mind was blank. Tears, now, of frustration.

"The gates are opening, slowly. They are wide open now, and there, in the opening, is a gift for you. What is your gift?"

I tried to think of a gift. First I put my botany beau in the empty space in my mind. Too superficial. I visualized a Sunday School depiction of Jesus – pale-skinned in flowing robes and a golden halo around his head. Too clichéd. I couldn't see anything else. My frustration returned. Even greater was the disappointment. There was no gift for me.

The host was now telling us to carry our gift back, enveloped in the white light, back to the rose. I barely followed along, overwhelmed by a potent mixture of yearning, disappointment, and failure. It was my fault there was no gift for me. I didn't deserve one. I couldn't even *imagine* one.

The host asked us to open our eyes. "Now we'll go around the room, so each of you can describe your experience and the gift you received."

I didn't register what the others said, too worried about admitting my failure. All too soon it was my turn. "I had the strange experience of anticipating what you were going to say about the rose being red and the white light."

"I've never started off with those images before. I think I must have got this visualization for you."

To my great embarrassment, a loud sob rose out of me. I covered my face with my hands and felt Asante's arms come around me. "I want to be carried up in the White Light," I wept. The yearning was overwhelming. Even at camp, I had never longed for Jesus the way I now yearned to be carried up in the Light. If I had been alone with Asante, I would have given in to my tears completely. Instead, I calmed myself, drew back from her arms, and turned back to the host. I spoke with an almost little-girl sense of shame. "I wasn't able to imagine the gates of heaven or the gift."

He said, simply, "You got your gift before you arrived."

———

I STAND ON THE HIGH shore, coffee mug cradled in hands, and watch the tiny figure of Motor Guy load up and launch his canoe on the other side of the lake. The boat glides along the opposite shore and disappears around the bend to the take-out. Unnaturally fast for a canoe but not too fast for me.

———

MA– RA– NA– THA–. I repeated the word in silent, drawn-out syllables. I was sitting on a chair, in a darkened room, at the first session of The Redeemer's new weekly Christian meditation group. I'd seen the notice shortly after attending the meditation with Asante, and, in spite of my growing doubts, the church context still felt safer and more familiar. So here I was, on a winter Tuesday evening, in a circle with a dozen other parishioners.

When we arrived, the new assistant, a fatherly man with blunt, kind features, explained that we would simply sit for twenty minutes and silently repeat the mantra "maranatha." It was, he said, an Aramaic word meaning "Our Lord, come!" or "Our Lord is coming." Repeating it was just to give the mind something to do, since the mind likes to be thinking. "Meditation isn't about making anything happen," he told us. "The basic aim is to learn to be aware of what *is*. It's about coming to our centre, which is where we find God."

I liked that: God in my centre, not up in the sky. I liked that I could have relief from my obsessing mind. Most of all I liked that I wasn't to analyze my meditations and that when I realized my mind was wandering, I was (as Asante's friend had also said) gently to bring it back to saying the mantra. No beating myself up for getting absorbed in some concern or fantasy and forgetting to repeat the word.

Before we began, the assistant pressed play on a cassette tape recorder so we could hear a short talk by a Benedictine monk named John Main. His sonorous British voice lulled me (as no doubt intended) into stillness.

Soft music began to play, signalling the end of the meditation. And then we got up to go home. No discussion of beliefs (or guilty non-beliefs), no analysis, no talk at all. I loved it.

━━◆━━

I CARRY THE BREAKFAST dishes into the woods to wash them in a pot of water mixed with a few drops of biodegradable soap. Crouched down over the soft mossy forest floor, I put my ears on high alert. A bird sings two long notes. Leaves rustle. From close by comes a faint, high-pitched whine. It sounds eerily human. Is someone there? I stay stock still, heart thumping. The moan comes again, and then a creaking sound, from straight above. I look up to see one pine tree sway against another. I let out a breath.

I emerge (unscathed) from the woods to find the morning breeze has become a waves-whipped-into-white-caps wind. I hold my hair back and survey the wild sea. Today was supposed to be Portage-into-Manitou-Lake Day. It's one thing to get caught in a headwind. It's another to start out in one, especially when I don't have to. I will stay put and fulfill my Life's Purpose.

———●

MY LIFE'S PURPOSE became clear when I was ten. I'm not sure what the trigger was, though *Harriet the Spy* was a definite influence. Like the ten-year-old main character in this children's novel, I took to heart the nanny's advice that if you want to be a writer, you have to write everything down. Harriet begins to carry around a composition notebook, writing brutally honest things about the friends and family members she spies on (aided by a flashlight and other spy tools). Inspired, I bought a little blue Alco lock-and-key diary and a flashlight. My spy career, writing nasty (and frankly contrived) things about my teacher and classmates, didn't last (though one could argue every writer is a spy). The flashlight was put to better use in under-the-covers reading after bedtime prayers. And I started to write stories after school – my first a mystery styled after Enid Blyton's *Secret Seven* series that was impressively solved in fifteen pages. (A couple of years later I bought myself another little Alco diary – this one emerald green – and thus began my lifelong journaling habit.)

So I had it figured out before puberty. I would get married, have children, and write novels. My husband would support me, as my father supported our family.

This vision has undergone various surgeries over the years. The husband (financially supporting or not) has eluded me. I (happily) earn my own living. And I made the decision (which, sadly, ended my last relationship) not to have kids. I knew if I did I wouldn't write another word for twenty years. And I really don't need any more excuses to procrastinate.

———●

I LEAN BACK IN the Crazy Creek chair and open the notebook to review the results of my cottage-hopping productivity, pages filled with messy handwriting – in indelible pen – much of it crossed out. It's not that easy to write the story of a murdered friend.

We met in the early 1990s, Louise Ellis and I. By then I had started a freelance editing business and moved from Toronto to Chelsea, Quebec, near Ottawa. Louise was the contracted writer of the Canada Post annual yearbook and I her editor. We began to have long phone conversations that went well beyond work-related matters. She too was looking for a soulmate, someone who shared her spiritual view of the world, someone who wanted to grow and heal with her. A year or so after we met she confided she was in a relationship with a convict named Brett Morgan and they'd been together two years. He had been convicted of manslaughter but had served his time, and she was advocating for his release. A few months after she shared this with me, Brett came to live with her. And not quite a year after that, Louise went missing. I happened to find her car, abandoned on a rural road not far from my house. That night, after dealing with Brett and the police, I had a dream like no other I'd ever had, more like a visitation. An old school friend came and told me where to search – and to write it in a book. I woke up immediately and wrote down the dream messages in my journal. Then, as bidden, I recorded everything from the evening, every odd thing Brett had said and done. It was only later, after a harrowing ten-week search for Louise, that I realized the instruction to write it in a book had a much larger meaning than recording a witness account in my journal. I was to write her story. But to tell it with empathy, I needed to understand what had motivated her to get involved with Brett. And I didn't understand.

I still don't. I thought it would help to get away from the distractions of home, but the cottage-hopping writing vacation has been a mixed success. My preoccupation with the writing has made me a bad house guest. The blood rushes to my cheeks as I recall the number of times I walked into the cottage this past week after an afternoon on a writing rock to find everyone already in the middle of before-dinner drinks, or the kitchen humming with meal preparations when I was on my way out for a post-writing run. Did I postpone my run? Ask what I could do? No. Something propelled me out the door, even as the Critical Chorus berated me: *You should stay and help in the kitchen. You're a terrible guest. You'll never be invited back.*

I've felt guilty for as long as I can remember. Certainly the Church confirmed my essential human guilt. Even today, years after leaving the Church, and an equal number of years working hard to go easier on myself, the guilt-confirming words of the prayers we intoned during Sunday services still resonate. My rational mind may now know I'm not a "miserable offender," filled with "manifold sins and wickedness," but there are too many days when something I "ought to have done" or "ought not to have done" leaves me in no doubt that I'm "not worthy so much as to gather up the crumbs" under God's (or my family's) table.

These four days are a welcome respite from my terrible-house-guest guilt, even as the Chorus is now on my case for procrastination.

The guilty scribe gets to work.

The sun is high in the sky. I've been scribbling for an hour and am restless. A paddle to a portage for a hike would do the trick. The wind, though, is gusting harder – hard enough to give the windsurfer out on the lake a good run. He tacks back and forth across the water, on his way, I suddenly know, to me. Part of me is wary. Another part is happy at the prospect. Maybe I want someone to talk to after almost forty-eight hours of self-imposed solitude. How dangerous can a windsurfer be? If the wind blows him over, the wind will blow him away again.

Sure enough, his tack brings him into the bay. Once out of the wind near my little harbour, he slows and lowers the sail. And I see who it is.

I relax and make my way down to say hello to the man who complimented my paddling abilities from his dock the other day.

He doesn't disembark, just crouches on his board near shore. Now that he's closer, I see creases in the corners of his eyes when he smiles.

"I came to see how you're doing – and to invite you for tea or a meal. There's a whole clan of us over there." He waves back at the other shore. "At least twenty of us. You're welcome to join us if you get lonely or want some company. My name's Frank, by the way."

"I'm Brenda. And thank you for the offer. That's very nice of you. I'm doing fine actually. Better than I thought I would." I appreciate his sensitivity in mentioning the large clan.

"I do see solo paddlers going by now and then, but not very often. It takes a certain confidence to come here camping on your own."

"Confidence – ha! I lie awake all night listening for bears."

"All the more power to you for coming out here then," says Frank. "You've got the best site on the lake, you know. The locals call it Smokey Bear Point." At the look of horror on my face, he adds, "It was named for a *fire*."

I know I won't take him up on his invitation. Still, as he catches a departing breeze, it relieves me to know I have an ally (and his entire clan) on the lake. It makes up for the departed wolf of Wolfe Bay.

The waves seem marginally smaller now and the wind not quite so fierce. Out on the water an aluminum boat heads my way, propelled by a shirtless man, hand on the throttle. Good God, does every man on the lake know I'm here? Maybe it's the park warden come to check my camping permit. Though the warden would surely have a shirt on.

The boater skirts around the point, sees me on the rock and raises a hand. I wave back. And then – is the wind that much stronger and cooler around the point? – he reaches for his shirt. A moment later he turns the boat around, and I see the badge on the shoulder.

By the time he has nosed into my little harbour, I'm standing just above it, arms crossed over my chest. "That looks more official." My cheeky greeting takes me aback. I'm usually respectful of authority.

The warden steps out onto the rocks. He's tall and lean, with close-cropped salt and pepper hair and Vandyke beard. Despite the salt part of his hair, he doesn't look so old, maybe in his early forties. "I've come to check camping permits and such."

In a decade of interior camping in Algonquin, no one has ever checked my permit. "And you want me to get mine?" I can't seem to stop myself from the familiarity. Something about his energy seems to invite it.

"Yes, please." Then, in a less officious tone, as he follows me up the slope, "How's the condition of the site?"

"Perfect – except for the overly civilized picnic table."

He laughs. "I know what you mean. It's only because it's on a head lake where people arrive with everything but the kitchen sink. The interior sites are more rustic."

I retrieve my permit and hand it over. He doesn't comment on the number of campers indicated on the pink slip. He says, "You picked a good lake to come to on the long weekend. Not so busy up here."

"I know, I was here about five years ago. It's beautiful. Though I think I found the only site on the lake that has rock. I was expecting it to be more like the Temagami region. It's not that much farther north."

His eyes light up. "Oh, yes! Temagami! There's nothing like it, is there, even with all the cottages. I was just there a few weeks ago."

"Get out. I was just there with my niece. Where did you go?"

"We got flown in to – "

"*Flown* in. Oh, you *bastard*. Show me where." I reach for my plastic map case and pull the Temagami map out from under the one for Algonquin. I barely notice I've sworn at a man in uniform with a billy club dangling from his belt.

The man in uniform laughs, reaches for the map and spreads it on the picnic table. We hold down the corners, heads close together while he traces his route with a finger. I show him the shorter route Harriet and I took a little closer to civilization.

He steps back from the picnic table and glances into the hemlock grove. "Wow, that's some tent you've got there – you sure you're not harbouring fugitives?"

He is turning back around, he is smiling at me with warm hazel eyes, and I am opening my mouth to tell him the story of Brenda's Palace, when a supersonic jet of a thought zings through my brain: *This is the man I'm going to marry.*

Where did *that* come from? I don't even know his name. He could be married already for all I know.

To give myself time to recover I ask him how long he's been a warden.

"A warden? Only two years. But I've been a ranger for over twenty – since my early twenties. I do campsite and trail maintenance, as well as enforce park rules. I think of myself more as a ranger than a warden."

Free-spirited ranger does seem to suit him better. He laughs when I describe the image I had of the big mean warden arriving to boot me off the site if I stayed more nights than I paid for. "I'm not really into enforcing the rules. I love this job because I love being in the park."

He's not, he admits, even on duty. "I only came out because it's such a beautiful day and I had nothing else to do." He leans back against the end of the rickety picnic table, arms folded in a relaxed way, apparently in no rush to leave. "I don't live up here permanently. I'm filling in for the regular warden this summer. A sweet old lady is renting me a cottage. But she's having family up this weekend, so I made myself scarce."

I look past him out on the lake and nod at the empty aluminum boat that has begun to drift away from shore. "You might be staying longer than you planned."

He swivels his head around. "Darn. I really should learn to tie up that boat."

"I take it this isn't the first time this has happened."

He confesses it isn't.

"Then I guess you're used to swimming for it," I tease.

Instead, we each grab an end of my canoe and carry it down to the water, where I hand the ranger the spare paddle. "Good thing I brought it."

The wind has pushed his boat far out into the lake, and it takes several minutes to reach. When we come alongside, a disembodied voice is speaking from the bottom. Startled, I glance in and realize it's a two-way radio.

I hold onto the side, and the ranger climbs in. I fully expect him to say goodbye. Instead he says, "I better check in to see if anyone's been trying to get hold of me."

There ensues a lengthy conversation, during which the ranger fails to mention his current location and status. The other ranger's voice sounds almost Irish.

"Ottawa Valley," the ranger explains when he's done. He does a wicked imitation in a falsetto: "Yeah, I cleared dem logs off the trail like you axed me to. I'm from de Valley, eh?"

I laugh. "Where did *you* grow up?"

His turn to laugh. "The Valley. On a farm south of the park."

I want to ask him why he doesn't sound like a Valley lad, especially when he reveals he didn't finish high school. "I never paid attention. I was always reading a book hidden under my desk."

We glance up to see a large black storm cloud has blown over our heads and another is on the way. We've drifted far from the campsite.

"Well, I guess I'll be going now. Happy paddling back to your site."

I tighten my grip on the motorboat. "I think not."

"Just getting you back for the 'swim for it' remark."

Side by side, we keep hold of each other's boat while he takes us back, at a slow, safe speed, to my campsite, where he readily accepts an invitation to supper.

We dine at the picnic table (it is convenient), then I excuse myself to go to the biffy, where I decide it's time for a post-prandial on a sunset rock. When I return, the ranger is already in place on the west-facing ledge, the tin mug beside him.

I sit down beside him. "You read my mind."

We pass the mug back and forth. I tell him about the novel and the real story behind it, including the dream that propelled my search. I tell him about the dreams I've continued to have about Louise. "This will probably sound weird, but I feel she's guiding my writing." I look at him, unsure how he will receive this.

"I wouldn't discount it."

Something like joy floods through me. Not many men I know give credence to dreams.

He shares his dilemma of whether to take the job up here permanently or return to his old job where he would have more time in the woods. "It will become clear to me," he says calmly.

I rejoice to hear this too: a man who listens to his interior voice.

I learn he loves not only to canoe but also, like me, to cross-country ski and bike. He loves to visit the city and eat in good restaurants. Clearly he loves wine – he's consumed much of mine. The similarities, the incredible ease, the meeting of minds, our teasing familiarity are entirely explained when I discover we're both Geminis – born two days if six years apart. Gemini – sign of the twins – is an astrological sign associated with the mind. Little wonder there has been such an immediate connection between us.

We go on to share our respective relationship histories and status. I'm relieved to hear his marriage ended years ago and he has two grown children. There was, he says, another long-term relationship as well. Now, he says, there's an old friend he's in close contact with out west, "very close contact."

This admission doesn't faze me. "I have friends like that. I have this propensity for attracting men who then run like hell in the opposite direction, and we end up 'just friends' – just friends but close friends."

He throws back his head and laughs. He has a great laugh. Warm and sympathetic, not mocking. "You mean run from the 'C' word?"

"Exactly. First there's the I word – interest. Then the R word. Then the C word, then the M word." I count them on my fingers.

"Don't forget the P word," says the ranger. "And there's the H word too – hope."

I bring the conversation back to safer waters. "Hey, now you're here I can ask you. How do people get away with driving in to the interior lakes? Yesterday when I was stopped for lunch at the narrows, I saw a pickup truck drive over the bridge – "

He stares at me. "That was *me*. I was driving in to Mink Lake to do permit checks. So that was *you* at that beach. I saw you. I *waved*, and you didn't wave back. I thought you were a snob."

"I'm not a snob. I never saw you wave. There was too much glare in the glass. I almost went for a walk on the railway line, just before you drove by."

"So we could have met yesterday. If I'd seen you walking on the railway, I definitely would have rolled down my window to talk to you."

"And never got to your destination."

"Not the way you talk. Actually, I would have said 'hop in' and taken you with me."

"And defeated the whole purpose of my being out here. I'm supposed to *carry* the canoe."

"You see, we were meant to meet. If not yesterday, then today. It's fate."

I've never met a man who talks this way, who talks about fate and things that eventually become clear to him and who doesn't discount the novel-writing guidance of a ghost. A man who talks the way I think. A man I've waited all my adult life to meet.

Down at the little harbour, he lingers.

On impulse, I ask if he'd like to come back for dinner tomorrow. He accepts with gratifying enthusiasm. "I'm on duty. I'll swing by at the end of the day." Before he leaves he assures me no bears have been reported in this part of the park this summer.

In the tent I force myself to read so I won't obsess about the ranger. I'm reading *The Color Purple*, and not for the first time. That first time, a decade ago, had a more profound effect on my perception of God than any of my university religion courses, or even my newfound meditation. Like me at the time, the main character, Celie, is trying to "chase that old white man" out of her head and has support from a wise, nurturing friend, Shug, who tells her, "God ain't a he or a she, but a It... I believe God is everything... Everything that is or ever was or ever will be."

It might have been Asante speaking to *me*. Seeing the words printed on the page like that made one thing clear: I wasn't finding "It" in the Church. ("It" might be found in meditation but I didn't need church to meditate.) One Sunday morning, the rector announced to the congregation that he was leaving to go to another church. My immediate thought was, "I'm leaving too." And not to go to another church.

It wasn't a loss of faith – more an acknowledgement of (Christian) faith already lost. It was a calling. A calling I'd never felt *in* the Church. A call to seek a God who was more expansive than the God the Church contained.

The God who left the Church with me when I was twenty-five didn't have a name, or a persona, or a physical image. "He" didn't even have a gender, though I didn't think I could call God "It," like Shug.

My own wise, nurturing friend Asante had other suggestions: "the Divine," "the White Light," "the Universe." In spite of its New Agey sound, we agreed we liked the Universe best. It didn't bring an image to mind and, as Asante pointed out, it encompassed everything in creation, even ourselves.

Now, in my dark, cavernous palace of a tent, I ask the Universe to keep the non-existent bears at bay. Then I give in to fantasies about my delightful dinner guest, which also keep sleep at bay.

I'm awake at dawn. A rarity for me. And not just lie-in-bed awake but out-of-the-tent-wide-awake awake. From the high east-facing rock, I watch the sun peek its glowing head in the rosy sky above the dark mass of trees. Slowly, surely, it sends a shimmering path of gold across the mirrored surface of the lake. I've seen the liquid silver path of the rising moon over water but never the liquid gold path of rising sun. Just before the glittering bridge reaches the shore below, the breeze comes up and fragments it into the zillion sparks of a July First sparkler. I spread my arms, primordial sun worshipper on the shore of the world, and greet the day. I can't help feeling I'm standing at the dawn of a new life. The natural world speaks in compelling clichés.

It's Portage-into-Manitou-Lake Day – the day to find where my boundaries lie. It's not new territory. Roz and I were here five years ago. We didn't camp on Kioshkokwi but pushed down the lake and through the Amable du Fond River to a campsite located just before the 1,355-metre portage into Manitou.

WE CONTEMPLATED the daunting portage all evening and again the next morning over breakfast. It was by far our longest in several years canoeing together.

"Wouldn't it be nice," we mused over tea and oatmeal, "if someone portaging in the other direction picked up our remaining packs on their return trip and carried them for us so we didn't have to make the second trip?" We laughed at the fantasy.

It was a short paddle to the portage. We started down the trail, me with canoe, Roz with food pack. About halfway, we met a bearded man with a canoe over his head, and a teenage boy who carried only paddles and life jackets. We exchanged hellos and continued in opposite directions. At the lake, I set the canoe down and noticed two big canvas packs farther down the beach that clearly awaited the return of the other portaging pair.

We were about to head back for the rest of our gear when Roz spotted a large overgrown raspberry patch beside the path. We took our time, savouring each burst of sweetness from the tiny berries. At last, we got back on the trail, and soon met up again with the father and son. We stared at them. Why on earth were they carrying a pack and paddles and life jackets back the way they had come? The father had to say, in thick German accent, "This is yours?"

Embarrassed, grateful, and delighted, we relieved them of their – *our* – burden.

On the short trek back to the beach to get on our way, I heard another voice altogether, the voice of Jesus as I'd never heard it before. Clear as a bell: *Ask, and you will receive.*

———

LIKE ALL ALGONQUIN portages, the trail over to the Amable du Fond River is marked by a rectangular yellow sign nailed to a tree. The sign has the black silhouette of a figure with an upside-down canoe where his head should be. Below the canoehead, the distance and bodies of water at each end are marked, in this case Kioshkokwi to Amable du Fond River, 265 metres.

I multiply the portage distance by three, to account for the number of times I'll have to walk the trail, first with barrel, then boat. The barrel has a padded harness that makes carrying something rigidly convex marginally more comfortable. I make no requests for Good Samaritans to carry my gear. On this first portage I've ever done on my own, the point is to do it myself.

The short walk with harnessed Blue is no big deal. I head back for my Scott Wilderness canoe. At sixty-five-pounds, it's too wide and heavy for me to flip up onto my shoulders. I grasp the gunwales on either side of the bow, and turn the boat over while raising the bow over my head. Then I walk backwards underneath, sliding my hands along the gunwales until the yoke cups my neck. Not nearly as elegant as a classic flip but, hey, I'm self-sufficient.

The river at the other end seems shallower than on the trip with Roz. It has a gravel bottom and I use the paddle like a pole to propel the boat forward.

Not far up the river I glimpse the next portage sign on a tree beside a steep sandy slope that disappears into the woods. In the shallows just below the slope looms something large, dark, and ungainly. The large rack on its head gives away the identity of the dark ungainly thing. Before me is the largest bull moose I've ever seen.

I stop poling a respectful (and safe) distance away. I'm at once awestruck by his magnificence and dismayed as he legs it up the sandy slope and onto the path. *My* path.

I thump paddle on gunwales but there is no answering charge into the bush – just a twitch of ears among the leaves. What to do? Advance or retreat?

I climb out and stand in the calf-deep water, eyes trained on twitching ears. My last encounter with a moose was only a few lakes from here, with Roz, the evening after we manifested pack carriers on the Manitou portage, and I have no desire to repeat *that*.

WE WERE CAMPED across from a creek that the map showed could be navigated a kilometre or two to a portage. Roz declared she wanted to see a moose and her baby, so we cleaned up the dinner things and followed the winding ways of the creek in the luminescent evening light.

Just beyond the portage, the river became blocked with logs and boulders, and we turned around, only to find our way blocked again. This time by a moose. A cow. She stood in the middle of the creek, her horse-like mouth dripping water and long grasses.

A cow moose dines in the creek off Biggar Lake, 1993

Neither Roz nor I spoke or moved. The cow seemed to assess us, then retreated out of sight in the thick alders.

With some trepidation, we glided the canoe past where she had stood.

A rustle in the bushes up ahead brought us again up short. Out from the trees on the other side of the creek stepped a gangly moose calf.

From behind came a louder rustling. We swivelled our heads. The cow had come back out of *her* bush. We were now caught between a mother and her baby.

No one moved.

Then Baby stepped back in the bush, out of sight.

That's when Mama charged.

"*Paddle, Roz!*"

There's nothing more unnerving, not even a bull moose blocking the portage when you're out in a canoe by yourself, than being a small creature in the stern of a canoe chased by an angry mother moose. Since I didn't get any hoof marks imprinted in my skull, I assume she just wanted to scare us away from her offspring. Mission accomplished. We hightailed it out of the creek.

Be still our banging hearts.

Ask, and you will surely receive. But be careful what you ask for. It's definitely not recommended to come between a mother moose and her young.

M Y HOPE NOW, as I stand in the river a short distance from the portage trail and twitching moose ears, is for a couple of burly portagers to arrive from the other direction and startle him away.

After a few minutes of no activity, human or ungulate, I make the decision to retreat. I'm here to find my limits, not push them beyond my comfort zone. Bending down to turn the boat around, I tell myself being out here at all is pushing my limits. There are other portages on other parts of the lake to try. The moose sighting is a bonus.

I slosh through the water, guiding the boat ahead of me, and compose the story to tell my dinner guest.

Back on shore at the previous put-in, I'm taken aback to see an upside-down canoe on legs make its way through the trees beside the river from the direction of the next portage. Behind it strides a woman with a bulky pack. I climb the slope from the water to see a path I didn't notice before – a continuation of the portage for use when the water levels on this stretch of river are too low for navigation, as they very nearly are now. If portagers have come this way, past the other take-out, then the moose has surely vamoosed. My hope, though not quite a prayer, has been answered. *Thank you.*

I lean against the still-warm rock, bathed and dressed in my finest sarong. There's a tin cup of ruby liquid in my hand and a feeling of accomplishment in my heart. I'm zonked from lack of sleep and the day's exertions, which included a walk with the food barrel over the 1,355-metre portage to the Manitou beach and raspberry patch for a picnic, and back. Fatigue is more than cancelled out by anticipation.

While I wait, I pull out my journal. Frank the windsurfer was right. It did take a certain confidence to come here. And with each portage crossed and each wind battled, that confidence has grown. I now declare that as far as capabilities go, I'm ready for a real solo trip. But what about my confidence in the Universe to keep me safe? What about those nerves of mine?

I pour more wine and ponder. The sun slips behind a wide band of blackish-grey.

Every night in the tent I've sent a prayer to the heavens, and my prayer, it dawns on me, has been answered. Every night I've been kept safe 'til morning light and (unasked but obliged anyway) every day 'til evening dark. The secret seems to be in the detachment that accompanies the asking. You ask for someone to carry your pack and forget about it, you don't count on it happening. You ask to see a moose and place your attention on navigating the river. You hope for other portagers to come along and you make an alternate plan.

You ask to be kept safe. You put yourself in the hands of the Universe. Or whatever you call God. And God sends agents – windsurfers and wardens – to let you know you're safe from bears. God keeps the wolves at bay too, even sends them home.

It comes to me there is something to be gleaned from Mr. Motorized Canoe hanging around. I've been so focused on my ursine nemesis

I forgot to take anything else into consideration. Maybe Motor Guy was sent to remind me to create prayerful boundaries against *all* potentially harmful influences, not just the ones prowling about in my imagination.

I look up from my journal. The bank of cloud has widened, blackening more of the sky.

There's no question the ranger's visit has settled down my jittery phantom companion – not just with his reassurances about bears but by his very (benevolent, male) presence and the anticipation of his return, which has distracted me from other thoughts. It's my mind that imagines it hears things or is afraid something is going to pop out of the bush. It seems to me being safe isn't as important as *knowing* you're safe.

If nothing else comes of last night's visit, I tell the Merlot, if the park ranger doesn't come back, then at least he's done that for me. But disappointment lurks under my gratitude.

The light has all but faded when I close my journal. No sunset today – none visible on Kioshkokwi anyway. The brooding bank of cloud has moved up over my head, slowly but surely overtaking the pale sky. For the last several hours I've strained to hear the distant whine of a motor, sound that only yesterday was a source of exasperation.

The coolness and twilight send me into the tent. The wine and no dinner send me into a funk. Impossible to summon even a semblance of detachment. I blame the wine in my empty stomach. He's been delayed, I tell myself. He changed his mind when he saw the weather. He got cold feet.

I don't really buy that last possibility. Most likely he got delayed and doesn't want to risk the weather. I despair though that if he doesn't show up we won't connect again before my departure tomorrow. Was it really just a moment to enjoy and release? Someone to take away my preoccupation with phantom bears?

The answer arrives in the faint hum of motor that breaks the dark silence of the lake.

The lake is remarkably calm for midday, the hour I told Cathy I would arrive at the Smoke Lake landing. I'll call her from a pay phone. She'll forgive the delay when she hears the reason.

I paddle without effort. The canoe and my heart are full, my cheeks and ribs sore. I've never giggled with a man before. Giggling is usually reserved for girlfriends and mothers and sisters. We've exchanged email addresses and phone numbers and promised to keep in touch.

The road is not, however, entirely open and free, and when he arrived he was anxious to set the record straight. "It's sitting in idle," he said of his relationship with the woman out west. "I don't know where it's going. But" – he looked at me with that steady gaze of his – "now I have compelling reason to find out."

I heard him out calmly, with detachment even (easier to summon now that he had arrived; something *had* come up at work, then he wasn't sure of his welcome and worried it was too late).

It took me aback when he produced a duffle bag and tent. But of course he would have to stay after such a late arrival. When rain began to spatter down, I suggested we set up his tent to eat in. It wouldn't be safe for him to sleep in afterward but there was, I added, gesturing to the hemlock grove, plenty of room in Brenda's Palace. It wasn't my intention to seduce him, though I wasn't averse to the idea. In an olive-green open-necked shirt instead of the geeky uniform he looked darned sexy. However, a chaste night was assured, or enforced, by a serious case of poison ivy he said covered most of his body.

He was in no rush to leave. "If the sun sets at nine, then midday isn't until three in the afternoon" was his irrefutable logic when I told him I was supposed to be at Cathy's by noon. His reluctance to leave, and his parting hug, dispelled any doubts I might have had of his interest.

Now I pull paddle joyfully through the water. If I haven't already fallen in love, I'm irrevocably on the way. I came to the park to find out if I can go solo. And found the one I want to go in tandem with the rest of my life.

The carrier of her own canoe (Photo: Cathy McLeod)

2

ON MY OWN, NOT ALONE

Smoke Lake around to Smoke Lake: August 7–12, 2000

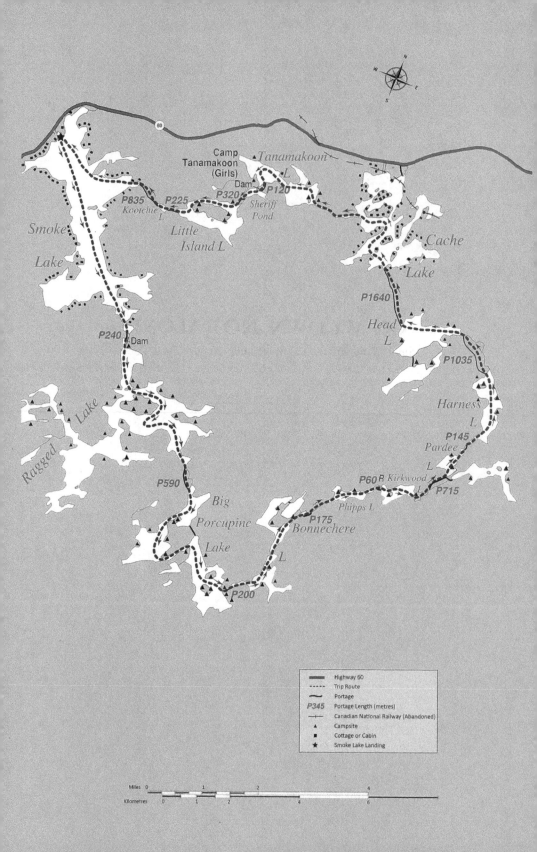

I PUSH OFF FROM the landing into blue-grey waters, a crosswind, and a potent mix of apprehension and exhilaration. With each glance behind, everything shrinks a little more, the cottagers and other trippers, cars and canoes, packs and luggage piled on the docks. The wind carries the voices inland until there's only the whistle of the breeze and buzz of an occasional motorboat.

Smoke Lake, so familiar from two previous canoe trips and my new annual visits to Cathy's cottage, is the obvious starting point for my first real solo canoe trip. And whether she's back from her sister's by then or not, I'm to spend my last night in the tiny cabin down at her shore. Ever since I first slept in the sweet one-room wooden structure two summers ago, I've secretly dubbed it "Brenda's Bunkie."

CATHY OPENED THE wooden screen door – so old the screen was real metal and badly warped – and I followed her inside. I took in the white-painted counter along the back wall, the tiny pot-bellied stove in the corner, the futon bed beside the big mullioned window overlooking the lake – and fell in love for a record second time in two days.

Cathy dumped my gear bag on the bed. She may not go on canoe trips anymore, and may be even shorter than I am, but she can haul packs around with the ease of a seasoned tripper. Perhaps to be expected by someone who went to camp every summer and on family canoeing expeditions right from the door of the cottage her parents still own across the lake. Now she's happy to have her own cottage and *not* go camping.

She took me up to the main cottage, a much newer building perched on the side of a hill. After the kids were in bed, we sat at either end of the overstuffed couch, swirling glasses of shiraz. When we arranged the visit I told her there was nothing to report about my love life. The weekend had proved me happily wrong.

Cathy and I have known each other since we were eight years old. We grew up next door to each other in a Toronto suburb and bonded over our shared love of books and dolls and miniatures and our shared crush on one boy in grade five and another in grade seven. Not to mention our shared mortification in being the first in the class to get our bras when we were ten and the next year our periods – and each at the same time. She was the first, and for many years only, person I ever showed my stories and, from the age of ten, became my keenest fan and most helpful critic. There could be no greater gift from a childhood friend. Her unwavering belief in me as a writer nurtured my belief in myself. Now that she's married with kids, she likes to live vicariously through my endless stream of romantic encounters, hopeful relationship starts, and painful breakups. She always takes in my story with gratifying enthusiasm or sympathy, whichever is required in the moment.

On the drive from Kioshkokwi, I had decided she was the only one I would confide in about the ranger. Usually when I meet a new romantic prospect, I tell the world. In this case, I didn't dare even write that rocket-ship-through-my-brain intuitive thought in my journal, and restrained myself from sharing that part with Cathy. The encounter felt too fragile, not weak but newborn. It felt like the energy would dissipate if I talked about it too much. It needed nurturing in the secret womb of my heart, and in the secret womb of the Universe. Not to mention the ranger's heart. Nothing could grow if all those secret places weren't in sync – and synchronicity didn't stand a chance given the existence of his relationship "sitting in idle" with the woman out west.

So now, while the propane lamps on the walls softly hissed and the bottle slowly emptied, Cathy drank in my tale with her usual attention and enthusiasm.

On my last day, bags packed for the next cottage destination, she showed me the bunkie's broken padlock. "We had to saw through the lock to get in, so we're just going to leave it on the latch so it *looks* secure. This would be a perfect place for you to write. Come and use it any time we're not here." She gave me a sly look. "I have a feeling you're going to be spending a lot of time in Algonquin."

"Shhhh!"

"Brenda! You can't tell me that was just a fleeting thing."

"It's out of my hands!"

"And it's better that way, no? You're the one always saying how important it is to let go."

"I've let go."

She gave a skeptical laugh. "Well, if you have, you're a stronger person than I am, Brenda Missen. But then, you always have been."

I wasn't so sure about that. In this case, though, I did feel strong. Strong and calm.

"Brenda's Bunkie" on Smoke Lake

I PROPEL THE CANOE down the lake. In the distance I can just make out the pine-clad point where, if I were on my way to Cathy's, I would turn into the east bay. So many associations with the ranger, across the lake and across the province.

I RETURNED TO MY rented house in west Quebec after my Ontario cottage-hopping writing vacation restless to move back to my home province. The part of Ontario that attracted me was Canadian Shield country, maybe around Haliburton or Frontenac. Work wasn't an issue; with the advent of email, physical proximity to my clients was no longer necessary. But I wanted to go with someone, especially since it would mean moving into relative isolation. I had no one particular in mind, though I was aware how opportune it would be to reconnect with an Algonquin Park ranger if he, by some miracle, became free.

He phoned, in October, after I had all but given up on him. He apologized for not having called sooner; he had broken his elbow and spent weeks in hospital. In one breath he said he wanted to come to visit, in the next that nothing had changed in his relationship status. I screwed up my courage and told him that he needed to resolve things in his current relationship before we saw each other, that I needed another male friend like I needed another hole in my head, that I had seen possibilities but they weren't possibilities under the existing circumstances. I told him in the past I had been willing to settle for less than I wanted but wasn't willing to do so anymore. I told him I wasn't trying to come between them. If it worked out I wished him well. If it didn't, I would welcome hearing from him.

I had never spoken with such forthrightness in my life. I had adopted new male friends, even some who might have unfinished business elsewhere, in a spirit of "openness" and in many cases secret hope. None of my current prospects were involved in or getting over a relationship. None had demonstrated a tenth of the ranger's receptivity, either.

"You're saying all the right things," he kept saying. "I didn't know how to approach it. I'm glad you did. You've given me a lot to ponder."

My heart was pounding when we hung up. I had no idea if I would ever hear from him again. I was afraid I had revealed too much, too soon. Yet under my surface agitation was an amazing calm. The calm of having power in a situation where you appear to have none. Of speaking your mind, setting your boundaries, being true to your heart. I had delivered a message, and it had been comprehended with a gratitude, enthusiasm, and admiration I was not expecting.

Christmas was coming, and I was still on my own and still in Chelsea. On the drive home from the chiropractor one day I spoke out loud to the windshield: "If you want to go, Brenda, just *go*. If you wait for someone to come along who wants to go with you, you may wait forever."

So I had already made the satisfying decision to go *some*where when the phone rang from a 705 area code a month into the new year. He had broken up with the woman out west. On February thirteenth, I drove to his winter quarters near Kioshkokwi Lake. That weekend's reunion led to many more. We skied, snowshoed, embraced, and giggled our way headlong into love.

THE MEMORIES SLIDE over me and recede, like the water off my paddle. I don't expect, or want, to run into him this week. Today I don't even miss him – a huge relief. There's no dampening my excitement. I'm out here, doing what I love most in the world: canoeing in this near wilderness called Algonquin.

I reach the sandy shore at the south end of the lake and my first and only portage of the day, an easy 240-metre carry-over to Ragged Lake. I get the canoe – a rented dedicated solo boat – on my head using the teepee method I used with my own on Kioshkokwi two summers ago. At forty pounds this one is two-thirds the weight and much easier to carry.

A cheerful couple are stacking a large pile of bags, coolers, and water jugs in their boat when I arrive back at the beginning of the portage. I hoist the big blue waterproof canoe bag onto my back. It contains a bunch of new gear I'm excited to put to use: a lighter tent, smaller one-burner stove, and compact sleeping bag.

The woman looks over at me. "You look like a veteran."

"Not a veteran *solo* canoer." Nevertheless, her compliment boosts my confidence.

When she asks where I'm headed I rhyme off the major lakes on my loop and she is gratifyingly impressed. She climbs into the waiting boat. "Keep safe out there now."

I wrangle the food barrel onto my front like a big and decidedly not snuggly baby carrier. The two packs, a cumbersome load, make me look like a roly-poly blue person. Too bad. I can't manage a pack with the canoe and don't want to do more portage relays than necessary.

The roly-poly blue person heads down the trail with a little jingle from what may be the most important piece of new gear, a small round chrome bell strapped to the barrel, whose sole job is to alert any bears that might happen to wander nearby.

I've got bears on the brain. At the permit office this morning, the attendant announced that one or two have been getting into campers' food north of Highway 60 – the road that bisects the park. She assured me the rangers are out there, setting live traps with fried bacon. This trip is south of the highway, which for some irrational reason makes me feel safe – as if an invisible fence prevents bears from crossing the road. Even if the bears do stay to the north, though, there's next week's trip to consider. I've booked the fourth annual Auntie Brenda/ Niece Harriet canoe trip in the very area the ursine gang is carrying out its food raids. I pray the rangers will have caught the offenders by the time we put in.

The middle of Ragged Lake is taken up by a huge island. On its south side I find home for the night. Within an hour, I have the new tent set up, wood collected, and fire lit for my one-pot store-bought rehydrated teriyaki noodle dinner. The sun makes its habitual evening way to the hills, casting a gold light over the campsite, including the tent. It's another "palace," not in size (it has half the floor space of Brenda's Palace and is less than half the weight) but in its royal colours of purple and gold.

In another hour I've devoured the noodles, washed the pot I also ate from to save on cleanup, brushed my teeth, washed my face, and stashed everything that might interest a bear in the food barrel, including soap and toothpaste in case it's a fastidious bear. Now I lean back in the camp chair near shore with my journal. What, I ask it, am I doing out here? I ask not in a doubting why-in-heaven's-name-did-I-come-out-here-anyway kind of way, but in a genuine questioning of purpose, of quest: what do I want from this week of relative solitude in the relative wilderness?

The answer flows out the end of my pen. I want to pay attention to my surroundings and be aware of – and grateful for – the rocks and boulders, the trees, and any and all animals and birds I meet on the way, except possibly bears. I want to "see" things I've never seen: the living energy of the Earth, the energy of the rocks and trees, the aura of my guardian angels, and the Presence that imbues everything. I want to know, experientially know, that I am not, am never alone. I want to rejoice, continually, in the company of angels and archangels, of trees and rocks, of winds and rains. I want the scales and veils to fall from my eyes. And the fear of bears to evaporate. I want to walk, to be fully, consciously aware of walking, with what Asante calls "the All who is in Everything."

A tall order, perhaps for a mere five days, but I figure five days in the bush is worth maybe five years of "real" life at home. And if none of my wishes for this week happens, it's enough, very much enough, simply to be here.

—————

I WAS STARTING TO get used to the fact that he knew, without the benefit of call display, that it was me. We talked every day, and when I could get away I made the three-hour drive to his place for the weekend or even a week (though I never got much work done). Shortly after our Valentine's Day reunion, we met up in Toronto, and I was delighted to find my bushman was equally at home in a city restaurant. Over calamari and Chianti, we discovered we shared a dream to live off-grid. I told him I'd always wanted to live in a log cabin, and he told me he *had* a log cabin, on a ridge in the highlands near where he grew up. We talked about embarking on a cross-park trip in Algonquin after the ice broke up. We were uncannily identical

(Gemini twins) in our tastes and favourites, everything from songs to pie flavour (he put me on the phone with his sister after I refused to believe raisin could be his favourite too). I had never felt such certainty I was meant to be with someone.

There was no doubt he felt the same. In one phone conversation when I confessed my doubt that he could so recently have loved someone else and now be loving me, he responded, "Everything I've experienced so far in my life, all the people I've experienced it with – the incredible people, yes, like the woman out west – everything has brought me to this moment and to you. We were meant to meet last August and to go on from there – to go on from *here*."

No one had ever said such a thing to me. Doubt evaporated into joy. And relief. I would not have to let go of this one.

By this time I was an old hand at "letting go." At least in the sense of surrendering potential relationships to the Universe to find out if they were meant to be. Perhaps not so much in the sense of releasing relationships that didn't work out. I had a tendency to hang on.

A poster I gave to my best friend in grade nine introduced me to the concept of letting go. It said, "If you love something set it free. If it comes back, it's yours. If it doesn't, it never was." It had an accompanying illustration of a bird sitting in the open door of a gilt cage.

My best friend and I both happened to love something. Some*one*. The *same* someone: our young, good-looking, long-haired, un-attainable history teacher. Every afternoon after school, we loaded up a plate of my friend's grandmother's baking and retreated to her bedroom, one of us curled up on the bed, the other in the mustard-coloured pod chair under the poster taped to her closet door. Between mouthfuls of exquisitely fattening squares of raspberry, chocolate, and pastry painstakingly spread in thin layers, we exchanged reports on our hunky hippie history teacher. How he had brushed by her, or squeezed the back of my neck, or yelled at us in class, or waved and smiled – "and he was at the other end of the hall, *everyone* saw – what do you think it *means*?"

We could exchange ideas for hours on what it meant. Which was, obviously, that he was in love with one of us. Which one was a matter of debate, and debate it we did. But it was a happy rivalry. Who else could so completely understand such love and longing for this cool hippie teacher? We shared the feelings as well as the object of those feelings. Who had no inkling he was being kept captive in my best friend's bedroom, let alone deprived of the choice to come back to us should we ever relinquish our hold on him. Which we had no intention of doing. It never occurred to us. Despite the urging of the poster over our heads.

When the ranger and I parted that August long weekend on Kioshkokwi, I did genuinely "let go" – I surrendered it to the Universe. I let go again after he phoned that fall. And the Universe brought him, eagerly, smittenly, back. And now there was no reason to surrender or release or stay the least bit detached. He was mine.

I DOZE AND WAKE, doze and wake. Not from nerves so much as the noise of hard-pricking rain on taut nylon. I wouldn't mind if it rained every night. What bear in its right mind would prowl around in the pouring rain?

The stirring up-and-down-the-scales song of a thrush permeates my early morning dreams. It seems to sing for hours. When daylight arrives, it stops abruptly and into the sudden silence comes a musical "glook." My wake-up call from Raven.

The raven inevitably reminds me of the ranger.

HE TRAMPED AHEAD of me on snowshoes on a warm, plus-five day, somewhere in the highlands, somewhere beyond the back of the farm where he grew up and down the road from his log cabin. It was a day of mixed sun and cloud and sudden warm breezes. I was dressed in the ranger's (on me knee-length) green Algonquin Park hoody and my own black vest, blue gaiters and red Roots Winter Olympic Games cap. Without the benefit of trails, he led me through field and bush and over hills and into woods. I didn't know how he knew where to go. I had to remind myself he had spent his whole life roaming this land.

It was my third visit, this time to his mother's home. She was away and he was here on a break from work. My own work wasn't getting done. We talked and laughed, drank wine, skied on Algonquin's groomed trails, and sang along to CDs in the car (the only hitch being we both wanted to do the harmonies).

Today, he seemed subdued. The previous week we'd met up again in Toronto to have dinner with his friends. I thought it had gone well until the ranger confessed his embarrassment and horror at what he called my "over the top" exuberance. I was too loud, he said, "too much."

I extended my stride to fit my snowshoes into his tracks and worried he was having second thoughts about "us." Worried about our recent painful conversations about my social behaviour. Did his friends, too, think I was too much? I had felt so instantly comfortable with them I had just been my joking, laughing self. My face burned in shame at the memory and what they might be thinking of me.

We came to the end of the woods and the snow, unstrapped our snowshoes and waded through brittle brown grass out onto a high, bare ridge of rock. Far below lay a frozen white sea framed by high hills of untouched bush that extended for miles.

I tore my eyes from the vista to the ranger beside me. "I hate you. You grew up here."

"It's a marsh. A huge marsh." He pointed into the distance to two rivers that flowed through, one in, one out. "I first came up here when I was ten." He looked at me. "I only bring special people up here."

Relief flooded through me. He could not be having second thoughts.

We sat on the rock and I drank in the view. Beside me I could feel the ranger's appreciation of my appreciation of his special place. I met his eyes and my breath caught in my throat. His eyes held everything: light, sparkle, intelligence, understanding. Love for this sacred marsh. And love for me. I thought I saw that too.

He looked suddenly shy. "I never felt this with anyone else I've been with... and that is" – an embarrassed laugh – "that I want to marry you." Before I could respond he rushed on. "I don't even know what it means except it hit me along with a sound like a great whooshing wind this morning in bed before you were awake, and brought me down from my high to a much more level place. Am I scaring you?"

I shook my head. I was smiling and smiling. At last I could reveal the thought that had rocketed through my brain on Kioshkokwi seven months before. Synchronicity had finally caught up with us.

"When it came to me this morning that I want to spend the rest of my life with you," he said, "it had quite a sobering effect on me – I mean in a good way."

"I thought there was a change in you today. I wasn't sure what it was."

"So…" He took a breath. "Brenda Missen, will you marry me?"

"Yes!" I laughed against his mouth, now pressed against mine. "Yes, yes, and yes."

Movement in the sky caught our attention. Directly above soared a large black bird.

The bird, a raven, suddenly swooped. It hovered in one spot for seconds at a time, opened and closed its wings, circled around and did it all again. And again. An avian performance such as I had never seen before.

Long wonderful joyful minutes later, the raven folded and opened its wings one last time over our heads and flew off.

"Thank you!" the ranger called after it. He reached into the pack, pulled out a few crackers from our picnic, and crumbled them onto the rock. At my inquiring look he said simply, "It will find them later."

Engagement photo overlooking the marsh, 1999

"In some Indigenous cultures," said Asante, when I phoned to tell her about the ranger's proposal, "Raven is the herald from the Void, which is where Great Spirit – the Divine – lives. I would say the Divine danced at your betrothal. What a wonderful blessing."

A VIGOROUS NORTH WIND flaps the tent dry on my strung-up clothesline and then pushes the canoe and me down the lake. Navigating through a huge wetland, I belt out new lyrics to an old gospel tune.

> *All night, all day, O Lordy*
> *Ravens watching over me, my Lord*
> *All night, all day*
> *Ravens watching over me.*
>
> *When I'm paddling in my canoe, O Lordy*
> *Ravens watching over me, my Lord...*
>
> *When I'm snacking on my lunch...*
> *When I'm setting up my campsite...*
> *When I'm sleeping inside my tent...*
> *Ra-a-a-vens watching over me.*

IT WAS THE RANGER who spotted it. We were on cross-country skis out on solid, snow-covered Smoke Lake on another glorious March afternoon of above-zero temperatures under a blue, blue sky. It was a few days after his proposal. We had just delivered his signed contract for his old ranger job back in this part of the park.

We skied to the point of land that marks the entrance to Cathy's bay. White and red pines rose up from the point, lushly green amid the winter landscape. Out from shore and above the lake ice and snow protruded a peninsula of sun-bared rock that was begging to have picnic fixings and ski boots strewn about. And clothing. The unfettered ease with which I tossed my layers down beside the ranger's amazed me. In my staunchly conservative Anglican household, nakedness was a private, shameful thing kept hidden behind bedroom doors. "Petting" (anything below the neck) with a boy was strictly verboten, even with clothes intact. And I definitely wasn't supposed to have sex until I was married. My involvement with the not-yet-divorced man (and subsequent flings) had helped me shake off these ultra-conservative attitudes. Nevertheless, more than vestiges of self-consciousness remained, and it wasn't my habit to walk around naked in my own home, let alone in the great outdoors.

The ranger made it okay. He was so comfortable in his (bare) skin, he made it comfortable for me too – as if I had always sat my bare rump on bare rock and piled smoked trout and brie and cilantro on crackers and fed them to a naked, sparkling-eyed park ranger beside me. Warm sun beat down on us. There wasn't a breath of wind.

We laughed and teased each other and swigged smooth, perfectly aged Côtes du Rhône straight out of the bottle because we'd forgotten to pack the plastic wine glasses.

"You forgot on purpose," declared the ranger. "You hate plastic."

"I hate plastic, but I love you."

He gave me a half-mocking besotted look. "Course you do, Treasure."

It was his new term of endearment. Sometimes he shortened it to "Treazh." If I did something particularly nice, he'd say, "It's no wonder everyone in the whole world calls you Treasure." He uttered it with just the right amount of teasing irony to save it from sappiness. The endearment came from a tender love ballad called "If I Needed You." We both knew this Townes Van Zandt song from a Lyle Lovett CD we discovered we each owned, and when I told the ranger it was my favourite on the CD, he teared up. Of the nearly two dozen tracks, it was his favourite too. We sang along with Lyle in the car, and whenever we got to the last lines – about a treasure the poor could find – the ranger gave exaggerated emphasis to the word "treasure."

Satiated now with food and wine, the ranger laid his Treasure gently back on the Smoke Lake rock. The rock welcomed my warm spine along its warm spine and the ranger's warm body crouched between my knees. Under his delicate touch, my whole body began to vibrate in tendrils of exquisite sensation that seemed to emanate as much from the pines and rock and the watchful waxing moon high above the pine spires in the deep blue of the sky as from the passionate fingers and tongue of my beloved ranger.

Somewhere under the ice beside the rocky peninsula, the gurgling and glugging of languid wave after wave against the unseen shoreline mingled with my own moans. Then I couldn't hear anything except someone yelling her ecstasy into the space around the lake. Yells that ended in long drawn-out sobs. A release of so much joy in the gift of this man in my life, of joy in my connection to the rocks and the pines and the snow and the moon, and to the man who had his mouth on the most intimate part of me, teasing out sensations as if he had years, not just weeks, of familiarity with my body. I cried, for once, in utter joy rather than aching, painful longing for something that could never be with whoever was with me, no matter how much I wanted it to be. I was where I belonged, with whom I belonged. At last.

He lifted his head. "I love that you're expressing your emotion through your tears."

Smoke Lake picnic, March 1999

That made me cry more, that my raw emotional release didn't alarm him.

We rose and half dressed, and I got out my Pentax to capture on 35-millimetre film the sun-saturated exuberant sensuality of the day.

With the sinking of the sun came a chill, and we gathered up scattered clothes and ski boots and picnic remnants, dressed, loaded up the ranger's pack, and clicked boots back into skis.

We flew back up the lake, tree shadows leaning ever farther from shore to meet us.

Up ahead, the ranger suddenly stopped and bent over as if to examine something. I caught up to see a piece of driftwood embedded in the ice. Then I saw the knobby spines. Antlers!

The ranger pointed through the ice to the broad thick beam. "A moose rack."

We chipped away with the metal tips of our ski poles but got nowhere. "We could be here all night," said the ranger. "We don't have the right equipment. The rack's pretty stuck in there. We're only seeing a small part of it – it's probably this big." He spread his arms nearly a metre.

I was sad to have to leave it behind, though unsure why I wanted it so much. I was soon caught up in our race against the sun, which dropped ever closer to the hilltops the closer we got to the landing. We lost the race, but not by much. The car heater soon had us warmed up.

The phone was ringing when we came in the door. A few minutes into the conversation, I heard the ranger describe the moose rack and its location on the lake.

"Who was that?" I asked, when he hung up.

He named another ranger. "He's going to ski in tomorrow and get it."

"And whose rack will it be?"

"Well, his. He's the one going in for it."

I looked away so he wouldn't see my disappointment.

⸺

I PUSH THROUGH A crosswind to the narrows that separate the upper part of Big Porcupine from the lower part of the lake. The waves glint with white sparkly diamond light. When someone in our family got engaged, my grandmother would say, "She got her diamond." The expression amused me, and appalled me too. As if engagement was all about the goods. The ranger didn't give me a diamond, or any symbol of betrothal. At the time I didn't even notice. I've never liked diamonds, never cared about the ring. Having someone *care* enough to pledge to spend the rest of their life with me, that's another matter.

I enter the narrows and navigate an obstacle course of just-below-the-surface rocks that are hard to see in the sun-reflecting water. Many of the boulders are decorated in bits of green and white and red – souvenirs scraped from boat bottoms. I manage to complete the course adding only one or two souvenirs of my own.

Prime rocky campsite on Big Porcupine Lake, August 2000

Camp set up on the lower part of the lake, I mould myself between the rounded roots of a large white pine and revel in the stillness, both outside and in. For this one day, my brain has stopped trying to figure things out. Not that anything has changed. I haven't found resolution or, if I'm honest, completely let go. I'm still wondering what I did wrong. I feel betrayed, not just by the ranger but by my own intuition. My intuition told me this was "The One." Intuition found me the man who was himself intuitive and sensitive, who could often read my mind, who seemed to "get" the interior journey, the man who pledged himself to me (diamond or not) and wanted to lose himself with me here in the park. There's anger too. It's sitting on simmer on the back burner, and I'm waiting for it to simmer itself dry. When that happens forgiveness will come. You can't force forgiveness. You can only pray for it, be open to it. And wait. I'm praying. I'm open. I'm waiting.

FOR THE SECOND DAY in a row, there wasn't a cloud in the sky. This time we were on our way to a lake called Pinetree that was accessible from the highway but, the ranger assured me, very private. He parked his old red Tercel on the shoulder since the parking area wasn't plowed out. The portage sign was marked 1,885 metres. I gave a laugh. "No wonder it's private."

We strapped on snowshoes and tramped through deep snow into the woods. The trail had been broken for us. I stooped to examine the tracks. They looked like very large dog prints. Wolf, said the ranger.

The tracks led us past a creek and a gully and a beautiful interior rocky cliff. At last they veered off the trail, and moments later we popped out onto the shore of a stunning snow-encased bay lined with deep-velvet-green pine, spruce, and cedar. We found a ledge of sun-dried rock just along the shore from the trail. Our clothes were soon on the rock beside us.

The ranger pulled our picnic out of the pack. He cut an avocado in half, removed the pit, piled salsa in each indentation and squirted lime on top – camper guacamole. He handed me half but I reached for him instead. It was time to return the favour of the previous day.

Gratifying yells soon echoed off the trees and rocks around the bay.

Afterwards, we spooned guacamole into each other's mouths, laughed ourselves silly, burned ourselves under the hot spring sun. The ranger pointed across the bay. "There's a ridge up there that's part of the Leaf Lake cross-country ski trail system, just over that line of trees. I hope there were people up there. I hope they heard me."

I was horrified people might have heard and impressed by the ranger's total lack of shame.

In the late afternoon chill, we retraced our tracks out to the highway. I was unstrapping my snowshoes when the ranger let out an exclamation. From the back of the wagon he lifted an enormous moose antler.

My eyes filled with tears.

"He must have had a change of heart when he saw the car. I did tell him how much you liked it."

I held the rack in my hands, marvelling at the weight of it, the both rough and smooth feel of it, the number of points protruding from the broad curved beam. Definitely, said the ranger, a mature bull. I couldn't imagine balancing a double set of these on my head.

Asante loved the story of the moose rack. "I think it was a gift for both of you," she said. "Hang on a minute. I have to read something to you."

What she read was a remarkably apt passage about moose from a book called *Medicine Cards*. She had shown me the book and accompanying deck of cards during a visit I'd made to her Vancouver home the previous year. The cards were similar to a Tarot deck, except the illustrations were of animals, each one associated with certain symbolism or medicine from the perspective of Indigenous Peoples.

"I think you guys could get a lot from this book," said Asante. "Especially with all the time you're spending in the bush."

On my next trip to Ottawa, I bought a copy. At home I read the introduction, refreshing my memory about "medicine" – anything, the authors explain, that "improves one's connection to the Great Mystery and to all life," including through the healing of body, mind, or spirit, or the gaining of wisdom or understanding. All animals, they write, have distinctive habits and traits that can relay these healing messages if we pay attention. The book includes more than fifty animal summaries, derived from teachings handed down by elders of various nations. Teachings the authors feel need to be released beyond their own culture to help everyone understand our human connection to Mother Earth and all her creatures.

I found another book, too, *Animal-Speak: The Spiritual & Magical Powers of Creatures Great & Small* – a kind of animal dictionary with summaries of the biological characteristics of more than a hundred birds, mammals, insects, and reptiles, along with the different lore associated with each one in traditional cultures around the world. It seemed to me a perhaps unique combining of science and spirituality. A quote the author includes from Pawnee Chief Letakots-Lesa helped me make sense of the interconnection of people, animals, and the Creator:

> In the beginning of all things, wisdom and knowledge were with the animals, for Tirawa, the One Above, did not speak directly to man. He sent certain animals to tell men that he showed himself through the beasts, and that from them, and from the stars and the sun and the moon, should man learn... for all things tell of Tirawa.

With all the time I was now spending in the bush with the ranger, I resolved to pay more attention.

The ranger was gratifyingly receptive to these readings. And we were both amazed, and amused, by one paragraph in the *Medicine Cards*' description of Moose.

> The bellow of a male moose... represents his willingness to "tell the world" about his feelings. This... is not a seeking of approval, but rather an enjoyment of sharing because of the spontaneous explosion of joy that comes from the deepest part of one's being.

A LOUD SHRIEK JOLTS me awake. It goes on and on, seems to be moving right down the middle of the lake. Just a loon, I tell myself, a freaked-out loon.

For the second night in a row, rain beats down on the tent. The sound is deafening. Finally, I fall back to sleep. A snapping wakes me. A branch, I tell myself, breaking off a tree. *Not* a bear stomping through the underbrush toward my tent.

Just as I begin to doze off, the noisy rain starts again. Sleep doesn't return until faint grey tinges the sky.

The morning lake is a mirror. The rocks are warm. No campsites in view. No canoes. No winds. No rains. All is still and serene. And this lake, Harness, is as far from civilization as I'm going to get. Tonight will be spent on a lake that hosts a girls' camp. I may as well stick around awhile.

I spread out every piece of gear to send the night's soggy offerings back into the atmosphere and plunk myself and my journal down in the middle of it all. The bush, I'm discovering this week, isn't a place of loneliness, or even solitude. It's too alive, with rocks and trees, waters and winds, rains and thunder, and creatures, great and small – moose and muskrats and mosquitoes. Alive with conversation too, and not just with fellow portagers. It strikes me there's been a continuous dialogue going on, all day, every day, either silently in my head or aloud in my song. A dialogue between me and the environment and the elements. My waking thoughts have been one continuous prayer of gratitude and supplication. Supplication to the Earth to hold off the rain storms until I'm in safe territory, to grant me a good campsite, to keep the bears away. Gratitude for tailwinds and sun-warmed gear-drying rocks and bears kept away. Gratitude, too, for my strong legs and strong shoulders and my strong battered heart.

Serene Harness Lake, August 2000

THE FANTASY FOUND me somewhere on the highway on an April visit to the ranger. It followed in the wake of a long terrible phone conversation about all my male friends. He didn't know how to sort them out, who they were, how I felt about each one, how they felt about *me*. I knew why I had ended up with so many male friends but was at a loss how to explain to the ranger. On the highway, my mind made up a story that he became so wracked with unwarranted jealousy he broke off our relationship. I found a place on my own in rural Ontario and sank into a mourning far deeper than any I'd experienced in my long history of breakups. A constant sick feeling in my stomach prevented me from eating, and I began to physically waste away, as the ranger had when we were together because he was so eaten by jealousy. I became a complete recluse and, incidentally, a prolific author of literary novels. Months, or years, later, the ranger found me. In my mind I saw him walk up the long drive and imagined the sober meeting of our eyes.

That's as far as it went. No matter how many times I replayed it on the drive to the ranger's, the story got stuck at the moment our eyes met on the driveway. I could create neither a resumption of our relationship nor a final parting of the ways. It was like the needle of a record stuck in a groove.

I PICK MY CAREFUL WAY through the muddy rock garden of a trail over to Head Lake and find myself with the sudden hope that Cathy and the kids won't be at the cottage when I arrive tomorrow. I want to complete the whole trip on my own and have the bunkie to myself. Though it's a wonder that haven hasn't been spoiled for me.

I MADE THE DRIVE, canoe on car, from Chelsea to Smoke Lake to paddle to the bunkie for a few days to write. It was the middle of June, and Cathy and her family hadn't arrived yet for the summer. The ranger was to join me at the end of his work days. He could borrow a motorboat from the docks at the park hangar, which happened to be on Smoke too.

For the past couple of months he had been back at his old job, supervising a crew of junior rangers in trail clearing and campsite maintenance. Sometimes the park plane flew them to interior lakes and they camped out for the week. There had been more awkward moments between us, more censure from the ranger about my overly exuberant social self. I didn't know anymore what was appropriate and shrank into myself. After each social event I quizzed him: "Was I okay?" Even as he assured me I was, he seemed to grow more distant, and to avoid any conversation about our future. The last time we'd ventured there, many weeks before, was to muse on when we should get married. We had – no surprise given our ever-increasing mental connection – come up with the same date, the day between our birthdays. It even fell on a Saturday this year. At the time of our conversation it seemed so soon, only a couple of months away, yet I couldn't imagine waiting another year. Now that date had passed.

I docked at the bunkie, unpacked, and forced myself to work on chapter revisions.

At the sound of a motor in the bay I looked up. My guest puttered in with a pensive look, a cooler of beers, and a small bouquet of wildflowers in his travel mug.

I cooked pasta with marinara sauce in Cathy's fire pit.

"You look very at home cooking over a fire."

"You should come into the park with me, and you'll find out just how at home I am in the bush." I tried to keep the reproach out of my voice. Nearly July, and we still hadn't got into the park on a real trip. We had canoed together only twice and those only short day trips.

"I need to come to a different perspective on canoeing. When I first became a ranger I used to go in for ten nights at a time to do campsite maintenance with a partner. The trips I do now with my crew are shorter, but the last thing I want to do when I come out of the bush is go for a paddle." He gave me a look. "You don't want to hear this, do you?"

I gave a sad smile. This was a far cry from the enthusiasm he had exuded in the winter. His current unwillingness was understandable. But understanding doesn't necessarily lessen disappointment.

We ate supper by candlelight and mosquito whine. I drank too much wine because the ranger didn't share the bottle with me but stuck to his beer. When the bugs became too much, we carried the candles into the bunkie and lay down on the futon to watch the erratic flickers of light on the rough ceiling boards.

The wine gave me courage. I spoke to the flickering ceiling. "I've felt this distance between us and I don't know if it's my imagination or if you feel it too."

"It's not your imagination."

I turned to him in relief. "Do you know which one of us is the source?"

He rose on one elbow. "It's me. I don't know what it is. I've been trying to sort out where it's coming from. I didn't want to say anything until I figured it out."

"*Talk* to me. I'm going crazy in my head. Maybe talking will help you figure it out."

Silence.

"Does it have to do with our future? We haven't talked about getting married for a long time now."

He admitted our future was the root of the problem.

I hesitated, then put into words something I had considered saying for several weeks. "Would you like to be released from your marriage proposal?"

A long pause, and then, almost in a whisper, "Yes."

A calmness overtook me. "I release you."

He didn't respond.

"How do you feel?"

"Released."

"Released from what?"

"Not released *from*, released *to*. To a place where I can communicate with you again."

"Why didn't you *say* something?"

"I didn't feel I could, because, you know, I asked."

I took it a step further. "Would it bring you more relief if we don't assume we're going to move in together in the fall?"

Another pause, then, "Yes."

"Would it be better if I found my own place for the summer?"

He stopped me there.

We got up to get ready for bed. I felt agitated. I needed him to say something, to assure me he was still there.

Back in bed, candles extinguished, we lay in silence until I couldn't take it any longer. I spoke into the dark. "There are two things I want to tell you. I would rather have you than your proposal. And I would rather know you were *in* your heart than *have* your heart." The words came out as if spoken by someone else. I felt their impact on the ranger. Still, he said nothing.

"I've all but untied you from the dock and set you adrift," I said, near tears. "I need to know just how far adrift you're going."

That elicited a sympathetic squeeze on my arm. "Not that far."

"I need to hear *words* from you."

"I love you, you *know* that."

"I need to *hear* it." And I dissolved into tears.

He held me. "I need time to absorb what we've said."

"My big lesson in life *always* seems to be about letting go," I sobbed, "but I can't let go of you." I caught myself. "Unless. Unless it's what *you* want."

"It's *not* what I want. You're a fantastic person."

I could feel he meant it. It didn't help. The word "fantastic" felt so cold. The cold of a chasm that our conversation seemed to have only made wider.

I barely slept. I listened to the ranger's steady breathing and told myself the lesson was not about letting *him* go. It was, forever and continually, to let go of my attachment to the future. To live in the present moment, where life actually takes place. A hard place to live.

⟝━━⬥

A SHORT, WIDE CHANNEL of water separates Cache Lake from my destination on Tanamakoon. Thankfully the portages are over for the day. Eight kilometres of walking with a canoe and a double load of packs is enough.

At the end of the channel, a frog hops off a lily pad and kicks away under the water.

THREE SETS OF BUBBLE eyes faced me from a small indentation in a rock pooled with water. I sat just above it, on dry rock, on a warm morning in early July. The frogs, I hoped, had some special medicine for me. It was why I had brought my stressed-out self here to my mother's cousin's cottage in Haliburton: to heal. The plan when I sublet my room for this summer's writing vacation had been to spend it with the ranger, but being with him was just too painful.

Despite the pain, I was trying to stay open and loving. Really, I had no choice. Maybe for the first time in my life I was committed, for better or worse. I figured we were into the worse. I figured he just needed to retreat to a safer place and we could carry on, at a slower, more reasonable pace, to marriage.

To my own amazement, I slid into a mind-absorbing routine: morning meditation, spiritual reading, stretches, coffee, breakfast, three or four hours on my laptop, a break for a run and a swim, another few hours down on the rock by the water with notebook and pen. Dinner and an evening paddle with my cousin.

The frogs watched me open *Buddhism Plain and Simple*. The suggestion to do some reading on Buddhism had come from Asante, who thought I might benefit from the emphasis it places on waking up to the reality of what *is*. I had tried a book by a Tibetan author but found it hard going. This one, by an American Zen priest named Steve Hagen, put Buddhism into language I could understand. Enlightenment, said Hagen, is "nothing more or less than *seeing* things as they are rather than as we wish or believe them to be."

All I had to do when my mind got going was to bring myself back to seeing. Simply by *seeing* the state of my mind and my inclinations toward this and away from that, I was awake. There was some relief in this idea. I couldn't change the current circumstances with the ranger, *or* my mind's wild machinations, but I could *see*. I could see he was struggling with whether he could be with me and with issues that had nothing to do with me. I could see he was only half present when he *was* with me. Most of all, I could see that his half-presence was a source of great pain for me. I had nanoseconds of peace when I focused on "just seeing."

Evenings were spent attached to the phone cord attached to the old beige rotary-dial phone attached to my cousin's cottage wall. Our conversations went around in circles. I had no idea if we were going to survive. Whether we did or not, I still wanted to move back to Ontario and knew I needed to look for a place for myself for the fall.

My other calls were to Asante.

"Stop trying so hard," she counselled.

"But when I stop, I get into all the pain."

"I mean stop trying to change him. Accept him as he is, and I mean as he is right now."

"Even if he's not *there*?"

"Even then," she said gently. "You can make your own choice about that."

Would you use any of the following words to describe your condition: tired, overloaded, harried, frustrated, guilty, itchy, nervous, at a loss, empty, or weakened? If so, take a break and allow yourself to bathe in the waters of Frog medicine.

⸺

THE BEST CAMPSITE on Tanamakoon turns out to be located right across the bay from the girls' camp. I tell myself one night in a noisy camp bay won't kill me. Happily, the west side of the site has its own little bay, out of view and hearing of the camp, a bay that turns entirely, brilliantly gold, both sky and water, in the wake of the setting sun.

⸺

I TRIED AGAIN TO STAY with the ranger, after the third annual Auntie Brenda/Niece Harriet canoe trip in August, but he was still so distant. He offered me the use of his log cabin for the rest of my summer writing vacation. The cabin sits on a high ridge just a few kilometres (as the raven flies) from the ridge where he proposed to me. It faces a stunning view overlooking rugged hills surrounding a tiny snaking blue ribbon of creek that leads to one of the lakes in the vast marsh.

Sunrise mist over highland-surrounded marsh, 1999

On weekends, the ranger made the hour-long drive from the park. I almost preferred the time without him, when I could give my mind and heart a break from the long, exhausting conversations that went nowhere and the pain of feeling so blocked off from someone sitting in the same room. Through it all, he assured me he didn't want to break up.

If circumstances between us had been loving and harmonious, I would have been supremely content. I loved living off the grid. Every day I collected water from the rain barrel and stoked the fire in the big old cook stove to heat both the cabin and the water in the stove's reservoir. I used the heated water for the dishes and for the portable shower on the porch. In the evenings I lit the porch lanterns and the oil lamps inside, and read by their soft glow. I stored perishables in a cooler and replaced the ice every few days. I recharged my laptop battery from the car.

As I carried out these modern-pioneer tasks, it became clear this was the area where I wanted to live. It had nothing to do with my hopes for the ranger and me. I made sure I was honest with myself about that. I had hopes, no question, but if we broke up I knew I still wanted to move to the area. I had found my Ontario Canadian Shield country.

Once a week I made the winding drive down to the general store for the local paper to scan the classifieds for a rental. At the end of August I found it, a small winterized cottage on the river. Available October first.

I arranged to stay at the ranger's cabin until the end of September. In the middle of the month I drove back to Chelsea for a couple of days to attend to some business matters. I returned to the cabin to find a fuzzy pink slipper that wasn't mine wedged between the wall and the couch. When the ranger arrived that evening he admitted he had brought two young female work colleagues to see the cabin, and they had ended up spending the night. He was, he said, enjoying a new feeling of attraction with one of the young women, though nothing had "happened" and he wasn't even sure he wanted to pursue it.

His admission kicked me in the stomach. I couldn't bring myself to sleep with him. I couldn't sleep at all. I sat up in a chair and journaled by lamplight. Just before dawn, I dressed and made my slow, tear-streaked way down the long, deep-rutted lane to the county road below. On the narrow empty road, I walked north.

The wildflowers were my angels of comfort. They bloomed every which way at the road sides. I had never even noticed them before. As the sun rose, daylight coloured them into pinks and yellows, purples and whites. I stopped to admire their delicate petals, and, in a gesture even more unlike me, began to pick them: black-eyed Susans, red clover, white daisies, a few stalks of snake grass, and many I couldn't name. Each flower was another tear stopped, another consoling sight for my bruised heart. By the time the sun peaked over the tree tops, I had a huge bouquet.

I passed by a driveway that led to a white clapboard farmhouse. I walked on until I spotted a dilapidated box trailer parked in a field beyond a row of trees. Beside it sat a big grey boat of a car. Someone was moving about. I turned around, not wanting to meet anyone.

I hadn't got far past the farmhouse when the sound of a vehicle prompted me onto the shoulder. Instead of passing, the car came to a stop beside me. The big grey boat.

The driver rolled down the window, and a kindly weathered face with warm brown eyes behind thick black-rimmed glasses smiled. "Hello. Can I give you a lift?"

"Oh, no thanks, I'm just out for a morning walk." I gestured down the road and explained I was visiting the ranger.

The gentleman – for that is what he seemed, even wearing a faded lumberjack shirt and worn brimless cap – touched hand to cap and bade me good morning. To my astonishment, instead of driving on, he put the car into reverse. The sight of the car slowly backing up the road brought the first real smile to my face in days. Little risk of anyone colliding with him on this backroad so early in the morning.

The ranger was up, making coffee. He took in my exhausted, puffy-eyed face with a look of concern. I handed him the bouquet and told him about the man in the car on the road.

"That's Murray Prentice. He used to live in his car, but now he lives in a little trailer in my neighbours' field."

"He lived in his *car*?"

The ranger fished in the cupboard for a vase. "Not just any car – a two-seater Triumph Spitfire. He used to call it his moon module. It's still there in the field. I think it's only duct tape holding it together now."

"Moon module?" I was still trying to wrap my brain around the idea that someone could live in a car let alone a tiny sports car.

"Maybe because it went so fast he thought it could blast him to the moon. He kind of opted out of life after his wife left him. He had a long battle with drink, though I think he's put that behind him." He found what he was looking for – a mottled white ceramic jug – filled it with water, arranged the flowers in it and set it on a table on the porch. Amid all my pain, the bouquet, and the ranger's attention to it, brought me joy. And so did Murray Prentice, who had driven his big grey boat of a car out to offer the wildflower-laden lass a lift (and no doubt satisfy his curiosity) and then simply reversed back up the road to his trailer.

———

I STAND ON THE SHORE and make a futile attempt to capture the sky's golden splendour inside my camera. The colours fade to grey. Above me comes the distinctive whisper of wings. I look up to see a large black bird fly right over my head.

I call out a happy good night. I have become quite bonded with Raven this past year.

THE CAR WAS LOADED, the ranger at work. I was about to make the drive home to pack my life into a U-Haul and move to a cottage in this isolated area where he was practically the only person I knew. And it looked less and less like we were going to survive. I tried to keep the panic at bay.

I paused beside the car to take in the cabin's panoramic view one more time, the trees now turning to brilliant shades of red and gold. Would I ever look out over this view again? If I did, would I always associate it with this terrible pain?

Through the blur of tears something caught my eye. A large black bird had sailed in close to the ridge top. There it stayed, before me at eye level, making slow soaring circles just out from the ridge. Its underside was iridescent – somehow a pale black or even a deep dark velvet brown.

I stretched out my arms to the raven and wept anew, this time though in the way a child does at the arrival of a soothing parent. I felt the raven's love and solace at some level beyond my pain. They entered my being, not erasing the hurt but sitting with it, an equal but infinitely gentler Presence.

The raven flew off, and I called out my thank you. Then I got in the car and made the three-hour drive to Chelsea to pack up my life.

Raven magic is a powerful medicine that can give you the courage to enter the darkness of the void, which is the home of all that is not yet in form.

I HEAD TO THE EDGE of the dark woods to brush my teeth. The whisper of raven wings still echoes in my head. God, I have been learning this past year, is just there, wherever, in the world, or in your heart, you are. Cartwheeling in joy for your joy, or soaring in solace for your sorrow.

O UR RELATIONSHIP continued to crumble. I moved into my new home on the river in the fall and tried to stay open without having a breakdown. A permanent knot in my stomach prevented me from eating. Bedtime, which usually leads me into deep and uninterrupted sleep for eight or nine hours, became a time of dread, knowing I would wake up at 3:00 a.m. and lie awake prey to my thoughts. I had just moved to an isolated part of Ontario, two or three hours away from supportive friends and family. Just about the only person I knew was the man who had retreated so far it looked like we were going to break up for good.

He came over a few times. He got on the phone to find someone to plow my road through the winter and someone else to bring me ten cords of wood. He brought cedar lengths and split them into kindling for me. The one time he stayed for dinner, I couldn't eat.

My lack of appetite and sleep was sapping my strength. Usually a strong cyclist and skier, swimmer and hiker, now I could only go for unhurried walks in the woods. When each load of wood arrived, I had to pace myself, stacking slow row by slow row. My energy was depleted not just from these past few weeks but, it seemed, from a lifetime of "effort." A lifetime of my heart's efforts to love and please God – and half a lifetime trying to love and please my various boyfriends. It never occurred to me to let God or my partner love *me*. If I felt loved it was because I felt I had "earned" it by my efforts to be "good." To be "good enough." I didn't expect the ranger, or anyone, to love me when I was weak, when I was weepy or needy or jealous or insecure. I didn't feel like the ranger's treasure, and – a stunning realization – never had. Not because of anything he might or might not feel, but because the concept was too foreign. It was the joking way he'd spoken the endearment that had made it okay.

I placed another log on the row and the words from the *Book of Common Prayer* came, unbidden but all too naturally: *We are not worthy so much as to gather up the crumbs under thy Table.*

What was blocking me from receiving, it was now so obvious, was that ingrained sense of unworthiness that had been reinforced in prayer every Sunday in church for so many years. It was no wonder I had never felt like anyone's treasure. The negativity of that prayer had become ingrained, apparently, in the very fibre of my being. Never mind all the years of affirmations; I fundamentally didn't think I was worthy of having all that love and joy heaped on my head.

On my long, slow walks, I came up with a new tape to play over the old: *I am worthy so much as to share in all the abundance that is on thy table.* If I said it often enough maybe I would come to believe it. Though I knew it would take more than the repetition of positive affirmations. That was just treating the symptoms. It was time to truly, fundamentally know, in the core of my being, I was worthy of being loved. Time to allow myself to be cherished – treasured – just for being me. Just for being.

And so, over those fragile fall months, I tentatively opened myself up to being loved. And Mother Earth, and all her creatures, responded. I would look out my front window, to the oaks sheltering the house, to the crooked red pine on the shore doing its imitation of Tom Thomson's *West Wind* painting, to the blue waters of the wide river beyond the shoreline pines. And there it would be. I would go for slow walks in the woods, and stretch my head back to see the ravens and hawks flying overhead. I would look down and catch glimpses of the squirrels and porcupines and other creatures going about their lives in the woods around me. And there it would be. In everything – above me, below me, around me. Love. Caring. Protection.

ONLY ONE MORE night to go with flimsy nylon between me and the night-roving bears. I look up into a hole in the clouds where stars shine through and breathe from my diaphragm. It comes to me with certain knowledge: there are no bears lurking here.

The familiar gong of the bell pulls me out of sleep. It's the summer of 1975 and I'm curled up in my cozy blue flannel plaid-lined Canadian Tire sleeping bag on a narrow cot in a big canvas tent with my counsellor and tent mates. I pull the bag over my head. It's just cruel to wake up kids at seven during the summer holidays and send them down to wash in the cold lake. But, hey, wait a minute, our wake-up call is a shrill whistle, not a bell. Is it the breakfast gong? Have I slept in?

I sit up in alarm and take in my surroundings. Then I smile and snuggle back down into my Polarguard 3D nylon North Face bag on my thin air-filled Therm-a-Rest. This bell isn't gonging for my campmates and me at Pioneer Camp. This bell is across the lake, two dozen years later, rousing the girls at Camp Tanamakoon.

I WENT TO CAMP – an interdenominational, evangelical Christian camp my parents chose only because the neighbours' kids went – the first two weeks of July for six years. The irony of my faithful attendance is I didn't even like the camping part of camp – the canoeing or swimming or campcraft classes. I preferred the sedentary activities: Quiet Time in the tent before breakfast where we read the daily lesson from the *Keynotes* Bible study aid, Bible Study class after breakfast, and, my favourite, Rest Hour after lunch, when I could lie on my cot and read and write letters to friends and family. On Sunday mornings, we shook the wrinkles out of the one skirt or dress crammed in our duffle bag and walked around the lake, or paddled across it, to Chapel Point. Once each two-week session the preacher was Bernie Smith, a handsome Black man with a warm smile who was a world-renowned worship leader with Inter-Varsity Christian Fellowship, the organization that had founded Pioneer. He could make a Bible story that happened thousands of years ago sound like it could have happened today. He made Abraham talk like a hippie, saying "Hey, man" to God. He had us all laughing but his message was serious.

The message – one I had not heard in my church – was that we could have a personal relationship with Jesus. More than dying for our sins, Jesus was the Living Christ. That meant I could invite him into my heart and he would come to live inside me and guide my life. This, said Bernie Smith, was what Jesus meant when he said, "If any man would come after me, let him deny himself and take up his cross and follow me." Denying myself meant turning from my selfish ways and letting Jesus live through me. It meant accepting Jesus as my Personal Saviour.

I wanted earnestly to accept Jesus as my Saviour, and did accept him, too many times to count. It never seemed to take. I didn't have a story. One defining moment that changed my life. I longed for a story, like the other girls had.

Once or twice a session there was a special witnessing campfire. We gathered in the rustic lodge in our pyjamas and sat on blankets on the floor or on the mismatched sagging couches, and a counsellor or camper would stand up to tell how Jesus had come and melted their hard and selfish heart. They might recount some miracle that had accompanied the event, a dramatic healing or being literally knocked off their feet by a Higher Power. The stories were always moving. There would be sniffles around the room. Others would be inspired to give their own testimony. And we would all be urged, in a wash of emotion, to be witnesses for Christ. And I, also in a wash of emotion, would feel confused and left out. Did Jesus actually come to the other girls? Did they *see* him? How come I couldn't see him or feel his presence? It was a source of great, secret pain that Jesus never knocked me off my feet, or even just came and calmly answered my knock and came to live inside me. I felt I had been cheated out of a meaningful, personal experience of him because I had always gone to church, always tried to be good, to be unselfish and help others. Still, I beat myself up for not having a conversion experience, for obviously having too many doubts for Jesus to come to me.

I never spoke about this to anyone, and if I had my counsellors would have been shocked. I was an articulate and earnest participant in Bible Study. I had all the "right" answers. It was a failing in me, I knew, not in "the Way" laid out before me.

Yet, even as I longed for it, the idea scared me. If Jesus came to live inside me, what would happen to *me*?

———

What a friend we have in Jeee-sus
All our sins and griefs to bear
What a privilege to carrrrrry
Everything to God in prayer.

I warble the old-time hymn on my hunt for firewood; I promised myself a bannock baked over a campfire for breakfast. I interrupt my singing to address the woods: "Please, could you put some nice thick dry branches in my way that I can chop with the heel of my hiking boots?"

The woods comply. I drag several dead spindly spruce saplings back to camp. Beside the fire pit, I lean each thick branch against a rock and step down hard, snapping the brittle wood into kindling length. I gather twigs and birch bark and lay a fire.

Out of a zip-lock bag, I spoon a cup of flour premixed with baking powder, salt and sugar, combine it with water to make a sticky dough, and press it into the pot lid greased with melted butter. We baked something similar at camp, made from Bisquick. Doughboys, we called them. We wrapped a blob of the sticky dough around a stick and charred it over a fire we had to make ourselves in campcraft class (which one year was pretentiously renamed outdoor living).

The golden brown bannock flips easily out of the pan. The size of a very thick pancake but dense like bread. I slather half with butter and maple syrup (at camp it was margarine).

To get the morning sun I can't hide away in the little private bay. I make my way down to the shore that faces the camp. The other side of the lake is alive with laughter and high-pitched voices and shrill blows of a whistle. To my amazement, it doesn't bother me at all. It's friendly, happy noise. I sip coffee and eat bannock and lick leftover syrup off the plate. Cooking breakfast over a morning fire always gives me a great sense of satisfaction.

The whole trip has been satisfying. There's been "weather," yes, but after the rain always gear-drying winds. The portages have been easy, my fellow portagers friendly, and I haven't met a single bear. I can do this. I can be out here on my own. It hits me on the third sip of coffee, the *reason* I can be here. It's staring at me from across the lake: camp.

The revelation stuns me. My memories of Pioneer are mixed at best. But that's where it began – learning to swim, to canoe, to build campfires (nearly always, it seemed, in the rain), to waterproof my sleeping bag in a groundsheet and secure it with thick string wound in a complicated system of knots in the days before dry bags.

To have faith, too. There's no question my relationship with God got honed at camp, no matter what I might now think about my earnest, fundamentalist teenage self.

I carry dishes, pot of warm water, and biodegradable soap into the woods. Camping skills and faith, they've always been inextricably linked in my mind. It's another jolting revelation. The sacredness of camping was instilled into me at Pioneer.

Bending over the soapy dishes, I suddenly sit back on my heels and laugh out loud. If the camp leaders had been asked to predict which camper would most likely be out putting her tripping skills to use two dozen years later on her own, my name wouldn't even have made the list. My last summer as a camper, I skipped the intermediate canoeing classes where I would have perfected the art of "singling" (what we called soloing then). Our tent group snuck back into camp from the obligatory overnight at a site across the lake so we could sleep on our "luxurious" cots. And, crowning glory of my antipathy, I turned down the invitation to go on a three-day canoe trip. It was considered a great honour. I could think of no greater horror. I flatly refused in a way that surprises me now; I was not an assertive kid.

I scrub bits of burned bannock off the pot lid and muse that if the leaders had to base their prediction on who would have the *faith* to go into the backcountry on her own, it might have been a different story. They might have seen that the seeds were being sown on good soil – though they might not appreciate the unorthodox garden that has ultimately grown from those seeds.

I don't actually think of it as faith. Asante's word "knowing" is a good one. Doubts about Jesus aside, I've always had a knowing inside about my connection to the Divine source of my being, even as the years have changed my perception of it.

I carry the dishes back to the fire pit, steeped in memories. The wonder is I kept going back, every summer for six years. I got my Canadian Red Cross senior swimming badge and my junior canoeing and my advanced outdoor living. One day, the gods inside me must have known, I would be glad I'd learned such things.

The downpour and I dock at the same time. I run for the bunkie and twist the broken lock off the latch with a prayer of gratitude to the weather gods for holding back the rain until I got here. There's no sign of Cathy and kids. My solitude will continue.

Rain hammers down on the roof. I glance in the mirror on the back wall and am stunned by what greets me there. My eyes are bluer than I've ever seen them. Filled with luminous intensity. They look like portals to a blue-sky lake I've swallowed up inside.

The room suddenly brightens: the sun must be trying to peek through the rain clouds. I run out into the light sprinkle and, sure enough, stretched over the spruce spires at the marshy end of the bay next to Cathy's cottage glows an entire upside-down beaming smile of a rainbow. A rainbow that lasts, unheard of in my previous experience of rainbows, almost an hour.

Hour-long full rainbow over Smoke Lake, August 2000

With the rainbow comes release. I've done it: completed a canoe trip on my own. From the dock, I watch the sky's magic through smiling tears and speak my gratitude. I feel saturated with the Earth's Love. See it in every waving branch of every tree under the rainbow. Feel its energy in every rock and ripple of water, and especially in this glowing rainbow. Feel it inside me. I've just *seen* it, blazing out of my eyes.

Sleep comes immediately in the deluxe futon bed. Sometime later though, I wake. Through the mullioned window, a bright star shines in the black sky. It's soon overtaken by a curtain of what looks like rain. Except the curtain begins to shimmer…

I'm outside in a flash. Sure enough the whole (clear) sky is shimmering in white light. And it's cold! Back inside I go to pull on every piece of warm clothing in my sack. Outside again, I glance up from tying boot laces to see a shooting star. And another. The Perseids! I laugh out loud. The Universe has pulled out all the stops.

I snuggle under a fleece blanket in the deck chair to watch the show. Huge white curtains of light drift across the sky. The shimmering curtain transforms into the magnificent tail of a dove, then, briefly, the whole dove, and then, for the longest time, the wing of an angel. Accompanied by stars free-falling out of the sky. I count fourteen in half an hour.

Long after the lightshow fades, I stay wrapped under the blanket. Overwhelmed to have been woken up to receive this gift of northern lights after yesterday's prolonged rainbow. To have, yes, seen energies that are beyond my usual vision. My prayer for the week has truly been answered, and then some. More than seeing is understanding, in an even deeper experiential way, what that energy *is*: a Presence, a Love and Protection, that is eternal. And personal. I am loved more deeply and unconditionally than I ever could be by another human being. My Father, my Mother, my Creator, the source and sustenance of my being, is out here with me, watching over me every minute of the day and night. I see Him, black-winged against a blue sky. I feel Her in each conscious step on hallowed ground and in each paddle stroke on eternally flowing waterways.

The mist-coated morning seems to match my grogginess as I stumble up to the outhouse. A sudden splashing reaches my ears. Absently I put it down to shore-beating waves from the wake of a motorboat, though I haven't heard one. Then I hear moans. *Moans?*

I race down to the dock. The little marsh is enshrouded in an even thicker mist. A sudden parting reveals dark silhouettes of a moose cow and calf swimming to the portage across the bay. They step up onto the shore and disappear into the trees. They leave behind a commotion of splashing and moaning in the marsh. In the sun-shot mist I catch sight of a large head with a magnificent rack. I'm amazed. I've never known a bull to hang out with his family.

Invisible in the mist, Papa moose moans and splashes his way over to the portage trail, and I get another brief glimpse before he disappears into the bush after his family. Even though he's out of sight, I can still hear him moaning and groaning his way through the forest parallel to the shore, a moaning disembodied voice that might be the woods themselves sounding their joy.

Happy solo paddler, final day of Smoke Lake loop, August 2000

3

BUSH ANGELS

Canoe Lake to Little Otterslide Lake, plus unplanned
Head Lake: August 14–20, 2000

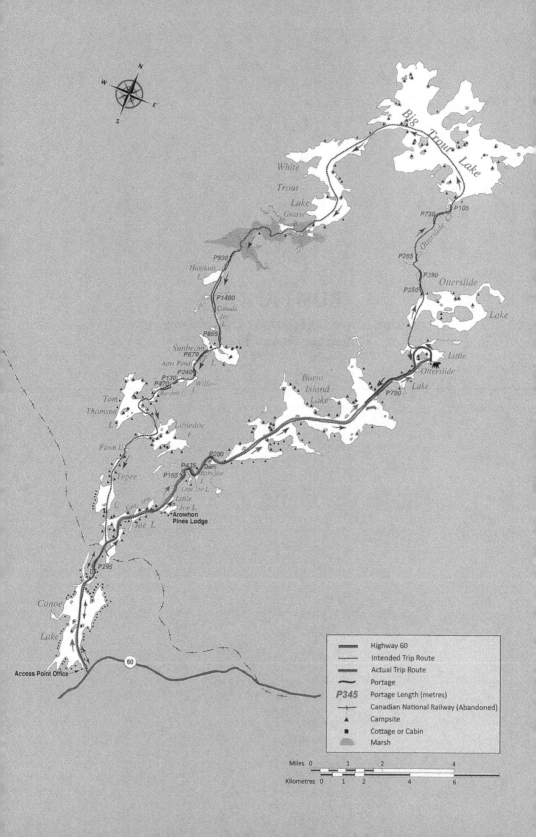

N
W E
S

Big Trout Lake

White
Trout
Lake
Grassy B.

P736
P105

P930
Hawkins L.

Otterslide Cr.

P265
P390
P250

Otterslide

P1400
Canada Jay

P855
Sunbeam L.
P670
Aster Pond
P240
P130
P470
Willow L.
Bartlett L.

Little
Otterslide
Lake
P790

Tom
Thomson
L.

Littledoe L.

Fawn L.

Burnt
Island
Lake

P200
P135 Dam
P165 *Babyliee*
Lost Joe L.

Tepee L.

East Arm

Little
Joe L.
**Arowhon
Pines Lodge**

Joe L.

P295

Canoe
Lake

Access Point Office

60

▬▬▬	Highway 60
··········	Intended Trip Route
▬ ▬ ▬	Actual Trip Route
〰	Portage
P345	Portage Length (metres)
┼┼┼	Canadian National Railway (Abandoned)
▲	Campsite
■	Cottage or Cabin
▧	Marsh

Miles 0   1   2   4
Kilometres 0   1   2   4   6

"COLOUR OF YOUR CANOE?" The park attendant's eyes are trained on the screen.

From the other side of the counter, Harriet and I watch her type the information for our permit. Under her sunhat, my niece reminds me of myself at fifteen, about to go off to summer camp. Though I would never have agreed to a week-long canoe trip with my aunt, even if I'd had one who went anywhere near a canoe. We don't look particularly related. Her skin is pale, where mine has a naturally high colour intensified by the sun, and her hair is thick and curly and brown.

"Tent fly colour?" "Licence plate?" The attendant types my responses.

I have a question of my own, a broken-record question I asked a week ago, before my solo trip from Smoke Lake, and again when I came out two days ago: "Have you caught those bears yet?"

The attendant looks up. "We still have bear problems."

"What exactly are the bear problems?"

"People are seeing bears, and bears are getting into food packs."

"Are people being attacked?"

"We've had no reports of that this summer." She assures us the wardens are on the job, trying to lure the bear into a live trap with fried bacon. (Only one bear now, I note.) She undoes her assurance by admitting the bear is going to every campsite except the one with the wardens' treats. "Make sure you burn all your burnable garbage and hang the rest with your food."

"We have a barrel," says Harriet.

"And I'll be hanging it," I add.

The attendant recites our lake destinations for the next six nights: "Joe, Little Otterslide, Big Trout, White Trout, Sunbeam, Tepee."

It's my most ambitious loop yet. Harriet may be only fifteen but she's proved her mettle on our three previous trips. Unfortunately, Little Otterslide is one of the lakes where the bears are carrying out their raids. It's not that unusual. This is the area of the park where all the novice campers come because the portages are so short.

"If you do see one," the attendant is saying. "try to make yourself look big. Use your paddles. Make a lot of noise. Bang on your pots and pans."

I don't tell her how unappealing this adversarial approach is, even if I could work up the nerve to confront a bear this way. I think of Asante's words: "Bless the bears." That was the subject line of her email response to my considerable indecision about where to go. By the time I arrived home from my solo trip it was too late to book another route – the park requires seventy-two hours' notice. Asante recounted how she'd spent several days in the mountains with a group from the drug rehabilitation centre in Vancouver where she now works as assistant counsellor. "We didn't know there were bears close by until one did a tour of the camp. We had food for twenty, and none was touched. I was in my tent and heard the bear walk by and I had no fear. That was amazing."

Her words brought resolve: we were not going to change our plans. It was time to face my fear – a fear so out of proportion with the harmony I otherwise feel in the back country. When we arrived at the Canoe Lake parking lot, I shared my resolve with Harriet. "We're going to send the bears benevolent you-stay-out-of-our-way-and-we'll-stay-out-of-yours messages. There's no reason we can't co-exist in harmony out there."

Harriet agreed. "And Mummy said she'd pray for us not to come to any harm."

"Asante said she would too. So," I took a brave breath, "let's go in and get our permit."

Out on the big lake, the winds are remarkably calm. Harriet leans back in her camping chair on the bow seat and draws her paddle through the water with long languid strokes. Pioneer Camp taught me to kneel, with just the edge of my bum on the seat, a position that creates a natural forward lean for an efficient stroke. I indulge my niece unless there's a strong wind that requires more effort and the stability that comes from sitting lower in the boat.

We're paddling a forty-five-pound rental. I've been looking to buy a boat about this weight for both solo and tandem trips. So far I haven't found anything I can remotely afford. The less a boat weighs, the more it costs.

I ask Harriet if she's put sunscreen on. I try not to sound too much like her mother, but her skin burns easily and she never seems to slather on enough. On the way to the portage, I teach her the song "Bears" I learned from a Lyle Lovett CD. It has a fun line about taking a bear out to lunch with you.

We reach the portage and Harriet jumps out to pull the bow up on shore. I point to the rope attached to the bow. "Don't forget to take the painter with you." She never remembers. It's become almost a joke between us. She waits for me to tell her to do pretty much everything – which on our first trip was a bit of a shock. My previous camping partners, adults, naturally took initiative. Not to mention Harriet went to summer camp (a regular secular one). I assumed that since she had all the requisite skills, she would apply them when necessary.

I lift the blue gear pack onto her back. She doesn't stagger under the weight. Just over five feet and slim but big-boned, she has an ox-like constitution similar to her auntie's. We set off down the trail and soon arrive at sparkling Joe Lake.

The first campsite we spot is vacant but we're put off by the sight of a plastic bag by the fire pit, no doubt filled with garbage. Not to mention the noisy group across the narrow channel. We keep on, only to find the next ten campsites are taken. We head back to the unoccupied site.

"The ranger was right. This really is the Wasaga Beach of campsite lakes," I comment, naming Ontario's most popular beach. Harriet knows all about my former relationship with the ranger. She may need instructions in camping tasks but her emotional maturity is far beyond her years. We've been sharing confidences since our first trip, three summers ago.

At the campsite, Harriet runs up the trail to find the biffy, and I pick up the plastic bag and peer inside. "Need any toilet paper? I've got two rolls here!"

"Nope!" she calls back. "There's another bagful up here!"

She returns from the biff. "Maybe it's a new service the park is providing."

"Or maybe the bears are pigging out so much they're in dire need."

Harriet doesn't have the teenage giggle that my sisters, my mom, and I (all of us well out of our teens) still have. Her laugh is an infectious guttural guffaw.

"One thing's sure," I add. "Some group of campers is cursing the counsellor who left behind their week's supply of T.P."

Harriet helps set up the tent. We ignore the rowdy group across the channel. On the bright side, the more noise (I tell myself), the less likely a bear will visit.

After supper we walk the barrel into the woods (I assure Harriet I'll hang it tomorrow on Little Otterslide), then I retrieve our towels for an evening dip. Lying on the ground by the tent entrance is a large black feather.

If Raven's assurance isn't enough, two loons arrive to fish in the waters just offshore. Their serene companionable circles calm me down.

Harriet on the second annual Auntie Brenda/Niece Harriet canoe trip, Temagami, 1998

FOR A CHANGE the ranger called *me*. And for a change I was calm. I didn't tell him I was still not eating or sleeping. I told him I had been dancing around the living room, which was true, and had returned to an even more solid sense of myself, which was becoming true. "There's nothing 'wrong' with me."

"No," he agreed.

"Well, I took a lot of harsh criticism from you this summer and I don't need it. I won't be going there again." Then, with a wry laugh: "I guess you can't have all the blame. I let it happen." When there was no response, I asked, "How are *you* doing?"

He told me about an overnight camping trip he'd made with a (male) friend and how warm it had been for mid-October. I waited for him to share some revelation he'd had on this overnight (why else tell me about it?) and tried very hard not to resent the fact that he'd gone camping with someone else when he'd rarely gone with me.

It soon became clear he was just making conversation. I knew I was going to be completely frustrated when we hung up. I took a breath. "I'm sure you're aware, every time we get together or talk on the phone, that I'm waiting for you to say something. Do you have anything you can offer me? Any thoughts about us?"

A long silence.

"No thoughts about us." My tone was dry. "Well, tell me this. Do you consider us to be together even though we're not seeing each other right now?"

Another silence.

"Be *honest*."

"That's hard."

"Why is it hard?"

The response came in an intense half-whisper: "Because I can't hurt you."

"You've been hurting me for months. If you know now you don't want it to continue, then you'd be setting me free by telling me."

Another silence.

"I'm not trying to force the issue. If you know, genuinely, you need more time, I'm willing to give it to you. Otherwise, set me free. I have emotional needs that haven't been met in months."

He spoke in that same intense half-whisper. "I set you free."

It stunned me for a split second. Then that still composed voice of mine that seemed to have a mind of its own spoke again. "Thank you. I set you free too. Now how," I half-joked, "do we say goodbye?"

"Just say good night," whispered the park ranger, who obviously wasn't expecting our breakup to be articulated this particular evening.

I whispered good night.

———

ALL MORNING WE'RE in and out of the boat, portaging our gear over the short trails that link up all the Joes: from Joe Lake over to Little Joe (where we paddle past the red-roofed cabins and octagonal log dining room of the Arowhon Pines resort) and from Little Joe over to Baby Joe.

We emerge from the narrows at the south end of huge Burnt Island Lake to see just how huge it is. What looks like the far shore in the far distance is a narrowing at only the halfway mark. It's at least eight or ten kilometres to the other end. An impressive tailwind helps us along. We're now well into the park interior. All quiet. No other canoes within view.

The silence is suddenly disturbed by a distinctive motorized whine. Harriet turns, her face as startled as mine. We look toward the sound and spot an aluminum motorboat in the distance.

"Where did *that* come from!" Harriet exclaims.

The boat veers in to the opposite shore, and the sole occupant steps out, dressed head to foot in a dark colour.

"Ah, must be one of the rangers on campsite cleanup duty. They stash a motorboat on the interior lakes for that. The park plane would have flown him in. This is the first time I've ever seen one in the interior. The ranger and I met on one of the head lakes."

Harriet feigns indignation. "Really, you'd think they could use a quiet canoe."

I laugh. "I guess the lake is just too big to expect them to make the rounds that way."

At last we arrive at the far end and set off down the portage under our respective loads. We're now entering the area of the bear raids. In case the bells aren't sufficient warning, I insist we make our presence known in song. From under the canoe, I do a reprise of Lyle Lovett's bear song.

Out on Little Otterslide, I consult the map. On the island up ahead are two sites, one of which has a red canoe pulled up on shore. "You have your choice," I tell Harriet. "We can camp at that site" – I point with my paddle to the vacant island site – "and fool ourselves that bears don't swim to islands. *Or,*" I aim the paddle at a campsite on the mainland, "we can camp over there with that gorgeous slope of rock."

Harriet, a niece after my own heart, chooses the site with rock.

We set up the tent and look longingly inside. We've been on the watery highway for eight hours. "How about a nap before dinner?"

Harriet's nod is enthusiastic. Then she looks concerned. "What about the barrel? Shouldn't we hang it?"

"Not yet. We're going to have dinner soon." Her concern, though, spurs me to walk the barrel down a little trail, where I find a small, perfect clearing by the water's edge. I set it down and join Harriet in the tent.

I haven't laid my head down for two minutes when the woods come alive with the most unholy snapping sounds.

Harriet and I sit bolt upright and stare at each other. In a dozen summers of tripping in the bush I've never heard anything like this. It sounds like someone is breaking limbs off the trees.

"It might be a moose. Sometimes they whack their rack against a tree, trying to rub the old velvet off." I don't quite believe my words.

I strain my ears, trying to determine the direction of the noise and listening for the telltale jingle of bear bell on barrel handle. *Please, please let me not hear a bell.*

My prayer goes unheard. Possibly it's drowned out by the racket – the racket and the unmistakable ringing of a little bell.

I can no longer deny it: a bear is ripping into my bear-proof food barrel.

Now look what you've done. A voice no external racket could ever drown out.

My worst nightmare is about to come true. I'm going to have to confront a bear. I turn to my teenage niece. "You have to come with me."

Harriet, bless her, puts her shoes on in record time.

We emerge gingerly from the tent and peer down the trail. All quiet now. We can't see anything. I venture a step or two farther down the path. And there it is. A black furry thing. It doesn't look very big, not from twenty metres.

I clap my hands. "Hey," I call out. "Go away."

("Oh sure," says Bear. "I think I'll have another power bar or twelve.")

We bang on the upside-down canoe.

("Hmm, distant thunder," muses Bear. "My, this is a tasty hunk of cheese. Mmm, five-year-old cheddar.")

At this point we're supposed to go yelling down the trail, brandishing paddles and banging on pots and pans, and the bear is supposed to run away in terror. That advice, of course, is for brawny six-foot males with nerves of steel. No one has provided the fine-print instructions for a short, lightweight auntie in charge of a similar-sized teenage niece. Besides, our one pot and lid are in the food barrel, behind enemy lines.

I intuit the instructions for five-foot females. We're to get in the canoe and paddle along the shore to the clearing, where we will bang on the gunwales from the safety of the boat. And if the bear gets mad instead of scared, we'll paddle like hell.

I hand my niece her life jacket and put on my own. We carry the canoe to the water and cruise covertly down the shore.

Suddenly, he's right before us, in a familiar clearing next to the shore, not four metres away. A big, healthy-looking beast, male judging from the size of him, who looks entirely unperturbed by our arrival. This isn't the enraged bear of my nightmares. He's not baring his teeth, or growling, or posturing on his hind legs. Nor is he the least bit bothered, even by the rock I'm ashamed to say I pull out of the shallows and toss into the pile of familiar-looking food spread around him. He is, simply, a bear – a big bear with a glossy black coat and a quintessential bear face. In the midst of my adrenalin rush and distress at his appropriation of our food, I'm filled with amazement. At this beautiful creature who simply looks at us looking at him. He has the same benign expression, I swear, as the Bear portrayed on the *Medicine Cards*. Except this bear isn't about to embark on a philosophical discussion of my interior life. This bear is here for the grub.

Medicine Cards **illustration of Bear**

IT SAT, UNMOVING, on the highway. My first thought was a car had run over it. Though why a frog should even be on the highway on a dusk-approaching afternoon in November I had no idea. It should, I thought, be hibernating at the bottom of a pond.

I was on my walk "around the block," which meant I'd walked, in my slow way, to the end of my road and over the short trail to the next cottage road, then out to the highway and back along the shoulder. The frog, fist-sized, sat near the median, just before the turn-off to my road.

It was a month after I'd forced the breakup out of the ranger. I had asked him not to call. Nevertheless, in the last few days I had become intensely aware of his presence, felt him wishing there was a way he could be there for me. I tried to tell myself it was a projection of my own longing, which was intense and unremitting. The scary truth was I couldn't fathom how I was going to live without him. It felt like part of myself was dying.

For all that I had steeped myself in the fairy tale that we get our fulfillment, even our very purpose and meaning, from the undying love and commitment of a soulmate, I never bought into the idea that you could literally die from a broken heart. It seemed extreme, and impractical. It was deeply disturbing now to find I was physically wasting away in the wake of this breakup, to realize I believed so strongly we were meant to be together that our separation was draining the life force out of me. I couldn't envision getting over him or connecting with anyone else. How could I find anyone more connected than we were? I could only envision myself continuing on here, on my own, in my beautiful, rugged, solitary paradise. The one thing I was looking forward to was Asante's visit. In less than two weeks I would pick her up at the Ottawa airport.

I stepped out to the middle of the empty highway and gently prodded the frog with my foot. As I did so, it hit me that I had already envisioned my current reality, in the car on one of my trips to visit the ranger in the spring. And that I might have brought that fantasy into reality with the sheer number of times I had reimagined it on the drive, trying to get past where the needle was "stuck," to some kind of resolution. I had to put a stop to it. I had no idea how.

The frog moved in a sluggish unfrog-like crawl. I crouched down, keeping an eye out for traffic. It didn't look hurt. I gave it another gentle nudge. "I don't want you to get run over. You need to get off the road, little friend. You need to go find a pond to hibernate in."

Beyond the shoulder was a marshy area. I nudged it in that direction and, when it was safely off the highway, left it to find its way.

The contrary position of Frog can denote an unwillingness on your part to wipe the mire out of your life... Negativity is drawn to you when you refuse to give yourself the time and space needed to assume a new viewpoint.

WE REACH THE SOUTH end of the island, and I hesitate. The site where I saw people camped is on the north side. I steer right, hoping this is the quicker way around. The Critical Chorus keeps up its silent but lethal rebukes. *Why didn't you listen to Harriet and hang the barrel? You shouldn't have brought Harriet on this route. You knew there were bear problems.* And the deadliest blow: *You're going to have to go out. You've ruined her trip.*

In the bow my niece paddles with a steady rhythm. "I'm sorry," I say to her back.

Harriet twists around and speaks in that wise-beyond-her-years way that pops out now and then. "It's not your fault, Auntie Brenda."

Yes, it is, chirps the Chorus. *You should have known better.*

It seems we're never going to reach the campsite. Clearly I chose the longer way. I hear about that too.

Unknowingly, Harriet interrupts the internal harangue. "I hope he leaves me my candied ginger. And he might at least leave us the packets of soup."

"Yes, some soup for the trip out tomorrow would be good." Secretly I can't imagine there will be any food left by the time he's done. Nor my new stove, which was in the barrel too.

At last, I spot a red canoe on shore. We head in and call out to the campers.

My heart sinks when I see them – a plump, affable couple who look to be in their fifties, not exactly what I have in mind for reinforcements. The man is grey-haired, balding. The woman beside him doesn't say a word but looks anxious when I tell my tale.

The man peers at me through thick glasses. "How big is the bear?"

"Big."

"There's nothing to do but wait for him to finish."

Near tears, I ask if we can camp with them and if they have any extra food, and he assures me we can come back when we've retrieved our gear. I steer the canoe on around the island, dismayed they didn't offer to come with us for moral support.

The next site is occupied too. When I call out to warn the campers, two men with bright friendly faces come down to the shore. They're definitely not brawny but that doesn't stop them from jumping in their canoe – I don't even have to ask. Paddling side by side across the channel, we're instantly laughing and joking about the park's crazy instructions for confronting a bear.

At our campsite they keep watch while Harriet and I do the quickest take-down in our canoe-trip history. Seeing the cautious way our bear guards, too, peer down the trail makes me feel better.

On the paddle back to the island, they offer us food and shelter for the night. I wish I could accept their offer but feel obligated to the other couple, who are expecting us back. I do accept their offer of morning coffee and a picnic lunch for the trip out. *Why* didn't I paddle this way around the island and reach them first?

To be fair, our hosts – Ted and Shelley – make us welcome. They feed us dried fruit and nuts and hot soup, and amusing (bear-free) stories around the campfire. Ted goes on a bit of a rant about how awful vegetarian food is, especially camp food. Harriet and I sneak surreptitious glances at each other. This may explain why we're not getting a real dinner.

Their unwillingness to provide more assistance becomes entirely understandable once I learn it's Shelley's first time on a canoe trip – not to mention in a canoe – and Ted has tripped only a few times himself. On top of everything else, they keep reaching out to kiss and hold hands and give each other smouldering looks (and, in Shelley's case, shy giggles). We've intruded on a romantic getaway.

Harriet and I retire early, partly from exhaustion, partly to give the couple some privacy.

Sleep is nowhere to be found. I'm too busy perfecting my levitation skills at each sound outside the tent – the rustles, I try to tell myself, of small creatures going about their nighttime business. Harriet, thankfully, sleeps through it all. She seems remarkably unperturbed by the whole event, while I worry I'm never going to be able to do another canoe trip by myself. I worry, too, about what awaits us tomorrow at our site, my barrel in shreds, my stove chewed to bits, maybe the bear himself back for a bit of breakfast. One thing's certain: there won't be any food left. This is the end of our trip. We'll have to paddle all the way out. A long day but doable. *It shouldn't have to be done.*

If bear has shown up in your life, ask yourself some important quest-
ions… Are you not seeing the core of good deep within all situations?
[No.] Are you being too critical of yourself or others? [Yes.]… Bear
medicine can teach you to go deep within so that you can make your
choices and decisions from a position of power.

I wake to the sound of the wind in the trees. Beside me, Harriet
slumbers on, mouth open, one arm flung above her head.

From outside the tent comes a loud high-pitched sound that makes
me jump. It's short and sharp, like an ambulance siren turned on and
abruptly off.

I scramble out in time to see a raven lift off from a tree stump right
next to the tent.

No life in our hosts' tent. As quietly as I can, I launch the canoe.
I don't want to miss my coffee fix. The waves are high, and I hug
the shore.

No one is stirring at the other campsite either. No coffee yet. A
tailwind pushes me across the channel toward our bear-invaded site. I
paddle with trepidation. I tell myself I don't have to get out if it doesn't
feel right, I can just inspect the mess from the water.

The wind pushes so hard it's difficult to keep the boat a safe
distance from shore. I manage to peer into the clearing and see no
one is stirring here either. I imagine the bear crashed out somewhere
not far away, unable to move.

A thick log sticking straight out from shore makes the perfect jetty. I
back the canoe in beside it so that if the bear comes back I'll be facing
the right way for a quick getaway.

With pounding heart I step out onto the log.

———

S HE STEPPED OFF the escalator into the baggage claim area, a
middle-aged woman with fine blond hair skimming her shoulders,
a high forehead even her bangs couldn't hide, and big glasses. She
wore a bright red bulky knit sweater down to her thighs, black
leggings, and turquoise cowboy boots. To anyone else she might have

looked quite eccentric. To me she was my beloved Asante, and she'd just arrived from Vancouver for a ten-day visit.

I rushed over and we reached for each other, laughing and tearing up, and then we stopped laughing and just held on, swaying in the sudden serenity of our embrace. I was in the arms of tangible Love and Compassion.

When we pulled back, I saw a look of concern briefly cross her face. I knew why. I'd had moments this fall of surrender, of joy, of staying put in the present. At best they were pauses, moments of reprieve in a steady downward spiral of both my emotional and my physical health.

Asante only knew the ranger and I had broken up. She was going through a difficult time in her job at the drug recovery centre, which was in internal upheaval, and I had been reluctant to burden her more. I was also afraid she would tell me in her gentle firm way to let go of my secret hopes, the relationship was over, there was a good reason it had come to an end, it had served its purpose, I had learned something important, and I would (she would never say "should") move on to something – and someone – more beneficial. This had always, under her previous tutelage, been how I'd got over previous breakups. I had always found a "reason" and learned a "lesson" and could move on to something "better." Could *be* someone better. But this old way no longer felt right. The catch was I didn't know what the new way was. I felt like a sluggish frog out of my element in the middle of a highway.

On the two-hour drive home from the airport, I prayed that if there was a way Asante could share her wisdom without my leaning on her and depleting her further, I would let myself be guided, even if she advised something I didn't want to hear.

In the evening, we sat on the landlord's ugly orange-flowered couch. Asante looked straight into my eyes. "How are you?"

I went to my bedroom and returned with a couple of envelopes. I pulled out a thick sheaf of photos and handed them over without a word. Asante had never met the ranger or even seen a photo of him. She took one look at the top one and said, "I think you guys are meant to be together." Then she breathed in, audibly, in a way that usually means she's connecting with something deep inside herself. She can take in a breath for longer than anyone I know – an ability honed through years of yoga training and teaching. She spread several of the photos on the couch and put her finger on one. "He's never been one hundred percent with you. Not even from the beginning. Not from what I see in these photos."

I picked up the photo, taken on the camera's self-timer. We stood on his snow-covered deck, embracing and laughing. Then I saw it. His smile looked genuine enough – he was definitely enjoying our time together – but he didn't look like he was truly "with" me in that embrace. He was striking a fun pose with a girl for the camera.

"I think you're meant to be together," Asante said again. "But it's not going to happen unless he opens his heart completely to you, which of course you know."

I poured out *my* heart then. I told her it didn't feel right to reconnect with him and it didn't feel right to move on.

"It doesn't have to be an either/or."

"What do I do?"

"Why don't you approach him with no preconceived notions. Start by lifting the communication ban. That will open the way for you to respond, moment by moment, to whatever the moment requires." She paused, then added, "Don't impose limitations on the future."

"You mean the Buddhists have it right?" The sudden tears in my eyes were more from massive relief at her support than trepidation at this call to walk into the pitch-black Void with open arms.

"Trust," she added. "That's all you need."

That made us laugh. How simple it sounded.

I opened the other, much thinner envelope. It contained a couple of self-portraits I had taken during a break in my wood stacking that fall. One had always disturbed me. I was sitting on the flat rock of the point overlooking the river, my head turned to look straight at the lens. On my unsmiling face was an expression I had never seen before. My features didn't even look like mine. I handed it to Asante. Only half joking, I asked, "Who is that, do you think?"

She peered at the photo and breathed out a long breath. "A pioneer," she said, at last. "A disillusioned, resigned, tough, pioneering kind of woman who's known too many hardships and losses and is resigned to living on her own." She gave it a closer look. "There's a hard resignation in her eyes to being alone – and continuing on alone – in her new isolated home on the river."

Her description alarmed me. And reminded me of that fantasy I had created in the car. I had never shared it with Asante before. I did now. "It feels like it's all come true. I do see myself staying on here on my own, and" – I gave a half-sobbing laugh – "I'm definitely not in good shape. It scares me."

She looked at me with grave concern. "I haven't wanted to say this but there's a near hopelessness in your eyes I've never seen before." She handed the photo back and her voice was tender. "You don't have to be that woman, you know."

A resigned, disillusioned pioneer woman, October 1999

I TIPTOE INTO the clearing and take in the mess. The barrel is not in shreds. There's only one bear-paw-sized hole, near the top. The harness has been removed, and the lid and the circular metal hinge that secures it are lying on the ground nearby. I can't believe the bear figured out how to unhinge the lid and take it off. I pick up the hinge and test it. It's not even broken. Clever bear!

There's barely a claw mark in the harness. I scrounge around for the extra green garbage bag I had stored in the barrel, put the harness back on the barrel and line it with the garbage bag to cover up the hole. It's going to be perfectly functional for our trip out. My spirits lift.

Now, where's my stove? Did he eat it? No, it's right at my feet, out of its little blue sack, still in one piece. The sack has only a few claw punctures. Careful bear!

I don't linger over these discoveries. I rush around, tossing strewn bags and food remains and dishes and pot and lid into the barrel. There, bless him, is my precious zip-lock bag of coffee, with nary a puncture mark, as well as a salvageable amount of bannock flour in a bag full of holes. And he didn't touch, beyond a claw mark here and there, any of our dried soups or pastas. Nor the bag of fresh pesto. With quiet delight, I realize we have enough food to get us out today without begging from the neighbours. Generous bear!

A stiff headwind hampers my progress back to the island. Digging in my paddle, I mentally compose a list of all the food the bear did devour.

Still no movement at the campsite of our friendly bear guards. Back at our hosts' campsite, Ted is boiling water on a two-burner Coleman, Shelley is pulling food out of a canvas pack, and Harriet is sitting on a log in her dazed first-thing-in-the-morning way. I regale them with a lively description of the picnic site while I make coffee and bake a breakfast bannock and cook up a Singapore Curry Noodle dish for our lunch on my stove, which is in perfect working order.

Standing over the hissing stove, I rhyme off the bear's dinner menu. "A pound and a half of five-year-old cheddar, two bags of tortilla wraps, half a pound of butter, two large bags of granola, one large bag of trail mix, one bag of pistachio nuts and about thirty dollars' worth of energy bars – wrappers and all."

In a grand finale, I produce the candied ginger for Harriet. She clutches the bag with a cry of delight. "He saved it for me!"

I PROBABLY SHOULDN'T tell you this." It was a pale December morning halfway through our visit, and we were standing at the counter making breakfast.

"You know you can't say something like that and then not tell me!"

"I feel his spirit hovering over your house," Asante said, at last. "It feels as if he's expanded it to cover the whole property."

I knew why she'd hesitated, afraid it would set me back. But this protective gesture (from a man who likely also felt no small amount of guilt for abandoning me to the "wilderness" on my own) touched me in a place deep inside. I didn't doubt for a moment the truth of it. Not only because I knew Asante's intuitive abilities, but because it explained my own sense of his presence. And here it was, his essence, his psychic energy, his spirit, whatever you wanted to call it, stretched out over my home, the way a bird extends a wing over its young, demonstrating his caring that he could not, for whatever reason, show me in person.

In the evening, Asante and I sat facing each other on the couch and mused on the protective nature of men. I had never given much thought to it, though it was there in my father and in all the male authority figures in my life. It had often come in the form of stern "thou shalt nots," intended to prevent me from hurting myself or others. Now Asante spoke about the caring impulse under the protective instinct. Her own boyfriend was phoning her at work more often and wanted her to call him when she got home at night. "He worries the guys are going to hurt me." She meant the clients she worked with at the drug recovery centre. "I appreciate his concern but it drives me crazy. I know I'm safe."

That got us wondering. How do women – strong women – let their men express their instinctively protective nature when we don't "need" it?

I continued to ponder the question in bed. I didn't need a husband and protector to watch over me to make me feel safe. The idea of someone *caring* enough to watch over me – that was something entirely different. It became, in fact, a growing yearning, long after I'd driven Asante back to Ottawa for a teary goodbye at the airport – the yearning made all the more powerful by the way it meshed with my own new willingness and openness to let myself be loved. They became entwined in my mind: protection and love. Protection as a *demonstration* of love. Maybe what was required of me was a willingness to be cared for in a protective way. Ask, and you will receive. But be *willing* to receive.

WE THANK TED and Shelley for their generosity as we launch our respective boats. We'll be travelling in the same direction as far as Baby Joe, where they plan to spend the night. Harriet and I soon fall behind as we detour over to the other campsite to thank our bear guards for their offer of coffee and food we no longer need.

We set off again, my spirits high. The waves are big but the wind is behind us, the sun shining. It looks like we'll have a tailwind all the way back down huge Burnt Island Lake.

"We still have four days," I say to Harriet's back. "You don't want to go home, do you?"

She turns and makes a face. "No. Do you?"

"No. I think we need to come back in – I do especially. Like getting back on a horse after you've fallen off. I was thinking we should go home for a couple of days, regroup, repack, and come back to the park for Friday and Saturday night. No one's expecting to hear from us 'til Sunday. I had a very safe week last week south of the highway. I was thinking we could rebook down there, maybe even just on one lake. Just to get our nerve back. What do you think?"

A vigorous nod.

"And I don't think we should phone your mom."

"Absolutely not. She'll only worry."

We arrive at the beginning of the portage in time to see Ted and Shelley head off with their gear. At the other end we meet up again. They've carried everything in one go and are about to load up the boat. Harriet and I have another relay to do. We say goodbye once again.

By the time we return to the lake, the sun has given way to heavy grey clouds. I glance out at the blackish water. The waves are huge and white-capped and now, alas, coming sideways. They'll hit the canoe broadside, which is far worse than head-on.

"We're going to have to hug the shore," I tell Harriet.

"Like we did on that big lake in Temagami."

"Exactly like then. I'm sorry. It's going to make our trip out even longer."

"That's okay."

I can see from her determined expression she means it. "You're a trooper."

I look out at the lake again. "Where do you think Ted and Shelley are? We should be able to see them." We scan close to the shores, where they should be paddling. There's no sign of them. No canoes at all.

At last I spot it: a tiny red dot of a boat bobbing up and down in the choppy whitecaps in the middle of the lake. "There they are. What the heck are they doing out *there*?"

We load the canoe and are about to get in when I glance out at the lake again. Something's not right. There's more red showing than there should be and what looks like two heads bobbing beside it. "Oh God. They've capsized. Quick, we've got to get out to them."

In seconds, we've launched the canoe.

"Kneel down low in the bow and paddle hard." I'm gratified to see my niece get on her knees and dig in. In seconds the boat is plowing through the waves faster than we've ever made it go. Even in the crosswind, it stays remarkably stable.

It takes a good ten minutes of hard paddling to reach the capsized couple, but only the first few strokes for everything to become crystal clear, only a few hard paddle strokes on a lake devoid of fellow travellers to realize I'm exactly where I'm supposed to be.

We reach the overturned canoe, and I'm relieved to see two heads – both in life jackets – above water. "Ted, Shelley! Are you okay?"

"We're okay!" Ted looks anxiously at Shelley.

"I'm okay." Her voice isn't quite as steady, but she's not panicking.

"You guys sure know how to get an auntie and her niece moving fast."

It's a godsend to already know their names and their canoeing and camping ability, to have established a rapport, and be able to joke with them and keep them calm. In the back of my mind, I hear one more voice – a gentle, forgiving one: *There was a reason for going the long way around the island after all.*

ON THE LAST night of her visit, I left Asante reading in bed to go down to the dock. I stood at the end, shivering despite my thick jacket. The bay was a pool of black ink. I looked up at the stars pricking through the dark blanket of sky. My own eyes pricked with tears. Something had broken free. I looked up and let it stream down my face: Gratitude for Asante's naturally healing presence, her gentleness, her wisdom. Gratitude to her for helping me to banish the hardened "pioneer" from inside me and bring "me" back. I still had a long climb back to health and wellbeing, but she had held out her arms and stopped the descent.

With Asante, angel of mercy, on my point, December 1999

THERE'S NO ROOM for Ted and Shelley in our boat. I never thought to take the gear out when we spotted them. Even if I had, I wouldn't be willing to endanger Harriet by trying to get them in. She's never performed a canoe rescue, and I haven't done one since camp, so many years ago. These conditions are no place to put my rusty skills to the test. We could all end up in the water.

The only thing we can do is tow them to the closest shore. I tie their boat to ours and instruct them to hang on. Harriet and I dig in with our paddles, but between the headwind and the weight on the back, we make no progress whatsoever.

"It's no use," I call out to Ted. "We'll have to go with the wind to the other shore."

"Whatever you think is best." I can tell from his voice and the way he looks at Shelley that he's trying to keep calm for her sake. We turn the canoes. My heart sinks when I see just how far the other shore is. It will take us forever. And the water is cold.

At that moment I spot first one canoe, then another, on their way out to us from the portage. Long moments later, the first boat arrives, thankfully empty of gear, the paddlers two lanky teenage boys. "We saw you from shore but it took us awhile to realize you were in trouble," says the one in the stern. He gestures behind him. "My dad's on his way."

"Thank God you're here. Help me get them in your boat." Harriet and I bring our canoe alongside theirs and hold on to their gunwales. I instruct the boys to lean toward mine to provide a brace. On the other side, Shelley struggles to climb in, then Ted. They sit in the middle, dripping and shivering.

I unbuckle my pack and pull out a fleece jacket for Shelley and trade my dry life jacket for her wet one. I give my Gore-Tex jacket to Ted. It doesn't nearly come around him but will at least provide a bit of warmth with his life jacket over it.

I turn to the boys. "Can you get them back to the portage?"

They set off just as the other boat arrives with the father – he introduces himself as Al – and another, younger teenage boy. In minutes, we have the overturned boat positioned perpendicular to their boat's midsection. As we did with the boys' boat, Harriet and I brace our boat alongside theirs for extra stability. Al leans forward from the stern to pull up on the bow of the overturned canoe. The trick is to get the bow up onto the gunwales, pull the boat halfway across, flip it over and slide it back in the water.

It comes out of the water much more easily than either of us expects. In seconds, it's righted in the water. Visible now beside it are two enormous canvas packs, which clearly weren't strapped to the boat but thankfully didn't sink.

Yet another canoe arrives, propelled by two young women, camp counsellors who apologize for not coming out sooner from their site. "We didn't realize what was going on."

They help us heave the sodden canvas packs into Al's boat and tie the empty canoe to it. We work quickly; the skies are threatening to open up any minute. The counsellors head back to their campsite before the rain comes.

Our progress back to the portage is hampered by an even gustier wind and the empty canoe dragging behind Al's. Driving rain pricks down on us. We pause to get Harriet's rain jacket on her and slog on.

By the time we arrive, the rain has stopped and Ted is standing on the beach, a sleeping bag wrapped around his shoulders. I order him out of his wet clothes and pull my fleece blanket out of my pack. Ted takes off his T-shirt and wraps the blanket around his shoulders with the sleeping bag over top.

I dig into the food barrel for my stove and find a packet of lentil soup. "How appropriate that we're making soup for you now," I joke, crouched beside the stove. "Talk about an immediate payback."

Ted chuckles and goes down the beach to check on Shelley.

I'm pouring soup into a mug when he wanders back. "I'm not doing so well."

I look up in alarm. He's unnaturally pale. "What are your symptoms?"

He puts a hand to his nose. "My nose feels cold, and my thoughts are slow." He holds out his right hand. "I can't feel my fingers."

Now I'm truly alarmed. I wrack my brains, trying to remember what I learned about hypothermia in the wilderness first aid course I took before my first trip with Harriet. I'm not quite willing to jump naked into a sleeping bag with him. I pull both sleeping bags out of my pack for him. Shelley hovers over him, looking distressed.

"Has anyone rubbed him down? He should be rubbed down." The voice belongs to a tall thin man I've never seen before. His imperious tone irritates me, even amid my relief at the arrival of more help – help that remembers more than I do about what to do for hypothermia. He turns out to be one of three adults leading a trip of nineteen teenagers from a church youth group. He dispatches the kids to the woods to collect firewood. Much sooner than I think possible, a bonfire is blazing at the edge of the woods beside the beach.

The youth group leader and I help Ted over to a log beside the fire. He's now complaining of numbness down his right arm and leg. He looks woozy and even paler than before, as if he's about to pass out. I'm terrified he might die.

FOUR MONTHS AFTER I forced the official breakup out of the park ranger, and two months after Asante's visit, detachment remained an empty boat floating in the middle of the lake, impossible to reach, let alone navigate. I took Asante's advice and lifted the communication ban, and even called the ranger to confess my hopes. His response came hurtling through the phone line, in a loud stern voice completely unlike him: "Abandon hope."

Long after I clicked off the phone, his words echoed in my head. They uncannily echoed a line from the *Tao Te Ching*, a little guide written by a sage named Lao Tzu twenty-five hundred years ago on how to live wisely. Louise gave me a copy for my birthday the year before she was murdered. Now that I was well into writing her story, I was finally reading it. "Hope," wrote Lao Tzu, "is as hollow as fear." He made hope sound like something we should give up – abandon – like fear. Hopes, he meant, are as illusory as fears. Hope is very closely related to "hanging on," and hanging on is the antithesis of "letting go." And letting go, just being, is the only way to be in this world without heaping needless suffering on our own heads.

I had all the theory down. Reality was a different matter. I prayed to be shown how to move on so I could embrace life again. Under my prayer, though, was something cold and dark, something I barely wanted to acknowledge. A secret dread that the new life I was being called to embrace was precisely *not* to find someone else but to remain on my own and – as Lao Tzu urged – love the world as myself so I could care for all things. And why should this idea fill me with such dread? Because my priorities were still skewed. I still didn't love God above everything and everyone, especially men.

Thankfully, work was distractingly busy. I had a new ongoing contract with the federal government to write success stories about Canadian exporters. One article about an international development organization that had introduced economic and social programs to Indigenous Peoples in other countries piqued my interest. The organization worked from a set of principles based on the traditional teachings of the Indigenous Peoples in North America. It isn't often I get to write about spiritual matters for bureaucratic clients.

The director was a member of two First Nations and a hereditary Chief and Elder. I emailed him the draft article, then worried I had misinterpreted the spiritual principles and he was going to tell me I had no business even trying to write about them.

"You did a great job," he said when he called. "You get what we're doing. So many other journalists who have written about us have got it all wrong." He wanted me to do other writing for him and was going to be in Ottawa on business. Would I travel there to meet him?

———

THE TRICK IS to warm him up gradually," says the youth group leader. I've privately dubbed him Hypothermia Guy. Something about his face – the set of his jaw maybe – makes him appear a man used to being obeyed. Notwithstanding his officiousness, there's no denying he came along just in time – has possibly saved Ted's life.

Al, Shelley, and I take turns rubbing his limbs. Every few minutes we get him to turn so each side of him gets warmed by the fire. "We have to rotisserie you."

Ted manages a smile at my joke.

On the other side of the fire, several kids from the youth group, and Harriet too I see, toss in branches to keep the fire just the right size. Shelley, in my polypropylene underwear and fleece, sits beside Ted with the mug of hot soup, making him sip from it.

"I know how much you love lentils, Ted," I tease.

He makes a face and manages a laugh, and I breathe in relief: he's going to be okay.

"The key is to warm him up gradually," says Hypothermia Guy, for what seems like the tenth time.

I leave Shelley to rub Ted's limbs and take Al aside to make plans. He's a pleasant-looking man with short dark hair and a pale face. His boys are younger versions, with friendly, keen-to-help demeanours. They've come up from Ann Arbor, Michigan, Al explains, and are on their way out today too. I tell him I don't think Ted and Shelley are in any shape to go anywhere, and he kindly agrees to stay with us here at the portage tonight. I'm worried about bears as well as Ted.

Al goes off to take a look at their gear.

At that moment, the sun comes out – the blessed sun. The colour has returned to Ted's face, and he can stand up. Shelley and I help him out to the sunny beach. It's three o'clock. Nearly two hours have passed since he told me he wasn't well.

Hypothermia Guy comes over. "Looks like he's going to be okay. We'll be on our way. We have to get up to Otterslide tonight."

He may have been irritating but my thanks are sincere. "You and your group came along right at the right time. We really appreciate all your help." I warn him about the bear.

The huge group heads off down the trail, and Al comes back, looking worried. "There's no way we can stay here. Their sleeping bags are soaking wet. *All* their gear is soaked – their clothes, their food. Nothing was waterproofed."

Dismayed, I try to think, pray for inspiration, for help. It comes to me that Harriet and I can paddle the few hours to the Arowhon Pines lodge on Little Joe Lake and phone for the park plane to come in for Ted and Shelley. I'll leave my tent and sleeping bags for them in case the plane can't get in today. Harriet and I can paddle on to the take-out and drive to my place for the night.

Al agrees to stay with them, and I call Harriet over to relay the plan. We're about to step in the canoe when we hear the whine of a motor – a motor attached to an aluminum boat heading, unbelievably, straight for the beach.

———

HE STRODE ACROSS the tiled floor of the Ottawa hotel lobby, a man with an imposing breadth of presence, if not imposing height, and a broad smile. I stood up and he took my hand, looked right into my eyes, and introduced himself. Then he apologized. He had an unexpected meeting. Could I come back in another hour?

Yes, I had errands I could run. I walked back to my car, climbed into the driver's seat, and burst into tears. I had no idea why.

Later, in the restaurant, we ordered lamb souvlaki and talked about his work and mine.

The restaurant emptied, and our plates, but we kept talking. As well as his international work, he was creating a resolution for

First Nations people – people like his own parents – who had been shamed, abused, and stripped of their language and cultural identity at residential schools. He spoke of the healing sessions he offered. "Telling their story helps them to heal and let go." He smiled. "Why are you looking at me like that? What do you need to let go of?"

The question and his smile – it seemed to know – jolted me into admission. Out came the history of my relationship, the intense connection I had felt with the ranger, our breakup and my inability to move on, even four months later. Story and tears poured out together. I was vaguely aware of bewildered waitstaff, who surely wanted to close up but didn't disturb us.

He listened intently. It was gratifying to be heard with such attentiveness. And embarrassing to display such emotion to a business client.

We paid the bill and walked in the frosty evening to my car, so I could drive him back to his hotel. I was about to start the engine, but he stopped me. "The healing," said my healer in the passenger seat, "is to cry."

"I'm tired of crying. I've been crying for months."

"It doesn't matter. You need to cry. And cry. And cry."

It was all too easy to comply. I bent over his lap from the driver's seat and felt gentle hands on my head. The feel of such gentle loving hands made me cry more. I heard words spoken rapidly in a language I didn't understand. I didn't need to understand the words to know he was praying. The prayers and hands urged more tears out of me. I cried until I thought I couldn't cry anymore, and cried more.

I don't know how long it was before I sat up. He looked at my tear-swollen face. "Your eyes are clearer now."

The words took me aback. Didn't my eyes look puffy and red? It was the first time I considered there might be physical benefits to tears. My eyes were obviously no longer clouded with the holding in of pain he had seen all too clearly. In his own I saw so much love and compassion I couldn't help telling him so, with heartfelt gratitude.

"What you see in my eyes is simply a reflection of what's in your own."

That pronouncement brought more tears, overwhelmed ones this time, as did all the things he went on to say to me in his gentle healing voice – things about myself that counteracted all the stern austere teachings and attitudes I had internalized from childhood. Things no male in my life – father, friend, lover – had ever been able to say (or I to hear). I was not a bad girl. I was a beloved child of the Creator. Beautiful, innocent, lovable, loved. *Worthy.* I felt understood, *known*, by this man who looked in my eyes and saw, and blessed, *me.* In that moment my mind and its ingrained attitudes and perceptions made a slow but inexorable change in course. Deep-seated patterns and beliefs were beginning to shift. Imperceptibly but surely, like a huge unwieldy ocean liner charting a new course.

I pulled up at the hotel and turned to my passenger. "I've had no idea how to let go of this relationship. The old ways weren't working. I was praying for the answer to come. After I left you this afternoon, I got back in my car and burst into tears. I was completely mystified. I think my soul knew my prayer was about to be answered."

He gave me his lopsided smile. "You had strong prayers – to bring me all the way from Alberta."

A YOUNG MAN in a blue coverall steps into the shallows and pulls the motorboat up on the beach. Red curly hair pokes out from a white brimmed hat, tied under his chin. I realize it's the ranger Harriet and I saw on his campsite maintenance rounds yesterday. (Only yesterday!)

"I was at the other end of the lake when a group of trippers paddled over and told me what was going on here. They came through the portage here awhile back."

It stuns me to hear that other trippers have gone through, that there was normal activity on the portage while we were dealing with our very abnormal activity. I explain the situation.

The red-headed ranger reaches into the boat and produces a radio – a perfectly wonderful radio.

Within ten minutes arrangements have been made for the park plane to fly in. And I've wangled seats for Harriet and me as well, by offering to take Ted to the hospital, since Shelley, it turns out, doesn't drive. The plane can take only one canoe at a time on the pontoons, but the ranger confirms the pilot can fly in tomorrow for mine. We can pick it up when we come back to the park.

I apologize to Al for abandoning him, and thank him for all his help. "Be careful," I say as we're leaving. "But," I smile, "I think the bear will leave you alone."

The park's de Havilland Turbo Beaver, with a canoe on the pontoon

The emergency doctor proclaims Ted to be exhausted but fine and to have got good care in the bush.

Back in the Canoe Lake parking lot an hour later, Ted shakes my hand. "You're our angels."

"Just returning the favour. Anyway, it wasn't only us. You had about thirty angels looking out for you today. And," I add, "one ursine angel."

THE REAL BLESSING of my Indigenous healer wasn't that he "healed" me, though he certainly was a catalyst for that healing. He didn't show me a new way to let go. There is only one way to let go, and that is to cry (and cry) and be done. At last I let myself cry freely, finally accepting the loss, not just feeling it. No, the gift of my Indigenous angel was that he showed me a new way to be in relationship. The love and compassion I saw in his eyes was, he had said that February night, simply a reflection of what was in my own. He pointed me to myself. Don't look to others for your happiness or wellbeing. Look to yourself. The rest will follow, as surely as the image in a mirror follows the person standing before it. He awakened me to a crucial truth: There's no knight in shining armour or even a wilderness-loving ranger in a canoe who is going to fulfill me. The wellspring of love is inside *me*. It was time, long past time, to tap into it.

A T THE PORTAGE over to our new lake in the "safe" part of the park, south of the Highway 60 corridor, Harriet and I run into the very two wardens who were on the bear-capture job. They haven't been successful, yet, they tell us. They're just taking a break.

The older one has shaggy grey hair and gun-metal-grey glasses. "We'll have to catch it," he says. "It's become a campsite bear – a nuisance bear."

"More like nuisance campers," I respond wryly, and we continue on our way. Now that I'm not anywhere in its vicinity, I'm relieved the bear has eluded capture.

In the evening, Harriet and I hang the new food barrel. We build up the campfire and pull our camping chairs close to rehash our twenty-four-hour adrenalin rush.

"I had a déjà vu when you asked if Ted and Shelley had extra food to give us," says Harriet. "When we were paddling down the big lake, I was daydreaming about what would happen if a bear got into our food and how we'd have to ask someone else to share with us."

"So *you* made it happen," I tease.

"Me! I wasn't the one singing about inviting a bear to lunch." She gives her wicked laugh, and flickers of firelight light up her heart-shaped face.

"I definitely won't be singing that one on portages anymore. Do you know why I asked you to put your life jacket on when we went to confront him in the boat?"

"I thought it was to make us look bigger."

"Ha, I never even thought of that. No, it was to give us extra padding in case he thought we looked more appetizing than the contents of the barrel."

"Hey, what did you mean when you told Ted he had an ursine angel looking out for him? You meant the bear, right?"

"Yes, the Latin name for bear is *ursus*. What I meant was if the bear hadn't got into our food we wouldn't have been travelling in that direction, and it would have taken a lot longer for someone to come to their aid. I was so mad at myself for ruining your trip, but we were exactly where we were meant to be."

Harriet nods as if that were never in question.

Before I slide off to sleep, I have a clear vision of how the bear looked at us, so benignly, so quintessentially bear-like, from the middle of his feast. In the pitch-black of the night, I suddenly see very clearly: Bear isn't an enemy to be feared but an ally, joining me in rising up against the real enemy, which, always, is within.

The "bear-proof" food barrel

(Photos: Garry Donaldson)

4

COMMUNION

Magnetewan Lake to Misty Lake and back: July 3–8, 2001

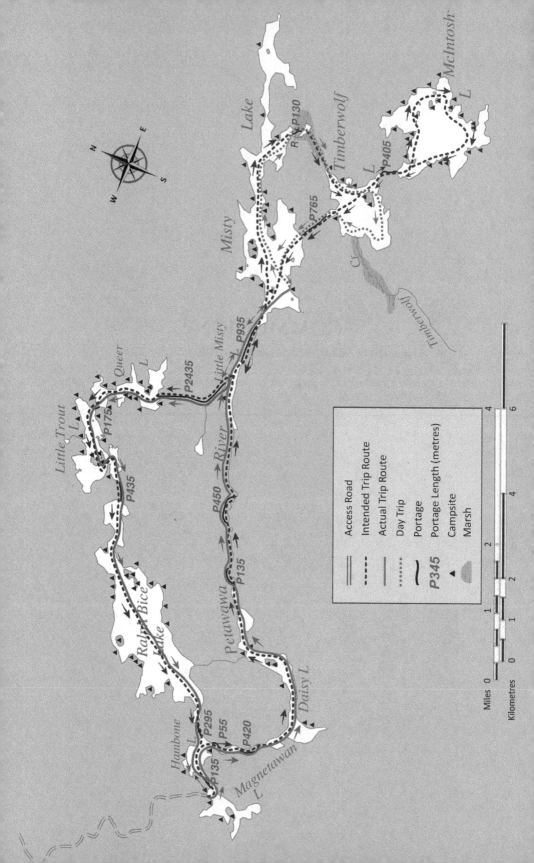

THE LOON PATROLS the waters just out from shore. He's not fishing, just looking around. I appreciate his company on this first evening of my six-day solo trip.

It took four hours in the car and nearly two hours in, and occasionally under, the canoe to get here to Daisy Lake, on the west side of Algonquin. I'm too exhausted to get the stove out. Lamb sausage leftovers from last night's dinner with my sister will do the trick.

The loon abandons his patrol and glides away across the lake. He's kept me company for a whole hour. I get the feeling he's been checking me out, though maybe checking up on me, too.

Minutes later, he's back, this time with his mate and their sweet downy brown baby. The three of them glide around not far from shore in the growing twilight.

Before dark, I carry my weighty purple twenty-litre dry bag – my new food pack – a short way into the woods to a large white pine. Two ends of a long rope dangle down from a high branch. The secret to getting a rope suspended from a high branch is to tie one end around a small rock, give it a good high toss over the branch and let the rock's weight pull the rope down the other side. I won't divulge how many tries this exercise took. My rock-tossing arm is out of practice.

I tie a secure knot around the food bag handle and pull down on the other end of the rope, hand over hand, until the bag is hanging a metre or so below the branch. Tension still tight on the rope, I circle the tree with it, round and round, tie off the rope, and say good night to the purple bag. It swings serenely above my head, safely out of bear's reach.

Inside the tent I check in with my inner bear-fear meter. It registers pretty much zero. I line the sleeping bag with a fleece blanket. Last weekend's heatwave ended in a radical plummet to near freezing. It's warmed up a bit since then but not so you'd know it's July.

I aim my headlamp at Annie Dillard's *For the Time Being*. I love the wonder-filled way Dillard experiences the natural world, right down to the level of earthworms and insects, and translates her experiences into thoughtful, often playful prose. Tonight I read her descriptions of the paleontological explorations of Pierre Teilhard de Chardin in the deserts of China and Mongolia in the 1920s. He was a man, she writes, who, "from the back of a jog-trotting mule,... could spot on stony ground a tiny rock that early man had chipped." He was also a mystic for whom the material world "dissolves at the edges and grows translucent" and is, as he put it himself, "entirely lit up from within."

I recall Teilhard de Chardin from one of my university religion courses. It took me aback to learn about a Jesuit priest who was also a paleontologist. It didn't seem a natural mix. (The Catholic authorities didn't think so either. They forbade him from teaching evolution and from publishing his work and effectively exiled him to China for two decades.) His theological ideas were, to my still-church-going university-aged self, perception jolting. Both church and camp had taught me to see, and live, through a dualistic lens, where all things "earthly," including our body and all its appetites (most especially sex), were bad. Very bad. And we were imprisoned in these bodily shells, and indeed in our whole earthly existence, until we (hopefully) made it to heaven. Anything "earthly," said Saint Paul and the other epistle writers, was "unspiritual, devilish."

That the Earth, and all earthly things, including my own bodily humanity, might not, after all, be the evil antithesis of all things "spiritual" is a perception I've continued to struggle with, long after having sloughed off most of my church beliefs. Tonight something inside me lights up as I read the paleontologist's writings, quoted in Dillard's book in my hands.

By means of all created things, without exception, the divine assails us, penetrates us, and molds us. We imagined it as distant and inaccessible, whereas in fact we live steeped in its burning layers.

I brave the morning chill to grope for my watch: nine-thirty. I've had a full twelve hours of sleep. Twelve much needed, and bear-fear-free, hours. I untangle myself from the blanket inside my sleeping bag and let my thoughts drift back to the delightful cause of my exhaustion.

———

HE ARRIVED ON the dot of ten, headlights flashing through the window. Nancy wished me luck.

"Don't wait up," I joked. I put on a warm jacket – it might have been July but the temperature had dropped more than twenty degrees during the day – and went outside.

He met me on the road just up from his vehicle. "Are you bundled up?" He had on a thick jacket himself. He gave an embarrassed glance up at the brightly lit house. "What must your sister be thinking of me?"

"She's actually quite sympathetic. To both of us."

"She's too kind."

He led the way across the grassy point and down the steps. Waves licked at the shore in the night wind. On the dock, he pulled the two Muskoka chairs together and when we sat down jiggled his crossed leg up and down and tapped the arm of the chair. Clearly ill at ease.

I wasn't that calm either. I had no real idea what to say. "I'm struggling again," I said finally. "I thought we had everything figured out, but you were being so flippant on the phone."

"I was just as frustrated as you, but couldn't really talk – there were a couple of others in the office. I called back because I knew you would spend your week in the bush stewing."

"This is exactly what makes it so excruciating. That you know these things about me. That you're so perceptive – and so willing, and able, to communicate the way you do." I looked at him helplessly.

"I'm in the same boat. I just want to be close to you. I'll be sitting on my deck and you'll suddenly be in my head, and I'll wonder, What's Brenda doing? I feel a connection with you."

There was more in his words than just an irresistible flirtation. There was something I thought I would never experience again, though the connection was completely different from the ranger. Of course. "I feel like you're a kindred spirit. So I'm muddling around, trying to find the elusive middle road, because I do want you in my life. I don't want you to disappear."

"I don't want to either. But I do worry my presence in your life will prevent you from being open to meeting someone else."

I gave a dismissive wave of my hand. "You don't need to worry about that. I *know* there's no hope for us – "

"For the foreseeable future."

"Don't *say* that. That's exactly the kind of thing that screws me up. That and your saying you might go on a canoe trip yourself this week and happen to run into me."

"Okay, sorry, I won't say those kinds of things anymore. Anyway, at least I get to go camping with you vicariously through my gear. Though you don't seem to need it. You already have everything. It's a huge turn-on, you know, your being such a gear girl."

"Outdoor stores are the most dangerous place for me and my wallet."

"Getting to know you has restored my faith in there being women it's worthwhile knowing and talking to. The women in my office, and the wives of the guys – I don't have the time of day for them. All they do is gossip."

"There are lots of women who don't gossip. You're hanging out with the wrong ones."

"Just as well. Being blindsided by one of you is more than enough."

———

I INTERRUPT MY reveries to dress. By the time I get coffee and granola into me, the sun has hidden itself behind ominous clouds. I wonder if I'll make it to the portage out of Daisy before the rain.

I've no sooner pulled the pack straps tight when the first drops tap down from a suddenly black sky. A clap of thunder makes me jump. I undo the pack and pull out rain jacket and blue hardware-store tarp.

I spread out the tarp, sit down on half and pull the other half over my head. Rain clatters down on the woven polyethylene.

Over the rain, the Critical Chorus makes itself heard. *Why didn't you get up and moving while the sun was still shining? You got twelve indulgent hours last night.* Then: *Why on earth did you pack up the tent? You should just stay put.* I tell these contrary – and contradictory – voices they have not been invited on this trip. I tell them it's perfectly fine I slept around the clock and packed up the tent. I tell them to go find their own campsite on another part of the lake and *stay there.* Then, since I'm in meditation position, the mantra comes, its repetitions punctuated by rumbles of thunder.

At last the storm moves on, and I launch the solo rental boat under heavy, dark skies. I keep both fleece and rain jacket on, glad I threw in extra layers at the last minute.

My eyes are on the skies but my mind is on the man I unknowingly blindsided on the highway that sunny Hallowe'en afternoon nearly two years ago.

———

I FILLED THE CAR with gas and picked up speed on the highway. The roads were dry and the weather mild for the end of October. The trick-or-treaters wouldn't have to wear raincoats or ski jackets over their costumes tonight. My weekend company had just left, a friend in wildlife conservation and his girlfriend. I was now off to find the school, not that far from my new home, where he and I had spent a weekend learning how to white-water paddle several years before. He had marked its location on a topographical map, which was spread out on the passenger seat.

The paddling school was the destination, but the real mission was to keep myself from spiralling into a post-weekend-company depression. It was only a couple of weeks since I'd forced the breakup with the ranger.

I glanced over at the topo map to see how many squares it was to the side road that led to the paddling school – two squares, two kilometres – and turned my eyes back to the highway. Just in time to see I had drifted over the double solid line. With a car coming straight at me. So close I could see the look of horror on the occupants' faces. I yanked on the wheel and swerved back into my own lane. The other car went sailing past. My overcompensation on the wheel sent me skidding to the shoulder. I yanked on the wheel again. Back across the road I went, nicking the guard rail. I pulled again, trying to lessen the correction. The steering wheel had a life of its own. Even just a small touch sent it swinging all the way in one direction, then all the way in the other. Thank God there were no other cars on the road. The Precidia zigzagged down the highway.

I don't know how many zigzagging minutes or seconds later, I had to face it: I wasn't coming out of this skid. I aimed the car for the ditch.

Hold on to me!

NO SOONER HAVE I got all my gear across the portage to the river when the skies crack apart again. Almost in sync with the thunder is a loud exclamation from a man who has just arrived at the end of the trail with his two adolescent sons. "Boys, look! A moose!"

Sure enough, knee-deep in the grasses beside the waterway is a bull moose. A young one, by the size of his antlers. Water drips off the velvety rack. He seems unperturbed by rain, thunder (and humans). Unlike the boys. At my invitation, they huddle under my tarp, looking soggy and miserable. I almost feel them wishing they'd never let their father talk them into this ludicrous excuse for a vacation. I hope this long wet cold hour won't put them off canoeing forever.

I WAS UPSIDE DOWN. Belted into the seat. The windshield shattered to complete opaqueness but intact. Engine still running. A white powder-like substance floated down before my eyes. I absorbed all this with a wild range of emotions. Alarm at what I thought must be microscopic bits of glass (I tried not to breathe it in). Amazement that the engine could still be running. And terror that the car, with its full tank, was going to explode. I had to get out. I pulled the key from the ignition, unbuckled the seatbelt and promptly hit my head on the ceiling. I was instantly overcome with claustrophobia. A space that was perfectly fine to drive in right side up was now unbearably confining. My own door was jammed, and a dark tangle of bushes pressed against the window. I looked over to the passenger side and there was my escape hatch – a gaping hole where the window had been. *Thank God.*

I scrambled out of the car and up the steep embankment to the empty highway. Where was everyone? Where were my rescuers? I sat down on the gravel shoulder, taking in great gulps of air. The sound of a vehicle brought me back to my feet. A small rust-coloured sedan pulled onto the shoulder from the direction I had come. The doors opened and two young men got out.

The passenger reached me first – dark hair, warm dark eyes. "Are you okay? We saw you go out of control. We came back. We're from the army base in Petawawa. We know first aid. You sure you're okay?"

I nodded. Who they were was beginning to register. They had seen me and come back because they were the young men I had nearly hit. "Oh my God, I'm so sorry. Are *you* okay?"

"We're fine. We had to swerve hard but we didn't go out of control." He rubbed my back. "Are you sure you're not hurt? My friend's gone to call the police." He gestured to a house beyond my car. I caught a glimpse of white siding beyond a row of cedar trees above the ditch. My car had landed practically in someone's front yard.

I sat back down on the shoulder and took in the sight of the Precidia. It lay on its roof, metal underbelly exposed to the sky like the underside of a giant mechanical turtle. The shape of the ditch exactly matched its top-side curve. I couldn't take my eyes off it. The way the ditch cradled it so perfectly had possibly saved the roof from crumpling in… and crushing me.

Every time I heard a car, I turned, hoping against hope to see a red Tercel. The deer hunt was about to begin, and the ranger's plan was to go to the cabin today. He would pass right by.

My bum was getting cold. I started to shiver. The sound of voices made me turn. Across the highway, the two young men were leaning in the open window of an SUV stopped on the shoulder. Their voices were animated, and the one who had gone to call the police was making a large zigzagging motion as he pointed down the highway.

The SUV door opened then, and the driver got out and crossed the empty highway. Although he wasn't dressed in any kind of uniform, my first thought was he must be some kind of off-duty officer – police or fire department or military. There was something in his bearing, an air of authority even the army guys didn't have. I got to my feet with some trepidation, and then let out a breath of relief. I was looking into the face of a man with kind eyes, a face a little younger than mine, nice looking as well as nice. No judgment here, only concern.

"They said you weren't hurt. Are you sure? I know first aid too if you need it. You shouldn't be sitting on that cold ground. Come and warm up in my car."

I let myself be led across the road. The warm upholstered passenger seat was a haven.

He stayed out on the highway, eyes on the road up ahead, then turned and spoke through the open driver's window. "Is anyone expecting you? Anyone you should contact?"

"No. I just moved to the area. I was just out for a drive."

"The police shouldn't be long now. Unfortunately, you're almost to the county line, pretty much as far as you could be from the detachment." He stood by the open window, stepping out every so often to peer down the empty highway.

"I don't want to hold you up."

He leaned in the driver window. "Hmm?"

It was oddly touching, this familiar way of asking me to repeat myself.

"I'm not in any rush. I'm a realtor in the area." He introduced himself. "I was just on my way home. I can wait 'til the police come. It may well be an officer I know. If it is, I'll give him shit for taking so long." A sudden grin sent creases down his cheeks.

I didn't tell him how much I dreaded the arrival of his friend. The last thing I needed was a stern rebuke from a bullish cop. I knew how dangerous my driving had been. I shuddered to think what would have happened if...

———

THE RAIN STOPS, the thunder recedes, and a sliver of blue hope shows in the sky. The moose is long gone. We launch our canoes into the river and call out goodbyes. Their boat with three paddlers soon pulls ahead of mine with just one paddler and disappears around a bend.

With every other stroke I glance over my shoulder to make sure another storm isn't sneaking up on me. Black clouds scoot over my head, considerately holding their bladders.

FROM THE FRONT seat of the police cruiser, I watched the constable direct the odd passing car around the tow truck. It was nearly dark now and he waved a red wand. He had already taken the army guys' statements and sent them on their way. My turn next.

The Mazda came slowly back onto its wheels and out of the ditch, as if reluctant to leave its resting spot. The constable, a thickset man with a crew cut, opened the cruiser door. "Anything you want out of your car before they tow it?"

The windowless passenger door creaked open only halfway. Inside, the black upholstery was coated in the powdered glass that had floated down on me when I'd landed. I reached in to pick up my wallet from the floor. I shook it open and bigger bits of glass from the blown-out window fell out. I glanced into the back and spotted the open box of Ivory Snow I kept in the car for the laundromat. I almost laughed out loud. The white powder on the upholstery that had floated down on me wasn't microscopic bits of windshield at all. It was laundry soap.

Back in the cruiser, the constable took my statement. Despite his tough appearance, no "attitude" emanated from him. He somehow made me feel entirely at ease – not like a bad girl who had done something incredibly stupid and dangerous – even when he flipped open a little book and said, in a gruff voice, "The bad news is in an accident someone's usually at fault."

He handed me the ticket (much reduced from what it could have been) and, unexpectedly, apologized. He couldn't take me home, he had another call to get to. But, he added, the real estate agent had offered. I hadn't even noticed the agent was still hanging around.

"He's a good guy, a snowboarding buddy of mine. He'll get you home safe. If you're okay with that. You sure you don't want to get checked out at the hospital?"

His concern touched me. "No, I'm fine, really. And that would be very nice of him, if he really doesn't mind."

We cruised through the village. I glanced at the dashboard clock. Six-thirty. Three hours since I had left home to do an hour's tour.

"Where were you headed for, anyway?" asked my driver.

When I told him, he proceeded to give me exact directions to the paddling school. "I've taken courses there too, though I mostly stick to flat water these days."

When I revealed I was a happy flat-water paddler too, and a cross-country skier, road cyclist, runner, and hiker, he became even more animated. He described some good hiking and running trails and how far it was to the Algonquin ski trails. He told me which local Internet service provider to sign up with and which grocery store in town was the better one. "I love the area. There's even a little ski hill. What? You don't downhill? My listings are miles apart, and I have a side-gig doing security checks on the cottages I've sold. I like being on the road."

He did seem entirely at ease behind the wheel. I hoped I would become at ease again too. I glanced down at the shifters, one for the four-wheel drive. "What kind of car is this?"

"A 4Runner. Toyota. An aging one at that."

I filed away the information. If there was a silver lining in this accident, it would be the purchase of a 4x4 to handle my hilly road this winter.

At my direction, he turned down the municipal road and a minute later paused at the fork to peer at the sign for my road. "I haven't sold any properties down here." I felt him memorizing the name. I felt waves of mild interest. Maybe understandable, given the similarities of our interests and love of the area. My internal response was *no*. The ranger and I weren't done. Even if we were, I was nowhere near ready to meet anyone new. Still, I didn't mind his knowing where I lived.

He stopped at the top of the hill, looked past me to the darkened house, then at me. "You're sure you're all right? You don't have a concussion from hitting your head on the ceiling?"

"No, just a bit of a headache."

"Can you get to the hospital if you need to?"

I gave a wry laugh and gestured to my empty driveway. "But I'll be fine."

Beside the car, I thanked him for all his kindness. I watched the taillights disappear around the bend at the bottom of the hill and wished I could have asked for a comforting hug.

I poured a Scotch and took the portable phone to the rocking chair. The alcohol filled my insides with a soothing burning warmth. Asante's line was busy. My parents were away, and I didn't want to interrupt my sisters' Sunday dinners. I tried Asante a few more times while my mind, always looking for the interior meaning of exterior events, tried to figure it out. I was determined to stay out of my usual negative thinking that I must have done something bad.

Asante apologized for the busy signal when I finally got through. "I was on the Internet all afternoon. And I'm sorry, Lovey, I can't talk long. Company's about to arrive."

Quickly I told her what had happened.

"Flipped out of control." She emphasized each word.

I knew what she was thinking. I spoke calmly. "I don't think my life is out of control. I think the car was meant to go, not me."

"That's my sense too. Thank God you weren't hurt." She apologized again for not being able to talk and suggested some herbal remedies to help me sleep.

As soon as I turned out the bedside light, images of the accident crashed into my brain. I turned the switch back on and reached for an old teddy bear.

I woke, not in the dark grey of early morning, but in the warm glow of the bedside lamp. I woke to hear words spoken clearly in my head: *You did die in the accident – it wasn't just about the car. You were out of control – you relinquished it to God and the angels when you asked them to hold on to you. The old Brenda died and a new Brenda was born.*

I lay in the warm light, suffused with sudden and surprising joy. The birthing imagery was perfect. I'd emerged upside down from the claustrophobic womb of my car. I'd been washed clean – not with microscopic bits of glass that would hurt me if inhaled but innocent baby soap. I'd just clutched a stuffed toy all night. And the accident had happened almost exactly nine months after the ranger and I had reconnected on the phone in the new year. A wonderful terrible gestation period.

After breakfast I worked up the nerve to call the insurance company. My last dealings with insurance, about a fender bender, had not been pleasant. I described the demise of the car to the agent, and braced myself for her reprimand.

"Are *you* all right?"

The response was so unexpected my eyes filled with tears.

It was the same with every agent I spoke to – two adjusters and my new local agent. No harsh judgment, only concern and some gentle teasing about the lengths some people will go to get a new vehicle.

In the afternoon I sat in the landlord's cedar Muskoka chair on the point, face to the sun. Onto my skin and through the fabric of my jacket I absorbed the rare November warmth, and back out to the world I beamed waves of utter gratitude. I was alive. Uninjured. Able to sit on this point and look out over the water. Thanks to the Divine Presence that had responded, unconditionally and immediately, to my spontaneous burst of prayer as the car somersaulted into the ditch. I had prayed to be held, and by God I had been held. For the first time in my life, I understood the meaning behind all the religious talk that had always made me squirm. I understood what it meant to "surrender to Jesus" – even as the words still made me cringe and I still didn't believe in Jesus. I wanted to keep surrendering. I had just learned (in a crash course) that the uncertainty of each moment isn't a place of darkness and deprivation. It's a place where every true need is met, even, or maybe especially, by strangers. I had been reborn into a world I had rarely experienced before, a world of unfailing kindness and compassion.

My smashed-up Precidia and passenger-window escape hatch, 1999

———————

I N THE LITTLE creek that leads from the portage out to Misty Lake, I glance over to see, not three metres away, Bull Moose Number Two. The impressive rack tells me this one is fully mature. He gives me an appraising look before plunging his head back to his underwater dinner.

Antlers, says Ted Andrews in *Animal-Speak*, are "ancient symbols of antennae – of crownings that activate the upper chakras of the head," the energy centres associated with intuition and connection with the Divine. "For anyone who aligns with Moose... a unique and sacred energy is opened."

Moose seems determined to align with *me* this week.

———————

G OD REALLY DOESN'T waste energy," said Asante from the passenger seat of my new Suzuki 4x4 after I picked her up at the airport for her visit that December. "You got a dramatic rebirth, and a new car just when you needed it."

I told her about the real estate agent, and she agreed it was good to know someone else in the area, someone who knew I was here on my own. She thought he sounded like someone I could trust if I ever needed him. That someone had checked on me a week after the accident. He pulled up in front of the house and rolled down the window when I came outside to meet him. The slight self-consciousness I sensed behind his casual confidence endeared me to him. I pointed out my new car and assured him I'd been checked out by a doctor. After a few minutes chatting he sped back down the hill to show a cottage in the next township.

———————

O UT ON THE BIG lake at last, I attach the water purifier to my Nalgene bottle and throw the hose over the side. Beyond a small island with a nondescript campsite that I reject, I spy a loon. She looks like she's swimming quite high out of the water. Suddenly wondering, I pull the agent's borrowed binoculars out of my fanny pack, grateful for the novelty of such magnified vision. Sure enough, two tiny babies are hitching a ride on the loon's back. I've never seen this familial phenomenon before. Finally I tear my eyes away from the sweet sight and pick up the water purifier again. Pumping, I pray for the most appropriate, beneficial, healing thing for all three of us: me, the agent... and his wife.

A NEW FRIEND IN the area filled me in on his marital status. It didn't bother me to hear he had a wife. I barely gave him a thought. We ran into each other occasionally in town over the next year and chatted easily, as people do who have common interests. He asked questions about my writing as if he were genuinely interested. He emailed to ask if I would edit his resumé – he was applying to a new volunteer organization that was to assist the police with search and rescue. I decided I had misread him. His concern for my wellbeing had been nothing more than neighbourliness.

So his phone call this spring, a year and a half after our Hallowe'en introduction, was unexpected. He was calling because he planned to be in my area the next day to show a property in the afternoon. He thought he would spend the morning canoeing in the marsh and wondered if he could use my dock as a launch point – and would I like to come? "I've heard you world-famous writers will look for any excuse to procrastinate. Thought I'd help out."

"We call it research. And that's very kind of you. I happily accept." I still had few friends in the area. It was a tight-knit rural community, and I didn't have the usual venues of church, work, or school to meet people. I made a split-second decision to accept the agent's friendship, trusting he had no ulterior motive.

He arrived at nine sharp with his own canoe, paddles, life jackets. And baby. "My wife's working today," he explained. "My schedule's more flexible. Saves on daycare."

"And it's never too early to get them in a canoe."

"My thoughts exactly."

The odd presence of the baby seemed to confirm his motives were benign and made our being together "safe."

He carried his boat down the concrete steps to the dock. I followed, amused. "You know there are already two boats here."

"Just a matter of personal preference." Then he saw the red cedar canvas on the dock – a score from the local classifieds. "We'll use yours next time. Looks like a beauty."

I liked the way he said "next time" with no hesitation.

"It's a beauty only for paddling from the dock. I'm still looking for a superlight for trips."

He gestured to his own. It was a nearly transparent composite of some kind with aluminum gunwales, designed to be used with a bent-shaft paddle.

I shook my head. "Has to be a Prospector with wooden gunwales."

"And therefore carbon fibre to keep the weight down. You must be made of money."

"Well, you know us world-famous writers."

He retrieved the baby from the car and plopped him into the boat in his baby life jacket. He was about ten months old, and had clearly inherited his bright eyes from his father and his smile from his mother, who by this time I had met at a few gatherings. She was tall, trim, and at least a decade younger than me.

Her husband held out a plastic-bladed bent-shaft paddle but I grabbed my own straight-bladed cherry-wood beavertail. "A matter of personal preference."

He shrugged and tried to hand me a life jacket.

I shook my head, amused. "I've got one of those too."

He held the boat for me, and we set off across the river. It was remarkably warm for nine o'clock in the morning, or for any time of day at the beginning of May. It had been known to snow at this time of year. We were in shorts and T-shirts.

The canoe seemed to inhibit conversation, partly because I had my back to the agent and partly, I thought, because we had never paddled together before. I wasn't used to being in the bow, where there are no breaks to do a corrective stroke.

Once in the marsh, we slowed to explore its channels, and conversation became easier. We talked canoes and tripping in Algonquin Park.

Back at the house I pulled out the park map and we compared favourite routes.

A week later he emailed to suggest a hike, but I was scheduled to make a trip to Ottawa. One email led to another and soon we were communicating almost daily.

———

I STAND ON A HIGH cliff of rock on my campsite, holding a steaming bowl of rehydrated chili, eyes trained on the marsh at the back of a small bay a few hundred metres away. Against the marsh greens a spot of brown seems to move. I put down the bowl to retrieve the binoculars. Sure enough, it's Moose Number Three. Another bull. In addition to its spiritual medicine, Moose, I recall from my time with the ranger, is a symbol of the sexual energies. No wonder so many are around this week...

———

I LAY IN BED READING. The usual quiet of the house and neighbourhood was broken by the sudden sound of an engine on the road. Headlights flashed through the living room. A cottage neighbour coming in late perhaps, though it wasn't cottage season yet. Minutes later, sounds of the car heading back down the hill. Who in the world?

From: the agent
To: brenda
Sent: Wednesday, May 16, 2001, 2:02 AM
Subject: Cottage patrols

Good morning... Drove down your road tonight on my security patrols. All quiet. Talk to you later.

I replied over morning coffee, and his response arrived in the afternoon. The way his words were inserted right into my email below mine in italics made it look like a conversation.

From: the agent
To: brenda
Sent: Wednesday, May 16, 2001, 4:18 PM
Subject: Re: Cottage patrols

So that was you on the road. Did you see my bedroom light on? (Okay you don't even know where my bedroom is.) *I do now! Next time I'll flash my high beams so you know it's me.*

NOT wanting to interfere with anyone's marriage, but if it's all cool, would continue to enjoy the occasional outing. Though I also don't want to get your wife's sensitivities up, so I'll trust you to do the appropriate thing. *Yeah, I better not tell her I know where your bedroom is.*

He began to drop in now and then, usually in the evening on his cottage patrols. The first time put me in a tizzy, wondering what his intentions were, but he went straight to the rocker, a respectable distance from my couch, and accepted a cup of tea in lieu of a beer or glass of wine. We debated canoe and paddle designs and snowboarding versus cross-country skiing.

Sometimes he called ahead, sometimes he just arrived at the door. I looked forward to his company and was secretly touched he was watching my road. It seemed to fit with my new willingness to accept the protective caring of a male in my life. His energy was fun and teasing and, yes, flirty, but safe flirty. When I tried again to have a serious conversation about our friendship and his intentions, he sidestepped it with a flippant remark.

———————

I UNZIP THE TENT to see a rain cloud abscond with the newly risen sun. I zip it up again. It's cold! I dig in my clothing bag — a compression sack also borrowed from the agent — and pull out all my polypropylene layers and red Olympics cap. Everything has a faint, familiar fragrance to it. I bury my nose in the clothes. The agent is instantly with me. Good god, does he spray his camping gear with cologne? Or has it simply taken on his scent? I don't usually like perfumes or scents but this one is subtle and masculine, and I've definitely never had such nice-smelling camping gear.

I COULDN'T BELIEVE he'd worked up the nerve to join us. My sisters and their children had come up for the weekend to celebrate the auspicious occasion of my fortieth birthday. I'd invited the agent to stop in if he was on cottage patrol but hadn't expected him to show up. Especially after a recent innuendo-laden conversation on my dock. Every time he left I was sure he would decide he shouldn't visit anymore and disappear. This time *I* felt he should disappear. Instead, here he was, shaking off the rain in my kitchen.

I hung up his dripping coat and led him into the darkened dining area, where there was much laughing and talking and eating around the table. The candlelight reflected off our half-empty champagne glasses. We had finished Kathryn's delicious lamb curry and were halfway through dessert.

I scrounged a chair and introduced him to my three sisters and the three nieces who were still up – Lynne's two little ones were already in bed. Six-year-old Sarah, Nancy's younger daughter and my goddaughter, couldn't stop giggling. I knew she thought he was my boyfriend.

That "boyfriend" let himself be served a slice of pie and accepted a glass of tonic without the gin. He seemed completely at ease, as if he'd always known my sisters. He and Lynne began to chat about raising kids.

When, much later, he rose to leave, I asked if he would drop Nancy and Sarah at the motel in the village where they were staying.

"No problem," he said in his cheery way. "I'll bring the truck up to the door."

I carried my half-sleeping goddaughter from the bedroom where she'd been tucked in with her cousins. The agent held the kitchen door open and stayed by my side, hand outstretched, flashlight lighting the way as I carried Sarah over the uneven, wet rock to the car. I felt an almost visceral feeling of being "Mother" and "Mate" in the company of "Male Protector." For the agent it was an entirely familiar role. For me, it was a moment sporting someone else's feathers. My sister's. Or his wife's.

He opened the backseat door, and I set Sarah down and buckled her in. As soon as I straightened up, the moment was gone. I was me again, the agent was the agent.

"Thank you for dropping by. You were very brave to expose yourself to all the giggling Missens."

He leaned down to my ear. "Happy Birthday."

I lay in bed, infused with poignant joy. His visit somehow cancelled out all the shallow flirting and sexual teasing of our recent encounters. His desire to join my family party, and his ability to do it with such ease, touched me in a place deep inside and left me with a yearning that had nothing to do with sex. A yearning to be cared for the way the agent made me feel so cared for – a yearning this domestic, married, unavailable family man could never fulfill.

I STAND ON THE pebbled shore, bundled up in five faintly fragrant layers. Gloves wouldn't be out of order, if I'd thought to bring them. Out on the lake, white-frosted waves rush from west to east. I survey the waves and send out a prayer to the Universe that on Sunday, four days from now, I'll have a calm, windless, I'll take even blisteringly hot, day to get across huge Ralph Bice, the last major lake before the take-out.

Today's destination is supposed to be McIntosh Lake, just a few hours away. I wonder if I should attempt it. I have to come back this way tomorrow anyway. My trip is roughly the shape of a figure eight, with Misty at the pivotal point. Maybe I should just stay put.

I have to smile, remembering the agent's suggestion that he might go on a solo trip himself and just happen to meet me at McIntosh. "If you come and find me in the bush," I warned, "I won't answer for the consequences." He looked so startled I had to laugh. That was the end of any suggestion he might go on a parallel trip. And the beginning of some secret, guilty fantasies he planted in my brain that have accompanied me, even if he hasn't. I haven't moved from this site but I'm accidentally running into him everywhere.

I WAS ON THE WAY to the laundromat, on a Thursday. My usual time to do laundry was during breaks in the blues jam I attended every Tuesday at the local tavern, but I'd given myself this past Tuesday off clothes-washing to enjoy another birthday celebration. To my great shock the agent had shown up. In the nearly two years I'd been a regular, he had never once come to the tavern. He'd looked so sexy in jeans and white T-shirt, I'd given myself permission to enjoy him and all the energy between us – which was palpable before he was even halfway through the crowd.

He bought me a beer and asked if I had met a recent contract deadline. It touched me that he remembered these things about my life. He refused to slow dance. Just as well. His goodbye hug was electric enough. Now, two days later, on the drive up the highway to town, I replayed that hug and fantasized he would just happen to pass by the laundromat and stop in.

I wasted no time getting the wash in. I had a phone interview for one of my company profiles in less than two hours. I sat on the bench outside to read the background material.

Loads transferred to the dryers, I resumed my reading on the bench. A car suddenly charged into the lot and braked to a halt beside mine. The driver wore dark glasses and a grin.

He got out and sat down beside me. "Is this your penance for all your birthday celebrations? I thought you liked to do your laundry while you were tarted up for the tavern?" He was quoting my tongue-in-cheek term for dressing up for blues night. "That was nice tarting the other night by the way."

"I ran out of underwear," I said and immediately regretted it.

He grinned. "Your thongs?"

"I don't wear thongs."

"No, that's my wife's thing."

"Too much information. Did you mention your tavern visit to her?"

"Yes."

"What about your Friday night visit with my family?"

"Definitely not."

"You know this puts me in an awkward position when I run into her. How do I know what she knows and what she doesn't know?"

"I'm telling her about every second visit."

"Be *serious*."

"Okay. I won't tell her about *any* visits."

I gave up. It was his business how open he was with his wife. I could, however, include the whole family in his visits. "What are you doing this weekend? I was thinking of having you guys over for a barbecue."

"Sorry, we're off to Ottawa to visit her folks. And I get to pick up my new mountain bike. If you're good, I'll let you try it out."

"You'd have to lower the seat *and* move it closer to the handlebars. I'm pretty short-waisted."

"Short-waisted." He repeated the word as if he'd never heard it before. "Do short-waisted people wear short-waisted underwear?"

"Stop asking about my underwear!"

He took a small calendar out of his pocket and flipped through it. "We could do the weekend of the twenty-third/twenty-fourth, if you really think you can handle the family."

"I think I can manage."

Suddenly I noticed the time. "Shit, get out of here. I've got to fold the laundry and get home. I've got an interview in half an hour."

As he was getting in the car, I made one last plea. "Do you think you could you at least tone down the flirting?"

"You flirt too."

"I know. I can't help rising to the bait."

"I'll keep reeling you in then."

"Get out of here. I'm late."

"Yes. Fold laundry. Drive home. Interview," he said and got in the car. Those simple words, indicating genuine interest in my life, eased some of my frustration.

The light on the answering machine was blinking when I came in the door. I pressed play. "Hi, thought I'd call while you're folding your *thongs* – to say I will not be telling about the laundromat visit. Repeat *not*." There was light laughter, then: "Okay, later."

From: the agent
To: brenda
Sent: Thursday June 07, 2001, 11:17 PM
Subject: Re: Roger to your message (and one from me)

As much as I enjoy your teasing behaviour and can't help responding, it's fucking me up a bit. *That was my sense, which was obvious today.* I hope we can tone down the flirting/sexual energy between us. *Agreed.* Beyond the "fun," I feel genuinely cared for by you (Yikes, you say.) *I'm not sure how to explain this part (even to myself) but basically I have had an affection or sense of caring for you since the very first time we met. I have met a variety of women in and out of wedlock and this unique situation has got me puzzled.* Can we find the middle road? *Here's today's paradox... I care for you too much to have a relationship beyond friendship. I feel we should meet in person as I am interested in discussing the possibility of a middle road.*

His admissions were overwhelming. Bittersweet. Here was someone who seemed to genuinely care for me, and was willing to communicate it, and I couldn't *have* him. Under all the pain and inner turmoil was a strange kind of joy. I hoped we *could* find the middle road, a way that involved neither retreat nor capitulation to the compelling attraction.

I took solace from an email from Asante, who was glad to hear me speak of the joy under the pain and reminded me that his arrival in my life as a caring friend with a natural authority and protective spirit was a gift. "He's a wonderful reflection of your own new ability to give generously to yourself, to be gentle with yourself. A true 'agent' of the Divine! LOL"

I TAKE MY COFFEE to the wind-sheltered side of the campsite. I brought along half of the restructured novel manuscript to review before my summer writing vacation formally begins next week. It's my journal, though, that I open. Before I can concentrate on the novel I have to empty my head of all agent-related emails, visits, and conversations of the past couple of weeks. Good thing I brought a fresh notebook.

At two o'clock it becomes official: I'm staying put. No McIntosh Lake today. It's the first time in the half-dozen years the park has required lake bookings that I haven't stuck to the plan. It's not as if hordes of canoe trippers are vying for my site. I've never seen the park so empty in July. Not that it's lonely. There's too much going on. The wind is a constant presence, the sun an eagerly anticipated guest. There's soup to heat up and slurp down, layers to peel off and put back on. And a brain to keep uncluttering in my journal.

Part of me feels it's a cop-out to stay. I brace myself for the Critical Chorus. My head remains blissfully silent. There are no "shoulds" on this trip. No beatings, no self-flagellation. The Chorus members who tried to stage a comeback on Daisy yesterday obviously heeded orders to find their own campsite. The weather will dictate my itinerary, not some critical, second-guessing voice in my head. I don't mind being dictated to by the weather. If I have a prayer for the week, it's to feel even more in my element out here in the bush, whether I'm McIntosh bound or windbound.

There *is* one voice in my head, a cheerful voice that sounds remarkably like my agent: *You wimp.* I just laugh at it. In its tone I hear nothing but teasing affection and acceptance of my decision. For all this, I have a bear to thank.

I dine again on the high rock facing the marsh. This time, two brown spots come into view. The binoculars reveal a cow and a calf – Moose Four and Five. I barely have time to enjoy them. Another dark cloud is already releasing its contents over the bay. I get everything covered or put away and zip myself into the tent just in time. I know I won't be confined for long. The brevity of the cloudbursts has nothing to do with the size of the clouds and everything to do with the speed of the wind blowing them through.

Through the plastic window in the fly I see the sun peek out from the other side of the cloud. The rain hasn't quite stopped. I don rain jacket and boots and head down to the shore to scout for evidence of God's promise not to destroy the earth by flood.

Sure enough, a full, glorious rainbow arcs right over the lake, ends touching down on opposite shores. Then, before my disbelieving eyes, the full rainbow moves right down the lake. I stand on the shore and watch in no small awe as it is drawn along by – and in – a wind-pushed rain cloud. It's the first time I've ever seen a rainbow on the move. It's a miraculous culmination of all the day's elements of rain, sunshine, wind.

As the graceful arc glides to the east, it occurs to me that at one moment, one end of that rainbow was right out there in front of my campsite, right at my feet. Seen by some imaginary person – or real moose – standing on the western shore. I am the pot of gold.

From: the agent
To: brenda
Sent: Thursday, June 28, 2001, 4:04 PM
Subject: your upcoming canoe trip

Your route sounds fine. I expect to have a detailed itinerary including dates as well as a telephone call when you are back at your car.

THE CALM ARRIVES at last and I take it to bed with me, a relief for body and ears. It's another cold night. I leave on two polypro layers and again wrap myself in the fleece blanket inside my sleeping bag. If there's no warm-bodied man *with* me, the next best thing is to have one request me to leave my route with him. I didn't even mind his dictator tendencies (he would say *benign* dictator), since I *wanted* to comply. There's something to be said for this male protective instinct – it's handy *and* fun. Besides, he's the perfect keeper of the route. He knows the park intimately and has search and rescue experience to boot. If I were in trouble, I know he would be in here like a shot.

THE PHONE RANG in the middle of dinner. "How goes the packing?" From the table, Nancy gestured not to rush the call. Now that she'd met him again, on two visits this weekend, she had nothing but understanding for my inability to shut the door on this unconventional but compelling friendship.

Conversation veered into a glib chat about "us." We seemed to be talking at cross-purposes. In the background I heard another phone ring. "I've got to take that." We hung up.

"Darn him!"

Nancy sent an amused sympathetic look my way. "He certainly is a tease."

"I thought we had everything figured out. Now I'm probably going to stew all week."

I put *Addicted to Love* into the video player. Halfway through, the phone rang again. Nancy laughed. "I wonder who that could be?"

I paused the movie and reached for the phone.

"Is there anything you need to talk to me about before you go off for a week in the bush?"

"That's probably a good idea," I managed to say.

"If you do, I'd rather talk in person. I'll meet you somewhere. Name your time and place. I'm working late so it doesn't matter what time."

"Well, we're in the middle of a movie at the moment." He burst out laughing when I told him what it was. "How about ten o'clock on my dock? Unless you prefer somewhere else."

"Dockside at ten."

I hung up the phone and stared at Nancy. "Did I *invent* this man?"

IT FEELS GOOD to be on the move again, even if just for a day trip. It's another mixed-up day: sun, cloud, breeze, calm, warmth, cold. I layer up, peel down, layer up again.

The wind rises. Mindful of the agent's email about the (life-jacketless) body of a twenty-seven-year-old that was pulled from a park lake last week, I put on my own life jacket and remove the heavy hiking boots. Sailing down the lake, I spot Moose Six and Seven, both cows, each supping in her own little marsh.

In the marshy narrows after the portage I manoeuvre around delicate yellow-cupped and white lotus-like water lilies. Just off to the side of the waterway is Moose Number Eight, thigh deep in the water.

Another cow. We keep a wary (and in my case also admiring) eye on each other. She's so perfect in her total unselfconsciousness about the inelegant hump behind her neck and her bulbous nose and her gangly (but useful) long legs.

The narrows spit me into Timberwolf Lake, where black clouds give way to blue sky and calm seas. And warmth! I peel down to tank top.

Making my way around the perimeter of the silent, still, serene lake, it dawns on me that perhaps the biggest legacy of all those summers spent at camp is the way God was "presented" in the wilderness. At Pioneer on Sunday mornings, we transported ourselves to church either on foot or in canoes. Our boats were red-painted cedar canvas, our paddles red-painted beavertails. Church was Chapel Point, whose walls were stately white pines, whose high arced ceiling was the sky, whose choir was a chorus of birds chirping in the tree branches. We read the Holy Word on a lakeshore lined with holy rock and shared our spiritual experiences around a campfire. No wonder I come to the woods – in a canoe – to experience the Sacred. No wonder I experience the Sacred in a canoe in the woods. And feel safe here. The woods are my church. Much more than church ever was.

THE REDEEMER'S rector stood behind the altar, a slim figure in a white robe who, behind his pointed black beard, looked both solemn and approachable. The wide sleeves of the robe fell away as he raised up the delicate hammered-silver plate I had many times passed to him in my former role as server during communion services. Plate held high, he announced to the congregation: "The gifts of God for the people of God."

His words were an invitation to partake in the Eucharist, to drink the wine and eat the delicate, white, flavourless, unleavened disks that lay on the silver plate. It was an invitation that in the Anglican Church is extended to all baptized Christians. But not, tonight, to me.

It was Christmas Eve during my third year of university. I sat near the back. Well spaced around me were people I'd never seen before. Each of us on our own. My fiancé (separated but not yet divorced) never came to church, though he was the reason for my unusual seat at the back. We'd been living together for several months now. Before making the decision to move in, I had gone to consult with my rector but he was away on vacation. The young assistant who met with me instead didn't seem concerned. My fiancé might not yet be legally free to marry but the divorce was in the works, and we were clearly committed to each other. This was the 1980s and the Church was loosening up on its stance against "living in sin." Satisfied I had the Church's blessing, I went ahead with the move. Then the rector came back from holiday.

One by one, starting with the front pews, the congregation members filed up to the altar. I listened to the choir sing the communion motets and remembered the way I had sat in the rector's office on the other side of his paper-strewn desk. We were not, he said, two single people who wanted to live together before marrying. Despite his legal separation, my fiancé was still legally married to another woman and so, in the eyes of the Church, said my rector, I was committing adultery. "Brenda, I can't in all conscience give you communion while you're living with him." He said it with infinite sadness and regret.

As I tried to absorb his words, he added, "I wouldn't blame you if you want to hit me."

The idea was so ludicrous I almost laughed. I felt betrayed, not angry. The blessing conveyed through his assistant had just been ripped away.

Muffled sounds of people getting to their feet a few rows ahead brought me out of my thoughts. I watched the line of bulky coats shuffle out of the pew and up the aisle. It was time for those in the row right in front of me to go up, and then those in my row, but none of us moved.

The rector's decision didn't spur me to yield to the authority of the Church, or, maybe more surprising, to leave. I was still some years away from giving a thought to the sacredness of the woods. Church was still an important part of my life, despite my doubts about its

Founder and my anger at its implication that only baptized Christians are "people of God" – despite, even, being denied the sacraments. I simply avoided the communion service and attended Morning Prayer instead. The rector and I continued to be on good terms. I knew he wished he could give me communion. We were caught between a rock and a hard Christian place.

PADDLING UP THE west side of Timberwolf, I pass by the marshy mouth of Timberwolf Creek and spot Moose Number Nine. Yet another cow. This is the most moose I've ever seen on one canoe trip. All of them solitary, except for the cow with her calf. Is there a sense among the solitary beasts that they're part of a larger moose congregation? Is there a communion of moose?

When Teilhard de Chardin was a stretcher-bearer during the First World War he had no bread or wine to offer at Mass. I learned this from Annie Dillard in the tent last night. He came up with the idea of offering up to God at sunrise each morning that one day's development, the "toil and sorrow of the world." And years later in China, Dillard quotes, he said his "Mass upon the altar of the whole earth" every day, "to divinize the new day."

My affection for Teilhard de Chardin and his way with words is growing every day.

A YEAR AFTER HE dropped his holy bombshell on me, the rector took me aside after the service one morning and handed me a letter. It was addressed to him from the governing body of the church and contained the recommendation that Brenda Missen be reinstated to the sacraments. I was mystified until he explained he had written to the bishop. It both amused and disturbed me to think that a group of older male clerics had sat around a meeting table discussing my sex life.

I returned to receiving communion as if nothing had changed. Though of course everything had.

———

I T'S A HARD PUSH up the lake. By the time I arrive back at my site I'm sweaty and in need of a bath. The water's too cold for a swim. I give myself a quick sponge bath and rinse my hair in the woods with a potful of shocking water. From the island campsite come voices, one high, one deep. "It's freezing!" "It's fine once you get in." "You first!" "I'll help you in." "Not that waay-ahhh!" A high shriek. Deep laughter.

The voices ignite a brief, intense yearning to be out here with someone. Someone like my agent. But not my agent. Will this experience elude me the rest of my life? I don't know. I'm just profoundly grateful it hasn't prevented me from being here.

Tonight in the tent, Annie Dillard reveals that the Jesuit paleontologist had a decades-long love relationship with a sculptor named Lucile Swan. His vows forbade him to consummate their relationship and, despite what he called "some difficult passages," he never broke them. I know someone else who has taken vows he will not break (despite suggestive comments to the contrary). Me, I identify with the sentiment Swan expressed in a journal entry Dillard sees fit to quote: "Friendship is no doubt the highest form of love – and also very difficult."

———

T HE WIND DIED, and the moon shone high in the sky. The sudden stillness of the night seemed to calm the agent sitting next to me on the dock. He stopped tapping and jiggling and spoke into the dark. "What has me blindsided is that I've been struck with intense feelings for you. I've felt them since the moment you came walking toward me on the highway. And I didn't even know your name. I wasn't looking to fall in love."

I couldn't speak. It was the closest he'd come to telling me he loved me.

The chill of the night seeped through my jacket. I made a mental note to pack extra layers. The agent must have seen me shiver. He got to his feet. "I've failed to consider your comfort. Let's go get you warmed up in the car. In fact, why don't we go for a drive? Unless you think you should get back to Nancy. I don't want to know what she must be thinking of me."

"Don't worry," I assured him again. "And we can go for a drive. I'm sure she's in bed."

I started up the concrete steps, very aware of him behind me. Suddenly I felt two hands on my hips, and before I knew it he had jumped me up to the next step. The instant after that he swept me right up into his arms, Rhett Butler style. Instinctively I wrapped mine around his neck, and he carried me up the steps as easily as if I were a child. His arms felt like home. A warm, embracing home. I had never, in forty years, felt anything like this kind of physical home. It didn't matter that we were both wearing thick bulky jackets. Some feeling, some warmth and comfort, radiated from his being. I felt *held*. I didn't want him to put me down. Ever.

A LITRE-SIZED Nalgene bottle full of near-boiling water makes an excellent, if not very cuddly, hot water bottle for a pair of cold feet on a cold July night.

IN THE SUV, the agent turned the heater to high. We drove up the moonlit highway in silence for several kilometres, then made small talk for several more. We were almost back to my road when he said, "If I *were* free… would you go out with me?"

"I haven't seen anything that would make me hesitate. I'd want to keep getting to know you. Two months isn't all that long a time to get to know someone."

"It's been two years, Brenda."

The words, spoken in such an understated tone, stunned me. I hadn't realized just how long he had been carrying around feelings for me. "But you disappeared for a long time."

"I disappeared intentionally, trying to clear my head of you. That didn't work, so I decided to try the other way – to get to know you."

"Hence the phone call to go canoeing this spring."

"I thought maybe I'd find some unredeeming quality. Nope."

Another long pause. We reached the fork before my cottage road. "I'm usually very private about my feelings. But you make it comfortable for me to talk about them."

At the turnaound spot, he backed in and cut the engine. He turned suddenly and in that impish, impetuous way of his said, "Ever made out in the backseat of a car?"

I had to laugh, even as I berated him for so quickly breaking his promise not to make provocative suggestions.

He looked at his watch. "I should get going." He turned away and, in a very small voice, spoke to the windshield. "Bye."

I thought he was joking but he didn't follow it up with his signature grin. I spoke gently. "Are you at least allowed to hug me?"

As if my words were a magnet, he reached over and pulled me into his arms. A hand stroked my hair with incredible gentleness. I felt a hand on my waist and then, briefly, sensually, on my hip. I pulled back and was so afraid we were going to kiss I buried my face in his coat. I could feel his desire. It seemed banked down with iron self-control that somehow emanated a tenderness I wasn't sure I had ever experienced before. I soaked it up like some starving orphan. It wasn't erotic or lustful, this holding. Not that the eroticism wasn't there; I had been in a state of arousal for the past two and a half hours. Enfolded in his arms, though, it was suddenly crystal clear that infatuation or sexual desire wasn't the driving force of our friendship. It was equally crystal clear that sex with this man would be at the incredible end of the spectrum – the genuinely-being-made-love-to, passionate end of the spectrum.

"This isn't fucking me up," I said, and heard him give a little laugh. A moment later, I added, "I hope this isn't fucking you up."

He assured me it wasn't.

"Think of it as the hug I wanted to ask for when you drove me home from my accident."

Moments later, I said, "I'm sorry." And then, calmly, with no expectation of hearing it back or need for him to do anything about it, "I love you."

He released me and kissed my cheek. "Have a good trip this week. And don't go getting eaten by a bear on me."

THE TRAIL THAT links Little Misty and Queer lakes is 2,435 metres, which means I'll be walking seven kilometres, my longest portage so far. The agent assured me it's flat and easy. I set a sedate pace with the canoe. On my head, the boat reminds me of an oversized moose rack. The thought makes me grin. Moose, bearer of the biggest antennae Nature can produce, is helping me to attune to the animating force of the Universe: Love. And so, I muse, as I tramp down the trail, is the agent. Because we can't have a "real" relationship, I can't turn him into my God, or look for my fulfillment in him. I haven't done anything to earn his affections. I already have them. Just for being me. The thought is as overwhelming as the super-large Kevlar antenna on my head.

One final push across wind-roughened Little Trout rewards me with a lovely south-facing campsite with a vast expanse of smooth-sloped rock and a lush hemlock interior. I'm almost too tired to enjoy it; in all, I've carried boat and gear nearly ten kilometres today. By eight o'clock I'm in bed. Which might just be part of the Bigger Plan to get Brenda up early and on the water before the winds come up on Ralph Bice – the daunting lake between me and the parking lot.

There's no payphone anywhere near that parking lot. When I pointed this out, the agent modified his "call me when you get back to your car" instruction to "call from the payphone at the outfitters when you return the canoe." In a post-dockside-chat email, he added that I should look for his vehicle in the East Beach area along the Highway 60 corridor. I didn't let on how much this non-solo participation in (or just after) my solo trip thrilled me.

Little Trout is not a quiet lake. Even in the tent set far back in the woods, I can hear the exuberance of the other sites – all of them, it seems, occupied. I insert earplugs to block out the sound of the campers and the wind and spare not one thought for the bears that will be able to sneak up on me.

I wake in the dark. The earplugs have fallen out and the wind is still howling – as are a group of campers somewhere on the lake. I grope for the little foam plugs and fall back to sleep.

At 5:20 I'm awake again. It's not yet sunrise but (I check, believe me I check) I'm awake. As in rested, ready to get up. I've had a full night's sleep before six in the morning.

It feels warm, even so early. Optimistically, I put my bathing suit on under my clothes. I have to dig for it in the very bottom of the no longer quite so fragrant clothes sack.

What greets me when I emerge from the tent isn't yet the sun but the moon, still high in the pale dawn sky, just past full. My first glimpse all week.

The best part of the morning is the quiet. The absence not just of voices but of wind. The lake is a mirror. Mist rises off the mirror. Balm to my soul.

So is the sun. Ah, the sun. It rises serenely, unimpeded, into a clear sky, a sky that's going to turn blue, blue, blue.

Rising so early I'm given the illusion of solitude, even on such a populated lake. I set my stove on the smooth flat shoreline rock out in the new sun and put water on to boil. The morning is so quiet the stove's hissing seems it will surely wake the lake. No one stirs.

I think the Universe must have misheard my request to *feel even more in my element* on this trip. It must have thought I wanted to *feel the elements more*. I've certainly been immersed. We've had an intense encounter, the weather and I, which has taken up a lot of mental and physical energy. Now, though, there's a deep internal quiet, as if the wind blew me clean inside, blew out all my distractions and preoccupations. Even my most major one. It's ridiculous to have this man so thoroughly in my mind and heart. Nevertheless I'm serene. Like the lake.

The fish are jumping, the frogs are serenading the sunrise, and suddenly there are ten loons on the water. I've never seen that kind of congregation except on Cathy's lake, where two or three dozen hang out together, for reasons unknown and contrary to the "two-loon-per-lake" rule. I sip hot caffeinated mud and watch the gathering. The loons swim around each other in unnameable patterns. Then, one after the other, five line up, like so many planes in succession on a runway, each calling out as they flap their wings and race along the water to take flight. I don't feel so bad anymore about making noise with the stove. Are the late-night revellers cursing in their sleeping bags? They're missing the show.

And what a show. Still following one another, the five airborne loons disappear beyond the tree tops. Moments later, they reappear, one by one, over the treeline, carving a wide unseen circle. They bank south in a fly-by right over my campsite, white bellies shining in the soft morning sunlight.

Gratitude swells inside for this awesome display. For this divinizing of the new day, as de Chardin might say. With that thought, it comes to me that all the birds and animals the different First Nations call totems – the loons and ravens, the moose and bears – are also sacraments. I see them with sudden clarity for what they are: "an outward and visible sign of an inward and spiritual grace." They bestow on us spontaneous, generous, and totally unexpected gifts from God. The earth is full of sacraments, living, breathing gifts of God. The four elements, the trees, the rocks, the plants – the very fabric of the Earth – they're all sacraments. We have only to become attuned to what they're pointing to – to the Grace and healing and nourishment they are ready to bestow on us – if, like Moose, we would extend our antennae and become attuned and aware. They're everywhere. Manifestations of the Love that animates the Universe. We live, as the paleontologist says, steeped in its burning layers – layers of fauna and flora, rock and earth, thought and feeling. Out here this week I've been partaking in a sacred communion with, and in, the elements (that word itself an alternate if no longer used term for the Eucharistic bread and wine, the Host). For the first time I "get" communion, as I never did in the ten years I received it, and the one I didn't, in church. Here, on this "altar of the whole earth," in this cathedral in, and of, the woods, I have been nourished, emptied of my self's preoccupations, filled with wellbeing, with peace. Grace.

The agent's love, too, is Grace at work. A gift in itself, despite some lingering interior conflict about its source. The Universe said, "Brenda needs love, send my special agent. Send him because he is so earthy and physical, so she will experience the holiness of physical being."

In our hands, in the hands of all of us, the world and life (our world, our life) are placed like a Host, ready to be charged with the divine influence…

Ralph Bice, which I have previously only battled – and with a paddling partner – on windy white-capped days, is a mirror. A hot, calm answer to prayer.

Hambone paradise harbour for my solo rental canoe, July 2001

The heat, the calm, the stillness permeate every stroke. And then I reach heaven.

Of all the names to call heaven, Hambone is not the first that springs to mind. But that's where I find it, on Hambone Lake, just before the take-out. Not a campsite but a private jut of rock off the main route, a perfect little picnic site with its own little harbour for the boat and a private lagoon for Brenda's Bath.

Clean from my swim I sit under the obligatory heavenly pine and eat the last of the now oily cheddar in a tortilla wrap. I revel in clean hair, bask in warmth. I feel so calm. As calm as Ralph Bice, as calm as the day.

I glance down into Hambone's mirror waters, and in the mirror I see my special agent waiting in his dark green 4Runner in a parking area along the Highway 60 corridor. I see an olive-green Suzuki pull into the lot and a (now clean) bush girl climb out and cross over to her agent. I hear him call out, "You made it! I'm so proud of you!" See him reach out his arms and swing her off her feet, in full view of passing cars, in a jubilant special agent hug.

I smile at this rejoicing reunion. I love what I see in the mirror.

After the bath, Hambone Lake, July 2001

5

IMPRISONED IN PARADISE

Pinetree Lake: August 19–23, 2001

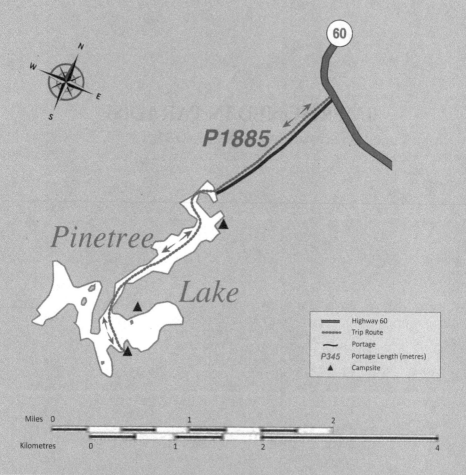

60

P1885

Pinetree

Lake

▬▬▬▬	Highway 60
••••••	Trip Route
〜〜〜	Portage
P345	Portage Length (metres)
▲	Campsite

Miles 0   1   2

Kilometres   0   1   2   4

R FZ. THE LETTERS ARE writ large in squeaky red indelible marker. So large I can smell them. The park attendant, wielder of the stinky marker, pushes the camping permit across the counter and points to the letters. "Initial here."

I'm amused he expects me to initial a code I've never seen before. "What's it stand for?"

"Restricted Fire Zone. It means no campfires are allowed in the park."

The rain is teeming down. I can barely see out to the highway.

He shrugs. "It's not enough to lift the ban. It will take several days of steady rain."

It's the first rain we've had since my Misty Lake canoe trip six weeks ago. Since then it's been so hot and dry the leaves on the small maple tree in my yard have turned brittle brown, the sumacs are drooping, and the pines are dropping needles in overdrive. We're in a level one drought.

In more modest-sized regular ink, I initial my agreement not to light a campfire. I've booked myself on Pinetree Lake for five nights to work on the novel I lugged around for six days for no reason on that last canoe trip. The attendant tells me I'll likely have the lake to myself.

Not ten minutes down the highway, I slow to look for the almost hidden entrance to the parking area. A couple of days after I arrived back from my July trip I shared its location with the agent.

H E PICKED ME UP at the tavern. It wasn't planned. It was blues night, and I wasn't having a good time. The ranger was there with some colleagues. We had previously got to the smiling-at-each-other-across-the-room stage; tonight he wouldn't meet my eye. A man I had briefly dated in the spring stayed at the other end of the bar. When I stepped outside during the break and saw the agent's car in the parking lot, I climbed in the passenger seat. "Where are we going?"

"To check on a cottage. The owners aren't coming up 'til next week."

We headed west on the highway, then drove several kilometres down a side road. I waited in the car while he checked the property. On the way out to the highway I told him my plan to go back into the park and was surprised he didn't know Pinetree.

We reached the highway. Instead of turning left, back to town, he turned right.

"Where are we going now?"

"To check out the Pinetree parking lot. If you're going in there I need to know where you'll be."

A jolt of pleasure at the benignly dictatorial protective tone.

In the tiny lot, he cut the engine and I described the nearly two-kilometre portage and what I remembered of the lake from two day-trips with the ranger (omitting a certain erotic picnic). We listened to Natalie Merchant on CD. Then his voice came out of the dark. "While you have me captive here, is there anything else you want to ask me?"

A moment of shock at such male willingness to communicate. I thought for a moment. "Did you come to any conclusions while I was away?"

"Conclusions?"

"You know, about us. I keep expecting you to take drastic action and decide you can't be in my life anymore."

He shook his head.

"Well, promise me if you decide you need to run you'll write me a little runaway note."

"I have no intention of running."

Relief at the words. "But is your wife okay with our friendship?"

"You don't have to worry about her being jealous. And you can drop around our house, you know."

"Well, that's nice to know. But that leads again to the awkwardness of what she knows and doesn't know."

"She knows we share a lot of interests. I've told her it's an activity-based friendship."

"Activity-based, okay. I guess I don't expect you to relate our entire conversations."

"No. I really don't want to explain the inexplicable emotional feelings I have for you." He looked out the window as if there were something to see in the dark. "I have this love-sick-puppy tendency to check my email every minute to see if there's a message from you. I try to tell myself we don't have to communicate *every* day."

"I'm in the same boat."

"I've been trying not so much to *explain* my feelings," he added, almost to himself, "as to quantify them. My expression of them to you has been rather disproportionate to how I feel."

I was too stunned to respond. What he *had* told me was overwhelming enough. And where did that leave his wife? Finally I said, "I think I need to hear from you, seriously, that you're committed to your marriage. I don't want part of my brain always going down the 'I wonder if...' road."

"I *am* committed. I know the only road open to us is what you call the middle road. Though" – he gave me that impish grin of his – "I have to wonder how wide it can be."

"I think it may already be wider than it should be. Should we even be here? Doesn't it bother you," I persisted, "that you don't tell her about most of our encounters?"

"No, that doesn't bother me. But I *am* struggling with whether I'm committing emotional adultery by loving two women at the same time."

As I tried to absorb his use of the L-word, he went on. "It's not your fault and it's nothing you need concern yourself with. This is my issue to deal with."

My heart was flooded with unexpected joy. My challenge – it was absolutely clear in this moment – was to accept his offer of friendship and also, totally unasked for, totally unearned, his love. I felt confident of the boundary we had set. If he had to set a stricter one, I would respect it, but it had to come from him. I would not assume I knew what his journey was. This was new.

———

THE RAIN HAS LET up to a friendly spit. I don't bother with the Gore-Tex jacket. I do put on my padded-shoulder life jacket and a rolled-up towel around my neck. The canoe and I set off down the narrow path into the woods at a plodding pace. My period is due any minute and I'm not carrying the lightest boat in the world. I opted to bring my own rather than rent a superlight, since I have only the one portage in and out – and since this will be our last voyage together. Next week I'm transporting her to new owners. She's been a faithful tub of a vessel but it's time to make way for a new, lighter, more manageable boat. I have my eye on a carbon-fibre-Kevlar Prospector, though it's way out of my budget. I'm prepared to sell the cedar canvas too.

My boots squelch in the mud, and I keep careful watch on my footing, amazed that just four days ago the path was dusty dry. Over that dusty path I shouldered not a boat but a baby.

———

THE AGENT'S SON in his lightweight backpack carrier was probably not even as heavy as the day pack on the agent's back. And he was carrying both the pack and his own long, sleek boat with enviable ease. We would not have to double back for any gear.

It was the agent who suggested we make the trip in. At first I thought he meant overnight.

He grinned. "I see that's got you all excited. But no, overnight is not an option."

So here we were on a day trip. He had sounded out his wife, who reportedly had not minded. She had even invited me to join them after for dinner.

We hiked over the exposed boulders in a dried-up stream bed and I chatted to Baby, who cooed his responses to the back of my head. We trekked deeper into the woods, crossed over more dried-up stream beds, and listened to the wind rustle the unnaturally dry leaves above. From behind, I felt the agent's eyes on my bare calves and, despite the heat, wished I'd worn long pants.

R AIN TAPS DOWN on the hull of the canoe on my head. It's been two and a half years since my first trek here, when the ranger and I trudged through deep snow in the tracks of a wolf. We returned weeks later, after the spring melt, with the canoe. I have to smile at the memory of how emotional the sight of my boat on his shoulders made me. I was certain I had found my One True Paddling Partner. I was happy to come in last week with the agent, to have refreshed my memory of the trail and lake, but it was, thankfully, no big deal he was canoe-carrier. Not that I feel entirely sanguine about our friendship. A month ago I felt so strong and sure. No more. Our hugs are becoming more intense and erotic, and I'm starting to feel no small amount of guilt.

Out on the water, exhaustion from the six kilometres of relays with five-hundred-pound canoe and packs dissipates and serenity descends on me like a gentle rain. The real rain has let up. It's nearly six o'clock. Not another soul on the lake. I look around. My Pinetree paradise is a deeply carved out, water-filled, unpolished jewel of granite whose high-sloped east shore is populated mostly with pines. Large swaths of bare rock show between the trees and undergrowth – unusual for Algonquin – and the slope, though steep, is hikeable.

I paddle on, eyes on the hill. The low bushes – blueberry bushes – are scorched from the drought. An ominous sight. If the blueberry crop has failed, the bears will be hungry. There's the added worry that when my period arrives I may be particularly attractive to hungry bears, though rationally I know there's no scientific evidence of this.

The lake narrows into one of my favourite places in the whole park, a long channel given shape by high mossy cliffs of rock. White pines cling to the rock. I let the boat drift to take in the sight and marvel at how pine trees can wrap their roots around granite and find nourishment in it.

The channel pops me out into the lower half of the lake. Straight ahead, on the far shore, the fluorescent orange sign with its tent symbol stands out like a beacon. The ranger and I found the site when we paddled in that spring. We didn't get out to explore, just admired it from the water and headed back before we lost the light.

Only one more hour of daylight. I scurry around to throw the food-pack rope over a large pine branch, set up tent and kitchen, chow down on a quick supper, and hang the pack.

Getting ready for bed, I discover my period has arrived. It's with exhausted relief that I sink onto my sleeping bag in the tent. "Thank you," I say out loud to Whoever might be listening. "Thank you for getting me here before my period arrived and before the rain comes back."

The words are no sooner out of my mouth when telltale sounds tap down on the nylon fly. As I told my niece on one trip after we zipped ourselves into the tent we'd just erected seconds before a deluge: "The elements and I have an arrangement."

THE AGENT AND his wife and I met up with a mutual friend in a neighbouring town to see a play. It was my idea. I was trying to suggest things the three of us could do together. This didn't stop the agent from flirting with me in the pub after the performance. His wife seemed not to notice. Still, I worried she was worried I was trying to steal her husband. On the drive home, I sat in their back seat beside the baby's car seat and brooded. It wasn't his wife I had to worry about. It was my own heart. For the first time I wondered just how badly I was fooling myself.

Home in bed I dreamt I was walking down a city street with a man. It was hazy who he was, except we liked each other. Suddenly, up ahead, loomed a large black animal, its shape cat-like. I pointed to it in amazement. A panther! The big black cat just stood on the street, waiting for us the way a dog would. No threat emanated from it. "It belongs to someone," I told my companion. "We have to go find its owner and return it home."

The phone woke me. I stumbled out to the kitchen and reached for the portable.

"Good morning, Sunshine!"

A pang of guilty joy at the sheer affection in his voice. It was time to say something. I let him ramble on about our evening outing, and said, "While I have you on the line."

"Uh oh."

"Yeah, I'm a bit messed up. I'll be blunt. I'm in love with you."

"Oh *barf*," said the agent.

If I hadn't been so stunned I would have burst out laughing.

"Are you serious?"

"Yes. I'm a little worried I'm not open to meeting anyone else."

"You told me not to worry about that."

"I know, and it was true when I told you, and it will probably be true again tomorrow, but right now..." Out the window I watched the whitecaps race down the river and around the point. "I just need a reality check. Need you to tell me you're not going to leave your wife for me."

"It's not my *intention*."

This was not reassuring.

"Even if I did leave her it wouldn't guarantee a relationship between us would work. You might hate living with me, you might not like my benign dictator."

"I know this sounds completely contradictory, but I also worry you're going to suddenly realize what we're doing is crazy and you'll go to the opposite extreme and run."

"I *could* go to extremes," he teased. "I *could* take that drastic action you keep talking about."

"I don't *want* you to go to extremes."

"I could become an asshole so you'd hate me."

"No!" I was half-laughing. "I don't *want* you to become an asshole!"

"In fact, I could solve everything by having an affair with you, and that would effectively end my marriage and also ruin any chance of anything happening with you." His voice dropped to a sexy whisper. "Brenda, I can't live without you. I can't hang up the phone because I already miss you."

Now I was giggling.

His voice returned to normal. "So are you okay now?"

"Yes. Thank you." And I was.

As soon as we hung up, the dream he had interrupted came back. I had no idea what panther signified. But my subconscious clearly did. I found an entry for it in *Animal-Speak* and was amazed to read that Panther holds the promise of rebirth and has ties to powerful sexual energies. It offers extra protection during a time of rebirth to face "offending malignancies of our life," aspects of ourselves we've "shoved to the back of the closet or pretended didn't exist."

The words reminded me of my car-flipping rebirth and the arrival of my protective agent. Something was clearly going on with that, something beyond the irresistible attraction between us, and here it was: "It may reflect a time of resolving old sexual issues, or it may simply reflect learning to embrace these energies as a true power without being judgmental."

My dream panther was tame, and needed to be returned to its home. Did I have the courage to take it there?

I OPEN MY EYES, far from rested. The rain, my cramps, and thoughts of a soggy-wet, blueberry-starved bear skulking about in search of a midnight snack kept me awake most of the night. I poke my head out of the tent. Everything – trees, rocks, tent – is wet, but it's no longer raining and not that cold. I dress and retrieve the food pack from the tree.

The stove is sluggish. The water seems to take twice as long to boil.

I've barely cleaned up the breakfast things when the rain returns. I crawl back into the tent, relieved not to have to pack up to go anywhere. I ignore the large zip-lock bag with the novel chapters I've come to rewrite, and reach for my journal.

HE SCRUTINIZED MY face when I opened the door. "Are you over your meltdown now?"

The indulgent tone kept the word from being a put-down. The concern in his eyes took my breath away. Who was this man who had so much affection and understanding for me, this man who could laugh me out of my angst?

"Come in?"

"Sorry. Gotta meet with a prospective buyer."

"Probably just as well. I should get back to the novel."

"I've been distracting you from it all summer. I feel guilty about that."

"I guess we both have a guilt thing going on, but about this I assure you there's no need. There's novel work and there's Brenda work. They're equally important, and you're definitely helping me with the latter."

He shook his head. "I'm not even going to ask. Anyway, I just stopped in to make a personal appraisal of your wellbeing."

"You're not worried about me, are you?"

"No, you seem fine." He laughed. "You sure have me fooled. But I have to fight my own tendency to want to reach for my cape."

He saw my blank look. "You know, Superman to the rescue. I'm learning to support you without becoming personally consumed."

I didn't have the nerve to ask what "rescuing" might entail. I was too overwhelmed by the idea of anyone *wanting* to rescue me. I kept my tone light. "Well, I think it's neat we're giving each other opportunities to break old patterns."

Usually in the lives of those with a panther totem, there either already exists or will soon arrive upon the scene an individual who will serve as teacher and nurturer and guide.

———

SEVERAL HOURS, one thunderstorm, a couple of breaks to stretch my legs, and forty-four pages later, I close the journal and massage my aching hand. If I could write fiction at this pace, the novel would be finished in no time.

Rain drums down on the tent. From the plastic bag, I remove the pile of notes and drafts of the scenes I've already written about my Louise and Brett characters. The magnitude of the task is daunting. Rereading the scenes makes me realize my narrator is too distant, too judging. *I* feel distanced. Even setting aside Brett's criminal background, I don't get Louise's attraction to him. And that's key to everything – to all the subsequent decisions that led her down her dark path. To tell her story with empathy I need to understand the attraction. But you can't force empathy. Like forgiveness, it comes by Grace. You can only stay open and pray for its arrival.

I stay open and prayerful all afternoon but the only thing that arrives is lethargy. The rhythmic dripping of rain on tent lulls me to sleep. Thunder wakes me up. I doze on and off for an hour. At six o'clock I force myself to sit up and read more notes. At seven I declare two hours a good day's "work." The thunderstorm has passed. I reach into the vestibule for my damp rain jacket and hiking boots and go in search of dinner hanging from a tree.

It's damply dark when I hoist the food pack back up into the sturdy white pine beside the water. Large feathery branches shelter me from the rain, which splatters out on the lake. I can almost hear the trees and bushes drinking. Greening up by the minute.

The downpour keeps me awake while a gang of intruders invades my brain. I thought my bearanoia was gone, but that was before the blueberry crop failed. Menstrual exhaustion battles it out with intruder fears, and in my half-asleep, half-alert state I manage to march an army of angels around the campsite, with a special forces detail encircling the tent, their wings so blindingly white they'll scorch anything, human or ursine, that dares to come near. At last I drop off to sleep.

The stove won't light. I try again. I even clean it. No go. I study the damp ground. Although it's been only a day and a half, not "several days," the ground looks sodden. I hunt around for only semi-sodden wood. These are, I reason, extenuating circumstances. If I don't get a coffee into me, I'll have a hammering headache by mid-afternoon that no amount of analgesic will alleviate, and then no writing will get done and there will be no reason to stay.

The fire refuses to light too. Even the small twigs and birch bark are saturated. I need dry kindling. Paper would be ideal. I bring out the big zip-lock bag and sort through old drafts and notes, looking for dispensable pages. Sadly, there are all too many – entire pages of crossed-out writing. There's no question I'm here to do a complete rewrite, not a simple edit.

Even the slightly humid crumpled-up pages of rejected writing aren't enough to catch the kindling. If they have any value, it's to assure me that under no circumstances are the woods in danger of igniting. The question pops into my head: *What would my special agent do?*

And there, voiced matter-of-factly in my ear, is his solution: *Pour stove fuel on it.*

It's never occurred to me to do such a thing before – either to use camp fuel or to consult a phantom companion. The combination is a blazing success. "That's an indication of my highest respect that I would ask what you would do in this situation," I say out loud to my ghostly adviser.

I do feel some measure of guilt for breaking my initialled vow not to light a fire until after three days of steady downpour. Not enough to stop me from going ahead. I keep the fire very small and make the most of it, boil water for coffee and bake a bannock for breakfast, cook up rice and beans for tonight's dinner and heat up water for the dishes. One frugal fire for the day. Which I douse thoroughly when I'm done.

I take a second cup of coffee over to the east-facing jut of rock beside the little landing harbour. The agent and Baby and I had our picnic on this point. The rock is out of the wind and faces what might well be my favourite view of all time. It begins with a lone spruce tree on a small point of land. Just beyond that, across a small channel of water, a long, sleek boat of an island, crewed by a line of pines. And beyond that, a high, steep slope of rock, treed with maple, poplar, and pine. Not nearly a mountain, not quite cliff, it's a towering slope whose rock surface, like the slope in the upper half of the lake, is visible through the trees. If you, God forbid, cut down all the trees, you would be left with one impressive, steep hump of bare granite. Not for the first time I wonder – how *do* trees grow out of rock?

The depth of the view, the unpoetic three-dimensionalness of it, draws me in, from spruce on point to pine-spired island, to steep hill beyond. And *up*. The tree spires in the foreground draw my eyes up the rock slope, whose own spires entice me to the top. The sky's the limit.

I take pen in hand to try to put into inadequate words what I could, if I had a large-format camera and a photographer's talent, capture in one thoughtful, well-composed click of a button. I feel a familiar tug of war between my pen that wants to capture the view in words and my feet that want to climb *into* the view.

WE FOUND A FLATTISH spot to spread out the blanket. Out of the backpack I pulled cheese and crackers and two Coronas that had managed to stay somewhat chilled in gel packs.

While the agent fed Baby, I slid the map out of its waterproof case, unfolded it, and turned it over to the descriptions of the park geology, fish, wildlife, and human history. And tips for canoe campers. I was immersed in the best way to string up a tarp when I felt the agent's head on my shoulder. "Read to me. I love being read to." His voice was sleepy.

Filled with quiet delight at this intimacy, I read the canoeing tips out loud. I skipped the section on how to avoid bear problems and what to do if you meet a predatory black bear (the very rare ones that are more interested in you than your food pack). I read to him about stormy weather until he sat up and stretched. "You could write the map tips yourself, Brenda."

A sudden gust of wind blew a corner of the blanket into Baby's face. We packed up the lunch things, picked up crying baby, and crossed through the dark cool interior of the site.

"Here's your tent site," said the agent when we reached a flattened clearing of darkened dirt a short distance from the fire pit. He marked out exactly where I should put my tent and which way the entrance should face for maximum view of the lake.

I jiggled Baby and shook my head. "So now you're trying to sell me a housing lot on Crown land."

FOR A CHANGE of scene, I take the novel notebook over to the rock that faces the main part of the lake and open to a fresh page. I do a lake watch and a sky watch. Is it going to rain? Is it warm enough for a bath? Is that a hawk soaring up there in the sky? That's definitely a gull bobbing out on the water. And look! Four loons! I watch them glide past in a graceful line.

Loon, always around water, is an ancient symbol for other levels of consciousness, dreams, and the astral plane (the state between this world and the next that Asante tells me can be accessed through the dream state). Loon, says Ted Andrews, can help me dive into my subconscious to understand myself – and by extension, I reason, my characters. Loon in multiples seems a guarantee of success.

I decide it's warm enough for a bath and retrieve my quick-dry towel from the tent.

———

THE AGENT LAID out a big beach towel emblazoned with an image of Buzz Lightyear at the top of the slope and lay Baby down on it. "Safer for him up here in the shade."

We spread our own towels on the warm rock by the water, keeping an eye on Baby, who seemed content to lie on his stomach and peer around at the lush green and dirt-brown campsite clearing around him, as if assessing future possibilities.

I peeled down to my bathing suit, slathered on sunscreen and lay back on the towel, self-conscious in my swimsuit. And even more conscious of the agent beside me in silky thin boxer-style bathing trunks. He was powerfully built – broad shouldered and well-biceped. Any signs of his "winter upholstery," as he amusingly called it, were gone.

We yakked away about our usual array of topics until Baby began to fuss. The agent climbed to the top of the rock and put him in the backpack carrier. By the time we launched the canoe, Baby had conked out. In sleep, his long lashes brushed his sweet face above his plump cheeks, and he looked enviably innocent, not a worry in the world.

———

CLEAN AND FRESH from my dip, I lie back down on the towel and marvel at how the agent and I lay so close beside each other on this same rock, and neither of us made a move, or even an innuendo. I didn't have one lustful thought. *Then*. It's only after our encounters that my fantasies get the better of me. I lust and fantasize, and stew in my guilt about lusting and fantasizing.

I pick up the novel notes. It's no use. I'm still too fidgety. Now that I'm reworking a whole different section of the novel, I tell myself, I have to ease in.

So here I am, out in the boat, easing in.

I make my way around the east bay lost in a fantasy about being on a canoe trip with the agent. I try to reign in my thoughts with the silent repetition of the mantra. I haven't meditated in nearly a year. Even after all this time, the word comes instantly back. I synchronize the drawn-out syllables with my paddle strokes – *Ma Ra* (dig, pull) *Na Tha* (slice forward) – and my breathing – *Ma Ra* (breathe in) *Na Tha* (breathe out).

Some traditions teach that to meditate you have to sit still in a quiet place, eyes closed, back straight. That's what I do at home. But meditation comes much more easily when my normally fidgety body is occupied with some repetitious activity my mind doesn't have to concentrate on, like paddling or swimming. I call it "meditation in motion." I thought the term was my own invention until Asante told me it's a description some practitioners give to Tai Chi or yoga, where moving through or holding different postures allows the body to enter a deep state of relaxation and the mind to become silent and aware. For me, the same holds true of paddling.

I meditate my way through a short channel into the west bay. Finally, my mind begins to focus on Louise. How am I going to get her character right when she was so different from me? Though maybe only in personality. Emotionally, maybe we weren't so different. She was so excited when she first told me about Brett. I know that excitement. My relationship with the ranger was nothing like Louise and Brett's in nature or circumstance, or *outcome*, but there *are* fundamental similarities: an intense initial attraction, a meeting of minds, and souls, and then the sudden stranger in my midst and the painful, mystifying retreat of that stranger.

And there it is, between one paddle stroke and the next: the key to the door. I just need to take those similarities and push them to their extremes – violent extremes that thankfully have never been part of my relationships.

The door unlocked at last, I spend the rest of the paddle creating fictional backgrounds for my true-life characters. There are lots of good writing rocks, but I don't stop. I'm keen to complete the circumnavigation of the bay, of my creative mind.

It's seven-thirty. On the swimming rock down by the water, the sun (sun!) beams over the calm, pale blue water. I'm arrayed in a sarong and tank top in the unexpected warmth, belly full of pre-cooked rice and beans with a side order of bannock and tahini, novel notebook full of the afternoon's thoughts and revelations. Out on a rock twenty metres or so from shore, a gull has been sitting for as long as I have. I'm pretty sure she's my muse.

I search my brain for a thought or idea I've missed recording. My brain, glory be, is still – a sure sign I've accomplished the day's work. Another sure sign is that my avian muse takes off, soaring away into the evening light on wings of gold.

I watch her go and realize, in no small awe, that I've solved a problem that's been with me from the very beginning of this endeavour – how to feel excited about, and empathy for, and able to portray, this one crucial relationship. For the solution, inward apologies but also infinite gratitude to the ranger. May he forgive me.

A HALF METRE OF wet March snow had fallen overnight. I waded more than skied through the drifts on the narrow woods trail beside the frozen river, ducking under spruce boughs weighed down with snow. At the top of the hill I paused under a branch, elated in the way only exercise elates me, breath coming hard, heart thudding, mind rejoicing in the soft, silent deep white beauty all around. It struck me that if the ranger hadn't ended our relationship, I would not be *here*. I would never have found my place on the river.

And that's when it came. Like a bird alighting on the snow-laden tree branch beside me. Forgiveness. It arrived when I wasn't focused on it or trying to make it happen. It arrived, out of the crisp sun-filled blue, with the realization that the ranger was the catalyst for a huge milestone in my life: the final dissolution of the fairy tale. I could look back now and see how our incredible mind connection had carried us away.

I took a swig from my water bottle and thought back to something my oldest sister had said – that we had conducted our relationship out of time and place, away from our real lives. It seemed to me now, standing under the snow-white spruce canopy, that we had conducted our relationship mostly on a "soul" level. It had taken place, metaphorically speaking, in a canoe on water, never landing on solid ground. It was when we brought it into the social realm that the cracks began to show. We had to deal with each other's personalities and friends and work schedules and habits – a far cry from purely connected minds and souls. Our minds were so connected, so often "one," it never occurred to me our hearts wouldn't, or couldn't, stay connected as well. No one was to blame. I could forgive him.

I planted poles in the deep snow and pushed off down the hill.

THERE'S NO RAIN to keep me awake but my brain is too full of new questions to sleep. Did Louise have any inkling of what was going to happen? Or did her intuition tell her to *be* with Brett, and did she, too, ultimately feel betrayed by it? She was an angry person, angrier than I've ever been. Did she come to a place of forgiving Brett before she died? Did she, perhaps more importantly, forgive herself? These are things I have yet to find out. In my own case, even as I've rejoiced at the arrival of peace in my heart toward the ranger, I'm aware there's still anger simmering. It's directed mostly at myself, for getting into one more short-lived relationship, and even more so for my "faulty" intuition. There's just no reconciling that powerful intuitive thought from three summers ago – that I was going to marry the ranger who had just arrived on my campsite – with my current status quo. I've spent years honing my intuition, it's always been a gift. How will I trust it again? And yet, I muse sleepily before I drift off, it must be somewhat trustworthy: I'm out here by myself...

A cooing loon reveille brings me out of the tent. It's eight o'clock in the morning and seven loons have gathered in the middle of the lake. I plant myself on a rock to watch.

The loons form a circle. A moment later several disappear under the water only to bob up almost immediately. All seven form a row, white breasts all facing me. Still in a row, they swim toward me. Just as I wonder how close they'll come to shore in this remarkable synchronized routine, they do a quarter turn, all at the same time, and form a single-file line. In silhouette, they glide up the bay, and I race to retrieve the agent's binoculars for a magnified view of the rest of the show.

Through the binoculars, I watch one loon separate from the others, look around and flap his wings vigorously along the water until he's airborne. He disappears over the treeline but, because he's a loon and it's a loon ritual, curves back around the lake, flying past his loon friends and me before he disappears for good.

And then there are six.

One disappears below the surface.

And then there are five.

Another goes to check on the one below.

And then there are four.

These four swim farther up the bay.

And then I have to go to the biffy.

The four are still hanging out in the middle of the bay when I arrive back. They line up, one after the other, flap their wings along the water runway, and lift into the air. Two disappear over the trees (forsaking loon ritual!). The last two grace me with a beautiful white-breasted fly-by over my campsite on their way around the lake.

And then there are none.

Except I know two are somewhere under the surface, somewhere in the lake. These two are the pair that belong to the lake, and sooner or later they'll reappear.

I build a modest breakfast fire. It blazes immediately without the help of camp fuel. I'm confident the woods are safe. No guilt. *Or* remorse.

"Remorse," writes B. Alan Wallace, my latest Buddhist mentor, "is sincerely focusing on a misdeed, taking responsibility for it, and regretting having done it… Guilt is an afflictive state of mind focused on the self as in, 'I am an unworthy person.'"

Asante puts it more bluntly: "Guilt is a useless emotion. It's just you feeling bad about something you've already done. It doesn't change anything."

My writing has always been the biggest source of this useless emotion. I've felt guilty for the way I procrastinate. Guilty for not being prolific. For not having one novel published by the age of forty. And now I have the agent to throw into the mix. Asante is right though. The guilt doesn't *change* anything. It doesn't spur me to do anything different. It just makes me feel bad. Which makes things worse. I've come a long way in silencing the Critical Chorus, but guilt feels even more deeply ingrained than the propensity to beat myself up. It's hot tar I can't seem to stop pouring over myself. And is even worse now because ever since Asante told me how useless it is, I feel I shouldn't feel guilty, which makes me feel guilty about feeling guilty.

I'm munching on fire-baked bannock on the shore when the two loons resurface.

The campsite at the north end of the lake is on such a steep slope there's barely a level place to sit. And nowhere quiet: a band of ravens is screaming at each other in a tree. Finally I settle on one of the few flat rocks down at the water and open my notebook. The plan is to sit here to write for several hours, and then reward my productive morning with a hike on the east shore slope. Somewhere beyond that slope is a ski trail. The same ski trail the ranger pointed out after bellowing his ecstasy into the little bay at the top of this very lake two years ago. The same ski trail the agent fantasized he would hike over to come for a visit this week. I can't help thinking what would happen if he did.

In spite of the ravens' continued screaming in the tree next door, I manage to scribble a three-page scene. Huge relief to get something down on paper besides ideas. Also frustration: I'm antsy for exercise. Oh to be a calm sort of person who sits and writes for six or eight hours straight, the way I imagine all the other writers in the world do.

I climb in the boat. The ravens have stopped their racket at last. My thoughts return to the agent. Are we committing what he calls "emotional adultery"?

—◆—

W E SPED BACK down the highway, canoe strapped on roof, Baby strapped in car seat. The agent made a mild comment about the frustration of being in such close proximity to me in a bathing suit on a towel in the hot sun.

"Well, at least you have an outlet."

"And you," he said mildly, "have an inlet."

I couldn't help laughing. "I mean at least you're getting sex."

"I have *no* outlet for our specific tension."

I shook my head. Our situations were not the same.

"Which leaves me with chocolate," he added.

I didn't share this addiction. There were many things I didn't share with the agent.

In the back seat, Baby woke up and began to cry. The agent murmured soothing words in the rear-view mirror, and the crying stopped.

I hesitated, then made up my mind. "After the ranger it was impossible to imagine I would ever find someone else who fit into my life so well. That feels naive now, but we were so alike, so connected we could read each other's minds. You and I share a lot of outdoor interests but you're not *like* me, you don't think like me, and that doesn't matter. And I've never let anyone else look out for me the way you do. With you I think I'm breaking old patterns."

"I wonder if I am too. My previous relationships always lasted three or four years, then I moved on. I wonder if I was simply repeating an old pattern – being attracted to you because my four years was up." Another glance at me. "It's not flattering to you to talk this way."

"I don't mind. I understand this kind of thinking. Besides, it doesn't strike me that way because it's not as if you set out to meet someone. Though I do wonder if I'm contributing to the problem by spending time with you."

"Contributing! You're the *source* of the problem."

I burst out laughing, "So maybe I've come along to help you break that pattern."

"Or maybe it's time to leave my marriage. She may well leave *me*. She talks about wanting to go back to Ottawa, and I have no intention of leaving here anytime soon."

I stayed silent while dismay and hope battled it out.

We were almost at his place when he spoke again. "My thoughts always come back to you, Brenda, like the needle on a compass."

"What direction am I?"

"You," he said, "are magnetic north."

———

I PUSH OFF WITH the paddle. The ravens – still blissfully silent – fly out from the trees and head down the shore toward the slopes I intend to climb. I count them as they go, seven in all. Two circle over my head as if to invite me to follow, then fly on to catch up with the others.

The boat glides along the shoreline below the steep slope, and I keep an eye out for a place to park it. From somewhere high on the hill comes a decidedly odd squawk.

Ravens have been known to make odd unraven-like sounds. Like the one last summer that made the sound of a brief high-pitched alarm or siren outside the tent the morning Harriet and I were soon to rescue our campsite hosts from a hypothermic spill. In retrospect, it was certainly a warning of the danger to come. The unexpected piercing sounds Raven is capable of making can also, I've read online, help bring about a shift in consciousness. If Bear was the catalyst for my shift into self-acceptance, I think Raven was there to shock it into my system. Which makes me wonder about these feelings of guilt I still carry around. Guilt isn't exactly a friend of self-acceptance. There's obviously more work to be done. The agent's love is so clearly a gift in my life. How do I reconcile the gift with the guilt?

———

H E STOOD AT the door. "I was working late. Figured you'd still be up. I brought you a present." He produced my paddle from behind his back, and my park permit. I had left both in his car.

I invited him in. Our previous evening with his wife had been easy and enjoyable. We'd entertained her with the events of the day. I appreciated that she'd let me share the company of her husband and her baby, though felt too awkward to say so. I hoped it came through that we had nothing to hide. She seemed determined – that was the word that came to mind – to accept me in their life. I admired, and appreciated, her for that. For not allowing jealousy to drive a possible wedge between herself and her husband. I suggested another barbecue at my place soon, and she seemed keen.

"You look tired," her husband observed now from the couch beside me. "But if you're offering, I'd love a cup of tea."

Two cups of tea and one friendly argument about optimum canoe designs and materials later, I glanced at the clock. After midnight. "Get out of here. I need to get to bed."

Near the door, he leaned back against the kitchen counter and continued to chat. I had a hard time keeping my eyes open.

"Okay, Sleepy," he said at last. "Get to bed." He reached across the three feet between us and placed his hands on my waist. There was a deliberateness and sensuality in the way he pulled me to him. His hands found bare skin under my T-shirt, and squeezed and caressed my lower back. I knew it felt strong and toned from all my canoeing. I felt a hand on the back of my neck and then in my hair. I wanted to pull back and kiss him. I put my own hands under his shirt.

He gave a small sigh of contentment. My own, silent responses were not so sanguine. He kissed my cheek. Then, softly, in my ear: "Are you all slumbery?"

I pulled back in astonishment. "Are you kidding? Just what kind of effect do you think you have on me?"

"Okay, wrong kind of hug," he said, and we both started to laugh. "You're supposed to be relaxing, not having an adrenalin rush." He turned me around and wrapped his arms across my ribs. I rested my hands over his forearms and let myself lean back into him. His voice was in my ear again. "Are you going to be all right?"

"Yes." Though I wasn't sure.

He took my hand in his and intertwined our fingers, and I realized it was the first time we had ever held hands. It felt even more intimate than our embrace. He took my other hand and drew both of our linked hands down to our sides. We stood that way for a long time, hands held at our sides, my back pressed against him. I became aware of a circle of steadily burning warmth in the small of my back. Desire burning in a steady, restrained way for me. It moved me profoundly, both the warmth and the restraint.

When I finally booted him out and went to bed I didn't, to my own surprise, lie awake in physical frustration. He had got me all slumbery after all.

———

A BOW-SHAPED CRACK in the rock makes the perfect little harbour for the canoe. I nose in and throw the rope over a dried-up shrub. On shore I scan the trees again. Are they up there?

It's not a relaxed climb. I'm suddenly all too aware of bears. Would a hungry bear make an odd unraven-like squawk to lure a human into the woods? I whistle. It helps, a little. I step around the rusty-red blueberry patches. Surely no bears will drop in if there are no berries? Could a bear mistake me for a blueberry?

The need to move wins out over my wimpy nerves. I keep to the bare rock, weaving around the sunburnt bushes, climbing higher. The climb brings me to a look-out that turns out to be the north arm of a small horseshoe-shaped bay. I scan the densely treed hillside at the back of the bay. Suddenly, from those trees emerges a band of birds. Black birds. Ravens. Seven.

Without a sound, they sail out over the horseshoe bay. They fly toward me, past me, at eye level with me, and on out over the lake. They disappear out of view around the bend. I watch them go, sorry I've disturbed them. Sorry to see them go.

Moments later, to my delight, they reappear, circling back at an unhurried graceful pace. They fly past me again, still at eye level, in a loose V-formation, and back into the trees at the back of the bay. All in a serene black-velvet whisper of wings.

I train eyes on the trees to see if they'll come back out. There isn't a squawk or a rustle. If I hadn't seen them go in, I would have no idea they were there.

———

NO OTHER BOATS were out to disturb the morning mirror surface of the river. Even alone in my canoe in daylight, I could still feel the agent's middle-of-the-night embrace. Halfway across to the marsh, I spoke to the river. "I love this man. He loves me. I like that he loves me. I'm in major internal conflict about it. He's married. And I feel guilty." At the word "guilty," the dam broke. My tears fell freely on the river.

The answering machine was blinking when I got back. "I felt some urgency to call you," said Asante's voice on the tape, "but I don't know why."

As soon as she answered the phone, tears flowed again, and I told her about the agent's prolonged sensual embrace. "I really need to hear from you that what I'm doing is okay."

"What you're doing is perfect." She spoke with absolute conviction. "And it's natural you'd have these moments of doubt, simply because of what you're working on – guilt itself."

"But why *am* I doing it? Why aren't I just saying it's wrong and withdrawing? It looks so wrong from the outside."

"Do you want to withdraw?"

"No. It doesn't feel wrong when I'm *with* him. It's afterwards I feel guilty about our sexual talk and, most of all, my sexual responses."

"I think you're shedding some deeply held beliefs about sex and your sexuality. About your own humanity."

I gave a teary laugh. "You mean that I'm only supposed to have sex within the bonds of holy matrimony, and then only to procreate?"

"That's the one. You've put yourself in this situation that seems wrong so you *can* shed those old beliefs – which I think are still sitting somewhere in your subconscious – and know you are an innocent sexual being. It's your guilt that makes you think you should withdraw."

"So what am I supposed to do?"

"You're already doing it. You're processing as you go along. That's what your panther dream was about. Panther, in the form of your incorrigible agent, has come to help you. Just respond, with your usual integrity, to each moment as it comes. There's nothing else you need to do. And you're doing amazingly well, I might add. I don't think I would have the stamina. I would have either had to withdraw or I would have succumbed to sex long ago."

"Well, that's something," I said, and wiped tears from my smiling face. Her words brought relief, and echoes of my other Buddhist mentor, Steve Hagen.

We can't use a hard and fast rule to deal with the dilemmas and uncertainties and ambiguities of life. A rule – any rule – would only open the door for relativism and contradiction. Nevertheless, we can see what's morally appropriate in each situation… It all has to do with our intention.

THE CLOUDS HAVE cleared again, the sky is pale evening blue, the lake tranquil. It's early evening, my favourite time of day, when the waters, and I, are still. I'm bathed and coiffed and waiting for a dinner guest to show up about now.

My evening companion is my journal. I describe the loons and the ravens, seven of each, in awesome and unusual displays. Seven is the number of the scribe, the number of the seeker in solitude. It strikes me that I've come out here, as a person under the influence of Seven does, to be alone, away from the crowds, to connect with Nature. Solitude is necessary for the scribe attempting to penetrate the mystery of her characters. I dredge further into my memory about Seven. Many things come in sacred sevens. There are seven wonders of the world. And of course the seven deadly sins. When it comes to days, the seventh is the day of rest. A day, the Psalmist might say, to "be still, and know that I am God."

"Be still, and know," the loons and ravens repeat now, in my head. "You can't write until you know. You can't know until you are still."

That's the real source of my conflict, my inability to sit still. The loons and ravens were moving though. The difference is that even in their motion they were calm, poised – meditating in motion maybe? Asante tells me real stillness isn't physical, it's mental. My restlessness is from trying to force a process that can't be forced. The more guilt I feel about not producing, the less I produce. I have to mull. I have to live with my characters in my head, find out who they are and how they would act, and I have to do it without judgment so I can tell their stories with empathy. I have to do the head work and the heart work before I can do the pen work. Be still, and know. Then the cacophonous raven squawking in your head will go away.

Twilight overtakes the evening, and I dig out soap and washcloth and make my way down to the shore for my evening ablutions. As much as I love this campsite, it's too much to be on one site for more than a couple of nights. I need to be on the move. My next writing trip will be a real trip but with short travel days that will give me time to move and time to write. The perfect solution for the not-quite-perfect Seven scribe.

Crouched on the rock, I watch the last of the light fade over the water and forgive myself for getting only two hours of "real" work done. More than enough work was accomplished today.

In the tent, I switch off the headlamp and am instantly asleep.

I'm attending a large family function. The event is some kind of religious, sacred family ritual. I wander through the crowds, looking for one of my cousins, who is gay. He's supposed to be directly involved in this ritual, which involves water, like a baptism, but is some other rite of passage. I know he will not – cannot – participate in this ritual, as sacred as it is. It goes against everything he is, against his very soul. Yet I hope he'll show up, at least to be with the family.

As I search, tears of incredible sadness and sorrow stream down my face, sorrow as I've never felt before. And empathy. I have, it seems, experienced something similar, some situation where I could not go along with a societal or familial expectation – though this family event is greater than "expectation." It's more of a deeply ingrained, deeply held and upheld ritual.

To my great joy, he arrives, and he's brought a barbecue and enough meat for a feast. I'm impressed at such a practical offering and so relieved he's come.

"You are so sensitive," he exclaims when he sees my tears. Which I cannot stop.

The rain is too much. I start to pack. I can't face another day confined to the tent or another day with no real exercise. And possibly no hot food or drink if the rain prevents me from making another illicit fire (which may be more elusive than illicit in this soggy weather). I'm also craving a steak.

The thought of red meat brings the dream back. The cousin in the dream is a real cousin, a decade older than me. We didn't get to know each other until I was in my early twenties. What brought us together was my relationship with the man who was separated but not divorced. There was suddenly a kinship between us – a kinship beyond blood – that we were both living a life outside the acceptance of our parents. After my relationship broke up, it was my cousin and his partner who took me into their home and saw me through the grief and introduced me to a new, different (fun!) life as a single young woman.

I launch and load the canoe in the rain and cross to the north channel. The dream is still so vivid, both in image and emotion, I could mine it for days. The most important thing seems to be my deep knowing that my cousin could not, would not, participate in the sacred ritual because it went against his very being. He was being true to himself, even though it caused untold pain to be separated from family and community. The message seems to be that even the most important religious or family ritual or societal belief is not as important as what one "knows" in one's soul. But where does that leave the "rules," the "right" and the "wrong"?

I stroke my way through the velvet-green channel into the north arm of the lake. The downpour is steady, but there are no winds to fight. In the middle of the calm upper lake the answer comes. It's my heart and conscience, my very soul, that "rule" me. The dream is a gift to remind me that my own soul – my Self, Asante would say – is the final authority for what is right for me, above and beyond any societal rule, law, ritual, or norm. Beyond guilt.

It's a shocking revelation. It feels almost sacrilegious. Steve Hagen, though, would tell me that in each situation I can *see* what is morally appropriate, that it has to do with my intention.

The dream reminds me of a story I read of the Buddha, who, watching a brahman make a ritual fire for worship, tells him that insight doesn't come by merely laying sticks on a fire: "You should trust to the truth that is within you to enrich your spiritual life and not to external rituals. Having departed from that way of doing things altogether, I kindle my fire within."

Each morning on my campsite this week I kindled a small fire. Doing so I broke the "rules." Under the circumstances – my broken stove, my need to cook food, the safety of the sodden conditions – it was entirely necessary and appropriate for me in that moment. I was careful. I neither made it a huge bonfire nor deprived myself entirely. The middle way.

The memory of those small fires reminds me of another "small fire" – the steady circle of warmth I felt when I leaned back against the agent in my kitchen, and all the fire there is between us. There is a sexual element to our relationship. Neither act on it, nor – more importantly for me – deny it. The middle way.

The rain lets up a little as the message sinks in. I've been looking at this friendship from the perspective that says it's "wrong," that says I shouldn't be hanging out with another woman's husband. The truth – my truth – is that I need to stay out of this perspective. The agent's protective, earthy, yes even flirtatious Panther presence in my life is absolutely right for me, right now. Here is precisely the opportunity to exorcise Guilt, in a broad general way, from my life. The challenge is to continue within the parameters of our stated, platonic boundaries – *and* to accept that I still have desires, thoughts, and physical responses. The key, it comes to me in weeping revelation, is to accept all my emotions, the so-called good and the so-called bad, the "offending malignancies" Panther fortifies me to face. To let them come, and go, without judgment, without guilt. To accept that this is what it means to be human. To accept my sexuality, my body, my humanity. My*self*.

The rain streams down again in earnest. The easy answer would be to stop the friendship so I won't be "tempted." Then I won't feel guilty. But that doesn't heal the guilt; it merely puts it into dormancy. Guilt then surfaces any time I cross a (strict) boundary, even in my mind. The reality of this situation, and every situation, is that I can trust my heart. I can trust myself to do the right thing. Moment by moment. Finally I understand what Asante has been trying to tell me. The hot tar of guilt I pour over myself really isn't necessary. In fact, it's harmful.

With each paddle stroke I feel calmer. Surer. It's time, long past time, to embrace my humanity.

In this past year since I truly let go of the ranger, it has felt like the huge unwieldy ocean liner that is my mind has slowly, almost imperceptibly, been changing course, slow degree by slow degree.

Milestone moments, like last year's self-accepting canoe rescue, are seared into my soul by the piercing call of Raven. Overall, it's a slow, inexorable process, one I have to sit in for a time, until the shift is complete. This trip has shown me how important the mulling stage is for my writing. Maybe the same is true for my life. Maybe the author of my life needs first to be still, to observe and mull, before she can participate in a new way, in her new, reborn life. The agent, married as he is, is part of that mulling. He points to the new view from the ocean liner as it changes course. A view I will climb into one day.

I look down into the blackish-grey waters beside the boat, and consider the infinite capacity of the Earth to absorb whatever we don't need anymore, whatever we want to release. Then I send Guilt, my prison warden, down under, to be subsumed. And continue my way up the middle of the lake to the portage.

Pinetree Lake's steep but hikeable slope

6

TUMBLING HOME

Smoke Lake: June 19–22, 2002

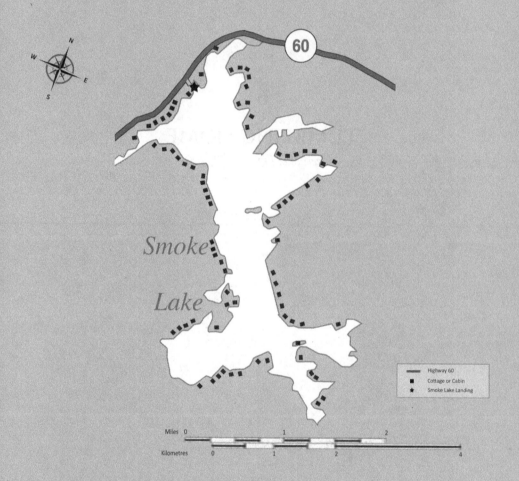

I HEAD OUT FROM the landing, boat loaded to the gunwales: canoe bag, food barrel, cooler, small knapsack, other miscellaneous bags, and... bicycle.

My intention was to leave it in the car. That changed after the agent called to say he had heard about some recent break-ins in Algonquin parking lots. He ended with a little friendly dictatorial advice: "Don't leave your valuables in the car."

I don't usually worry about such things, but when I arrived at Smoke Lake this afternoon his words were too fresh; they made it impossible for me to rely on my more usual approach to safety – which is to wrap protective White Light around the car. Easier to pop the bike into the boat.

I reach the flat rock where the ranger and I once enjoyed an exuberant late-winter picnic. Around the point, the wind pushes me into the east bay. Even with its oversized load, the boat is stable and tracks beautifully. Little wonder. I'm paddling the queen of canoes – a Prospector I've christened the *Empress*.

———

I FOUND HER AT an Ottawa outfitter I knew carried superlight Prospectors made from a carbon-fibre and Kevlar weave. I made the two-hour drive to the city in the spring, resigned to the fact that to get the lighter weight I would have to spend thirty-two hundred dollars plus tax. My intention was merely to have a look. I had already sold the Scott Wilderness. I would have to sell the cedar canvas too.

"I'm sorry, we have none in stock yet," said the salesman. "But there's a rental you can look at to give you an idea of what they're like." He took me outside, where several canoes leaned against each other at the side of the parking lot. He unearthed a red one streaked with long white scratches, as if a giant had scraped fingernails along the hull. He turned it over, and my eyes lit up at the sight of the wooden gunwales and seats. Exactly the boat and colour I was looking for.

"It's from last summer's rental fleet. We usually sell them off at the end of the season, but this one didn't go because someone tried to put their foot through it." He showed me a large patch, maybe a foot square, just behind the bow. "The hole didn't go right through – you can't see it on the outside and the boat doesn't leak, but it's not pretty. No one wanted it."

"Do you mind if I carry it around the parking lot?" I suddenly felt like my mom. When she went looking for a new car for the family, she would ask to see not the engine but the trunk. For our summer road trips, we needed a car with luggage room for six. I knew I should ask to take the boat for a test drive in the nearby Ottawa River, but I already knew how it would paddle – the Prospector is the quintessential wilderness-tripping canoe, designed to handle well and carry heavy loads. What I needed to know was how this forty-two-pound baby felt on my shoulders.

It felt good. The yoke settled around my neck as if custom moulded for it. I could have kept walking right out of the parking lot and down the street if not for the minor matter of ownership. I put the boat down beside the waiting salesman. "Why don't you sell me this one?"

"You'll have to negotiate with the owner. He stored it all winter, so I think he wants to put it through another rental season."

I negotiated. I got my canoe. I didn't pay thirty-two hundred dollars plus tax. I bless the person who tried to put a foot through the hull and saved the *Empress* for me.

＊

THE DOCK COMES into view first. On it a couple of lazy walruses are embracing in the sun. I glide in, and the walruses transform into two upside-down aluminum motorboats, one propped against the other. Beyond the docks, I catch a glimpse of the weathered wood porch railing and faded green screen door of Brenda's Bunkie – my wee home away from home for the next three or four days. I'm here to work on the novel, and to give Asante some space.

She's been my house guest for over a month now. She lost her job at the Vancouver drug recovery centre due to restructuring and packed her life into her car to come to Ontario to run a spiritual retreat. That fell through just after she arrived. There was no question I would take her in and for as long as she needed. My guest room is small, but Asante has a talent for arranging interior spaces, and she made room for most of the contents of her boxes. We set up her computer in the dining area and she began to check a website that lists positions with charitable organizations. Yesterday a job in Montana caught her eye and she applied.

I relieve the boat of its oversized load. The one drawback of Cathy's cottage is that there's nowhere to walk except up the short path to the outhouse. That's why I brought the bike. The nearly sixty-kilometre stretch of highway between the park gates has bike-friendly paved shoulders.

I slide the broken padlock off the latch, push open the door, and bring all my luggage inside to unpack. It's quite the luxury to have a cooler of meat, veggies, and ice here in Algonquin, not to mention china dishes, glass glasses, an espresso pot, and a pillow. When everything is set up, my new digs look so cozy and inviting I feel an almost physical sense of frustration, a finger jabbing at my chest. Why do I have this great life, where I can take off midweek to canoe into a cabin on a near wilderness lake, and no one to share it with?

Back out on the tiny sun-bleached wood porch, I reach into the cooler for a tin of tonic. The liquid sizzles and releases a faint spray of bubbles in the glass. I squeeze a quarter lime into it and add ice cubes. The ginless tonic reminds me inevitably of the agent. This was his drink of choice in my kitchen last summer. So much has altered between us since then.

Cozy Smoke Lake retreat

THE RIVER OUT my window sparkled in September morning sunlight. It was supposed to go up to twenty-two degrees. A great day to get in the boat.

I was pouring granola into a bowl when the phone rang. Automatically my thoughts went to the agent, hoping he had read my mind about canoeing. It wasn't likely. A conversation with his wife had spurred him to cut down on visits and emails. I didn't blame him, or her, but I missed him.

I checked the call display and saw it was an older friend in the area. I pressed the "on" button. "Good morning!"

"Did you see the TV this morning? You have to turn on the TV. It's just terrible. *Terrible.*" Her normally high voice was even higher in her distress.

Even as we hung up, I was switching on the landlord's fat old set. After a moment to warm up, the screen revealed the sky-reaching towers of New York's World Trade Center, one with thick dark smoke mushrooming from the upper storeys, the other with top floors in a blaze of flames. I stood in front of the screen, horrified, unbelieving. An hour later, before the world's eyes, the first tower disintegrated in a cloud of black smoke and dust and human terror. Half an hour later, the second followed.

I watched mind-reeling images that were replayed until they became mind numbing. Then I went outside into the warm, peaceful wonder of a day and sat in the Muskoka chair on the point. Feeling helpless. I closed my eyes, and prayer came, prayer for the Light to overcome the dark. With no assumptions or judgments about where, or in whom, Light and dark resided.

Through the day I responded to emails from family and friends and reached out to others. It felt important to connect. Though the person I wanted to connect with most was lamentably silent.

DESPITE THE RARITY of a real bed, sleep isn't any less disrupted than on a canoe trip. I drift in and out to the whine of mosquito in my ear.

And stew. This week Asante said, "If I were you, I'd be angry he came charging into your life last summer offering his love and then withdrew it." At the time I just gave a sad shrug. More than anger were familiar feelings of reproach and rejection, which I tried to suppress. Now, in the dark stuffy cabin, they push to the surface. I feel sorry for myself remembering how he barely spoke to me at a recent social gathering. Reproaches I haven't (thankfully) expressed to him pour out into the darkness: *Why haven't you been in touch? Why didn't you come to see me after the towers came down? Why didn't you ask about my new canoe when I hinted at it in May?* They're old and tiresome thought patterns I thought I had largely excised from my psyche. My rational daytime brain knows he's not solely responsible for our current situation and there's even some good in it – to have this void, to hold the space necessary for the creation of the new. Impossible, though, to stop the brain train from rumbling down familiar negative tracks in the middle of the night. I turn on the headlamp and reach for Steve Hagen.

*When you notice that your mind is caught up in longing and loathing –
leaning toward or away from something – don't try to stop it from
leaning... Just be aware when your mind is leaning... With practice and
attention to this moment, your mind will, of its own accord, lean less.*

A couple of thick black espressos alleviate my morning grogginess.
A blessed breeze on the dock keeps the bugs at bay. There's no rock
to sit on at Cathy's shore, and oddly I don't miss it. The aesthetics of
the cabin and its big mullioned window seem to make up for it. And
I know the rock isn't far under the surface layer of earth and bush. At
home last week I got in a rare mood to expose even more of my own
rock. I'm not usually one for yard work.

———

I STARTED WITH the shoreline slope beside the dock. At the bottom
of the steps, the first owner had poured a large concrete platform
over part of the rock. The second owner, my now former landlord,
subsequently bolted a dock to it. Each winter after I moved in, the
ice in the bay pushed the dock a little closer to shore, movement that
eventually, incredibly, caused the concrete to buckle. This spring I
hired someone to jackhammer the ugly platform into manageable
chunks and cart it away. Underneath lay a beautiful slab of rock. Now
I swept up all the pine needles and pulled grasses and soil from the
cracks and crevices. At the top of the steps, where the point overlooks
the water, I peeled away the scrubby plant life that had taken shallow
root over the granite. Late in the day, I lay down, exhausted, on the
bare rock, arms and legs spread as if I were about to make a snow
angel – an *earth* angel. The rock was a magnet, holding me pressed
against its smooth warmth.

Behind me, from the Muskoka chair, I heard Asante laugh. "You
remind me of me when I was little. When I was upset I would go across
the road to the field and lie down on the Earth and tell her everything.
Not that you're upset, but your lying there like that suddenly brought
back that image of myself lying in the field. It was just a natural thing
for me to do."

I knew she had grown up on a farm, but if I thought about her there at all it wasn't to imagine her outside, let alone lying on the dark prairie soil. In the twenty years I'd known her, she'd never been an outdoor person.

There was a gentle clink of ice against glass, and I sensed her taking a sip of iced tea. After a moment, she said, "The Earth lovingly absorbed everything I gave out. She was my 'other Mother.' She didn't say 'do this,' or 'do that,' or 'yes' or 'no.' She didn't say anything at all, but I felt fully accepted and loved by her. Her silent acceptance and love healed me of whatever pain I felt."

I sat up and turned around. "I love that. Your 'other Mother.' I'm surprised you don't live on the prairies anymore when you were so connected to the land."

"I've moved around to so many different places I feel at home wherever I am. My real home is inside myself."

I lay back down on the rock. "I know what you mean, though I do feel connected to some physical places more than others. Especially the Shield."

"Especially, I'd say, this very piece you're lying on."

At home on my shoreline rock

———•

THE CANADIAN SHIELD has been in my consciousness from the time I was small. I have rented-cottage memories of scrambling in bare feet over warm, lichen-covered rocks, loving the smoothness of the grey and the way the pale blue lichen was painted on. I thought the lichen was a loose, crumbly part of the rock surface. I had no idea what it was or what it was called. Nor what type of rock I was climbing on. Only later, in school, did I find out its Precambrian name and learn its composition of metamorphic and igneous rocks five hundred and seventy million years old. The oldest rocks in North America. Over those millions of years, the rocks rose and fell, got dragged along by continental ice sheets. A mind-boggling feat. Though I've seen the power of ice even at my own shore. If two-foot-thick ice that spans a small bay can push a dock bolted to cribs filled with rocks into a foot-thick platform and buckle the concrete, the capability of massive ice sheets to move huge rocks or scrape out tens of thousands of lake basins should come as no shock. When those glaciers retreated, they left behind a huge, solid, unshakable Shield. It's always brought me comfort, at some deep level, to know that half my country, and two-thirds of my province, is built on solid rock – including, now, my home on the river. My very own home.

———•

I'M THINKING OF buying a restaurant franchise," said my landlord. "If I do, I'll need to free up some capital. So I'm still thinking about selling."

"I'm still thinking of buying." It was the second time he'd asked in a month. I was playing it cool.

We went back and forth like that until the day in late fall when he said, "I'm getting closer to making a decision. Do you think you'll want to buy the house?"

"Jim! If you sell it, you know I'm going to buy it."

Not that I had cash for a down payment. The government, though, would allow me to borrow from my registered retirement savings plan as long as I paid it back over time. There was nowhere else in Central Ontario I would get waterfront property for the price Jim was asking.

It was an incredible opportunity. Even so, a niggling voice told me if I bought a house on my own, especially in this isolated part of Ontario, I would be resigning myself to life as a single woman. Was buying a house by myself an admission of relationship defeat?

———

THE WRITING GOES passably well, and at three-thirty I declare a break is in order. I change into cycling shorts, load the bike back into the *Empress*, and set off in diamond-glittered waters with a fantasy of running into the agent on the highway.

This persistent (unreasonable!) presence in my brain is really no surprise. Ever since that first prolonged teenage crush on my junior-high history teacher, I've always had a "man in my head," even if the man is barely or no longer or never was in my life. I've become marginally more sanguine about this ever-present male presence in my head. And at least am no longer turning him (whoever it is at the moment) into my God.

I reach the point out of the bay, and a sudden gust of wind tries to swing the boat around. I switch sides and dig in hard. I also take Steve Hagen up on his suggestion *not* to fight my mind's leanings but simply to watch them.

Lo and behold, within half a dozen strokes the agent slips away into the current, which sends up the chapter I'm working on. By this time I'm around the point and the wind is at my back. The *Empress* and I sail to the landing immersed in novel revisions.

From the phone booth in the parking lot, a quick call to my own home number reveals the good news that Asante has a phone interview tomorrow with the Montana organization. She's exuberant. We arrange another call in the afternoon so she can tell me how it went.

It's so hot even the breeze I create on the bike brings no relief. I speed down the highway, eyes peeled for dark rounded objects. June is the month turtles take their life into their hands to cross highways in search of a nesting site. In the car I make frequent stops to pick up a small painted turtle or clap behind a large snapper to get it safely to the other side. Asante and I have lent our assistance to several in the last few weeks, though none comes close to the turtle rescue I performed last September.

I WAS ON THE backroads, on my way to Ottawa. It was a couple of days after the horror of 9/11. Although I felt safe and protected in my sacred, isolated part of Ontario, the image of thousands trying to escape in the stairwells ("packed into a closet," one survivor put it) haunted me. I couldn't conceive of working on the hundredth floor of an office tower, or living in a high-rise. Even the thought made me feel claustrophobic and disconnected. I had to live, as Lao Tzu advised, "close to the ground." But there was something much larger to ponder than my own individual home or safety. Was this the beginning of greater terrorist attacks in the West? The airwaves were buzzing with talking-head commentary. I was struggling with the "them" against "us" thinking. Were we not all human? Were we not all full of internal conflicts? Were we in the West so "good"? And yet... an entire city, an entire country, had been violated.

In the *Tao*, evil is seen as an opaqueness, a self-absorption that doesn't let the Light in, not a force to be resisted. Jesus, too, said, "Resist not evil." But what does non-resistance really mean? I had no answers, only a renewed sense of urgency to connect more deeply with the natural world out my door. Not just for my own sake but somehow for the sake of the world. The answer seemed, somehow, to lie in, and with, the Earth. Perhaps she was everyone's "other Mother."

I emerged from the backroads and my thoughts, and merged onto the Trans-Canada. The two-lane highway wasn't busy yet with rush-hour traffic. Up ahead, something caught my eye. Something dome-shaped, maybe the size of a footstool, sat right on the centre line. I geared down and was nearly past when I saw, with a shock, what it was: September is not turtle-crossing-road month.

I made a U-turn on the empty highway and pulled over on the other shoulder. The turtle had clearly set out to cross the highway and had somehow avoided the cars from one direction only to realize that to finish the crossing would be suicidal. It now sat on the double solid line, paralyzed, I imagined, by fear.

Protection of my skirt made me reach for my leather jacket. I'm no stranger to the stream of pee a turtle who has been unceremoniously picked up can let loose (whether from fear or outrage, or both, I've never been sure). The stream from one this size was bound to be impressive.

By good fortune, or perhaps design, the turtle had picked a long straight stretch with excellent visibility in both directions. I looked both ways and clicked awkwardly in my high-heels out to the middle. When I reached the creature, I spread my jacket over its back as a kind of blanket, then grasped the edges of its shell through the soft leather with both hands and lifted. Cognizant of the waterfall to come, I held it as far out from my body as its weight would let me, and ran – as fast as my unaccustomed heels would let me – back to the shoulder.

I set my cargo on the gravel, caught my breath, looked down, and registered just what species of turtle sat inches from my bare toes. With its leathery, wrinkled forelegs and a tail lined with triangular crests, it might have stepped out of the dinosaur era. Its faded green shell, nearly half a metre long, looked as rough and solid as the Precambrian rock on my point. Its grizzled face was a lighter shade of green than the shell, and at the moment pulled back into the leathery folds of its neck while it surveyed me with tiny, intense eyes. There was no question: the creature I had just hefted off the highway was a very large snapping turtle.

I took a respectful high-heeled step back.

When you pick up one of the smaller species of turtle, its head and legs usually retract into its shell. The snapper isn't designed for retraction. Its protection is its bite. Amazingly this one had made no attempt to snap or to wriggle its powerful body out of my grasp. Nor did it snap at me now. Instead, we stood stock still, Snapper and I, one of us staring down, the other way up. Both of us, I suspected, in minor shock.

Beside us on the highway, a car whizzed by. Then another.

There was only a little turtle pee on the jacket. None on my skirt or legs. I thanked the turtle for its consideration, wished it a safe journey, and resumed my own.

"In Native American teachings," say the *Medicine Cards* authors, "Turtle is the oldest symbol for planet Earth." That seems very appropriate, given its prehistoric appearance. Turtle, with its hard shell, is also about the Earth's protection. She'll protect us and nurture us, Ted Andrews says, as long as we do the same for her. We can't "separate ourselves from what we do to the Earth."

I merged with four lanes of traffic on the 417, my mind back on the imploding towers. It struck me that we can't separate ourselves from what we do to each other either. Is there, I wondered, a way we can come to see, and honour, our connection to each other *despite* our differences? Not to fight but to protect and nurture each other, as the Earth does us. I could still see the way the snapper looked up at me from the side of the highway. It was humbling to have had the privilege of assisting such an imposing creature. I was grateful to have been there when it needed help, grateful it had *let* me help. I had a sudden vision of an Invisible Hand holding up traffic in both directions to allow the rescue mission to be carried out in safety – completing the circle of protection.

SOAKED IN THE sweat and joy of a good ride, I pull up beside my car in the lakeside parking lot and listen for the agent's warning voice. Nothing comes, so I load the bike in the back, cover it with a blanket, and surround the Suzuki in White Light. In my mind the protective light is dome-shaped and impenetrable, like an enormous turtle shell.

There's no one at the landing, not unusual for a Thursday in June. I propel the *Empress* out onto the now calm water, the sun a warm hand on my back. With no bulky bike cargo, I'm free to kneel closer to the side. The boat leans with me. There's little risk it will spill me out, thanks to the inward curve of its sides. This inward curve is a design feature with the lovely name of tumblehome. Tumblehome is what makes this tandem boat easy for a single person to paddle. The curve extends the cradle of the hull to the sides, which gives the boat extra stability when I lean it over (this kind of leaning entirely necessary and appropriate!). Tilting the boat this way puts the gunwales closer to the surface of the water so I don't have to reach as far with my paddle, which makes the boat easier to control on my own. It's one of the reasons I wanted a Prospector rather than a dedicated solo boat. It can be paddled either on my own or with someone else. In my imagination that someone else is in the boat with me. And this time we paddle in complete harmony – in my imagination anyway. Reality is a different story.

OUR CONVERSATION on the drive home from Pinetree Lake last summer changed everything. I latched onto the agent's idle musings that maybe his marriage had come to a natural end, that I fit in much more with his life here. This, combined with our reduced contact in the fall, brought my frustration to an untenable peak. The guilt, at least, was gone. In its place, though, came no peace, only a growing yearning to be with him. But anywhere we went in my imagination I slammed into a brick wall. The only solution I could think of was to ask for a moratorium in seeing each other. Just long enough to bring me back to equilibrium.

The bone-chilling November day I asked him over to tell him, he didn't take his jacket off, or even, oddly, his gloves. He sat close beside me on the couch and I dropped my bomb.

He looked sad. "I thought we had everything organized as to the nature of our relationship."

"I just need this time to get organized again." I paused. "It's felt to me like you've suppressed your feelings – and for good reasons – but it's still been a frustration to me."

He spoke slowly, thoughtfully. "I don't think I've suppressed them so much as tried to find an appropriate expression for them. And restrained myself from expressing them in ways I'd like to but aren't appropriate."

As relieved as I was to hear this, it didn't change anything. "It's different for you. You can leave here and go back to your family. I'm left simply wanting you to come back."

"I know." He said it with such feeling I couldn't help reaching for him. His arms came around me, and I clasped his wrist above his glove, the only bare skin I could find. My need to feel his skin was overwhelming, and surprising. It was nothing I had ever experienced before, this yearning for physical contact arising so purely from feeling. Not my ever-present need for affection but an expression of my specific feelings for this man. The natural next place for us to go was into physical, sexual intimacy. On a purely emotional level, that was right, not wrong. What *was* wrong was to deny it. And that was exactly what we had been doing for months, by mutual agreement.

Now, with his cheek pressed to mine and my hand encircling his warm solid wrist, the boundary had never felt stronger: a brick wall of wills and circumstances.

On the doorstep, he spoke gently. "I will honour your request, Brenda."

———

THE LAKE IS SO calm I head over to the west side to take the long way back to the bunkie. The route takes me past the beautiful square-timber cottage that belongs to Cathy's parents. It sits above a grassy clearing that slopes down to the shore. The building is much more appealing than my 1960s-era winterized cottage with its fake-panel interior, but I wouldn't trade properties for the world. The real estate mantra says it all. *Location, location, location.*

———

ON THE EVE OF New Year's Eve, Jim dropped in to clean the chimney, clear snow off the roof, and offer me the house in a private sale. "It's your fault I'm selling, you know," he said, mopping his forehead from his exertions. "You've stayed so long and enjoyed it so much and kept me from using it. And I know how much you appreciate it. That's why I feel comfortable selling to you."

We finished our tea, and I walked him out to his car. It was a clear sunny afternoon, not windy or too cold. The sight of his tire tracks on the just-plowed road reminded me of the agent. I'd lasted three weeks before emailing to tell him the moratorium was no longer necessary. So far, the only response I'd received was a double set of tire tracks imprinted on a dusting of snow on the road one morning before Christmas. Amid the relief that he was still watching out for me was a growing fear that he'd changed his mind about being friends. I was not detached. Not in the least. What my casually composed email had not said was how much I missed him.

Jim's voice brought me out of my thoughts. He spoke in a stammering way as if about to recite a speech. "Brenda, you look like you belong here." He waved his hand up to the oaks and pines. "You look like one of the trees."

It was the highest compliment anyone had ever paid me.

The bank would not grant pre-approval for a mortgage. My self-employment income and expense numbers didn't, the manager said, add up. It made no sense. For the last fifteen years I had paid the equivalent of a monthly mortgage payment in rent from that same self-employment income. I contacted another bank, and arranged for an independent appraisal. Maybe I really didn't want to buy on my own, maybe it really would be tantamount to resigning myself to the life of a single woman. But, maybe, that was my destiny. Maybe I really was being called to remain on my own, focused on my writing and my spiritual life. The thought depressed me. And so did the agent's continued silence.

The new year brought my period and a chest cold. The sound of a car on the road had me running to the bathroom to brush my hair, but no one came to the door. I looked out the window, afraid he hadn't stopped. No vehicle.

Then I spotted it, halfway up the icy hill at an awkward angle. Not the agent's 4Runner but a big boat of a car – the same 1980s Oldsmobile sedan that had been pressed into service to offer a lift to the weepy girl and her wildflowers on the road below the ranger's cabin that sleepless early morning three summers before.

It was no wonder the driver hadn't made it to the top. We'd had a freeze-up after a recent thaw, and my cold had deprived me of energy to sand the hill. And Murray Prentice's tires were bald. I put on coat and boots and lugged a bucket of sand down the icy hill.

By the time I reached him, Murray had the car backed down to the bottom and was making his own careful way up. He wore the same padded lumberjack shirt he'd worn that warm August morning. The same cool-looking flat-topped cap with no brim or ear coverings served as a toque. I invited him in for coffee.

It was my woodman who had officially introduced us. He was a cheerful man in his sixties, who lived with his wife on the farm where Murray's trailer was parked. In the fall, he delivered my wood a couple of cords at a time in the back of an old pickup, and talked about Murray. On delivery of the last load, he mentioned that Murray's faithful golden retriever had died, and Murray was lonelier than ever. Not long after that, I received my first visit. He had clearly told Murray about me, too.

I wasn't always up for company. Once or twice I'd gently told him it wasn't a good time. He left without any sign of taking it personally, and even as I felt badly, I appreciated it. I wanted to enjoy him in a genuine way, which meant I needed a certain energy – as I needed with all my older friends – an ability to set aside my own preoccupations and truly be there for him, "in my heart," Asante would have put it.

Today, my lack of physical energy put me in the perfect frame of mind for a visit.

Before he came in he sanded the hill with the contents of the bucket. When I opened the door to warn him about the icy steps, he reached for the heavy ice chipper.

"It's good therapy," he said when I cautioned him not to overdo it. He was, I'd calculated from things he told me, around eighty years old.

I left him to it, musing that most people would have said "exercise." For Murray it probably *was* therapy to be out of the tiny box trailer and doing something for someone else. Over the coffee preparations, I wiped away a few tears of appreciation for my new angel who was doing the chores I had no energy for.

He came in the house with an armful of wood from the shed, and we sat across from each other at my kitchen island. In true old-world gentleman style, he removed his cap. He looked closer to sixty-five than eighty, his face weathered but barely lined, his hair still mostly dark. He reminded me of my Uncle John, a laconic, stiff-gaited farmer with a kind heart. Murray had the same broad but lean bowlegged build and gentle aura about him – except that clouding the warmth of his eyes behind his black-rimmed glasses was bewildered pain. And he liked to talk. Or needed to. Especially about Casey.

He hadn't wanted her, he told me again this morning. Someone had given her to him. "But what an amazing dog she turned out to be. Smart. She'd show me something I'd left outside by accident. She helped me with chores too. She'd hold down one corner of the tarp when I was trying to get it over the car – I always cover it for the night in the winter. The trailer's not much but I made it comfortable for *her.*" His eyes misted over. "She got sick last summer. The vet gave me something for her, and next thing I know she's dead. I think whatever he gave her killed her. I've been thinking of writing a letter to that vet. He shouldn't get away with that." He looked at me with pleading in his eyes, as if I could undo what had been done.

It was heartbreaking how bereft he was, how unable to get over the loss – all his losses. The pain I was feeling the day I first met him, and that whole summer, was nothing compared with his lifetime of sorrows.

We got onto other topics, and he suddenly announced he played the fiddle. "I used to call the dances."

I was still absorbing the image of a much younger Murray calling dances when he stood up. "Well, I've taken up enough of your time. Thank you for the coffee, and your company. I'll go up to town and buy some food, maybe drop in on some other folks. Visiting's good. Makes the day go away."

I slowed to a stop on the county road, unsure I would be able to turn in to the field. There had been a snowfall overnight. The parking area was plowed out though, and I drove in, glad other people were looking out for Murray. I pulled up next to the big Oldsmobile, covered in its now snow-covered tarp.

The trailer looked shut up tight. The roof was also covered in a tarp, and its two small windows were boarded up against the cold. It was hard to believe anyone was inside, or could live in such a tiny box.

I wasn't used to "dropping in on folks," myself, but there was no way to call ahead and he'd given me an open invitation. If he wasn't up for company, that was fine. Mostly I wanted to check that he was okay. I'd barely seen him in a month. I knocked before I lost my nerve.

Murray opened the battered door in his trademark lumberjack shirt and any number of layers underneath. His face lit up. "Come in! I was just about to make a cup of tea."

He stepped back to give me room to step inside. The contrast with the bright sun was so great I had to pause to let my eyes adjust. And my nose. The dank, stale smell, though, was only to be expected in such a tiny space with boarded up windows in the middle of winter. One step took me to the only seat, a metal tubular kitchen chair with a torn vinyl cushion. I had to duck under a lit oil lamp that hung from a broomstick hooked to a bracket near the ceiling. The chair faced a bed covered in rumpled sleeping bags against the opposite wall. A tiny propane stove emitted heat through the open oven door.

Two steps from me, Murray boiled water at the stove. Over the sink beside him a rigged-up blowtorch was going full, scary blast. Murray was at least not freezing to death in here.

Beside the blowtorch hung a calendar, with a snowy scene for February. All but the last day of the month had been crossed off with big Xs. Days he'd made go away.

Murray pressed a chipped mug into my hand. I tried not to notice the crusty bits on the rim. The mug was, I told myself, as clean as he could get it under his living conditions. I took a sip. Good and hot.

Murray sat down on the bed and suddenly in his hands was a fiddle. "I haven't got the bow. It broke. And the fiddle got damaged by water. But she still plays." He began to pluck "Oh! Susanna."

He stood up then and plucked the rest of the song, and all but danced.

THE BREEZE COMES up for one more outing before bed but doesn't hinder the *Empress*'s stately progress across to the east side. Beside me along the shoreline, the trees sway and shake their glowing leaves. I'm mesmerized by their infinite textures and shapes and shades of golden green and the way they're packed in so densely: cedars wrapped in the arms of pines, vines curling up around trunks, smaller bushes pushing up through bigger ones. Amid the tangle, they look serene and still, even as they wave in the breeze. They seem so *accepting* – of all the tangle and the press of each other, of the weather conditions, of me in my canoe under the loving overhang of their branches.

Enveloped in all this acceptance, the *Empress* and I make our way back to the bunkie for supper.

I WASN'T HIDING," said the agent when I accused him of disappearing. "You were too."

It was one in the morning. I had just got back from blues night and was in bed with the phone to my ear. The agent had rung almost as soon as I'd got in the door. He was at his office catching up on paperwork, as he often did in the middle of the night. He was happy for me about the house offer and confident I would get a mortgage. He suggested the name of a company to inspect the house, gave his approval of the appraiser I'd contacted, and brushed off my apologies for not using his services. That we were having such an easy, cheerful, amicable, *normal* phone conversation seemed like a small miracle after so many silent weeks.

"It would be nice to see you," I said, mildly, before we hung up.

"I've tried to come to see you but you've had visitors lately, and I won't ask any questions about *that*."

His words stunned, pleased, and frustrated me. There was only one person my visitor could have been. Part of me wished I could string him along, make him think I was enjoying another kind of male company, but it wasn't in me. Amid my frustration was a tiny solid feeling of "rightness" that his attempts to drop in had coincided with Murray's visits.

After that he did drop in a couple of times, and sent the odd chatty email that sounded like the "old" agent. We saw each other at social gatherings. Sometimes he was friendly, sometimes he all but ignored me. As much as I continued to struggle with his absence, I knew one thing for sure (except during the occasional nighttime stew fest): his retreat was not a rejection of *me*. This was definitely new.

Thankfully I had house-buying matters to occupy my brain, especially after the unexpected phone call I received from the financial manager at my own bank. She had redone the numbers. "You're pre-approved for a mortgage!"

I called my parents to share the news. My father asked if I was committed to buying the house. I assured him I was and explained my plan to take the down payment out of my RRSP under the home buyers' plan.

"Don't do anything before you tell us."

I knew it wasn't idle conversation (my father never engaged in idle conversation). Nor was he one to order his adult children around (though he might make suggestions he thought you should take). I cheerfully promised I wouldn't do anything without letting them know.

Three days later, Jim brought over the legal offer with a closing date of March 28. He took the opportunity to give me a tour of the property. We were in the midst of another thaw, and it was easy to walk down to the water and up into the woods behind the house to locate each of the iron stakes that marked the four corners of the property. I had been living here two and a half years and never had any inkling of the boundaries. I was about to become the official caretaker of 1.26 acres of bush and a cleared point and three hundred feet of rocky waterfront.

At the last stake, in the still-leafless oak woods, Jim opened his arms to encompass the trees and the house on the slope below us. He spoke with exaggerated drama but also a hint of pride, and obvious happiness for me. "Brenda," he said, "you're a land baroness."

I stood on the granite ledge at the edge of the point and looked beyond the pines to the pale blue mush of ice dissolving imperceptibly in the bay. Behind me granular gritty snow lay in patches, but the rock under my boots was dry. I unzipped my parka. After a winter of frigid temperatures, plus six felt downright balmy. Tomorrow we would close the deal. Appraisal and inspection were done, mortgage and insurance arranged, legal papers signed, down payment in place (including an overwhelmingly generous gift from my parents), and I was about to become a land baroness. A much more appropriate word than landowner. We delude ourselves that anyone owns any part of the Earth. Not even the bank, though it was about to become mortgage holder.

Before me the crooked red pine that rises out of the rock on the shoreline below was doing its usual imitation of Tom Thomson's *West Wind*. It struck me how unselfconscious it was, how unapologetic that it was not straight and soaring like the pines on either side. It leaned like a solo paddler in a boat with good tumblehome – confident and sure. I breathed in its faint piney scent along with the spring-softened air. My leather hiking boots felt solid on the rock, connecting me to the Earth, sending my roots down deep. I felt like one of the trees. And suddenly it was crystal clear how they find nourishment in rock: it's the source of their being.

Gratitude to my about-to-be-former landlord swelled in my heart. All doubt was gone. I was not being called to retreat from the world; I was being given a gift to create a haven *in* the world, as I did on a small scale for Murray now and then, a haven of welcoming, nourishing energy for whoever might need it (as Asante would the next summer). I could have my solitude and share my solitary space. I could be hermit writer and social creature. I could lean with my pine tree, and steer surely, confidently, in total trust, close to my heart.

I looked out at the ice, remembering the way it had gleamed ghostly white under the beam of the previous night's nearly full moon. Tomorrow it would be full and at its closest point to the Earth – a so-called supermoon. It seemed a good omen. The planets too were in full support. Their alignment on my closing date was supposed to bode well for solid, long-term relationships. That reminded me of my dad, who had asked if I was "committed" to buying the house. And of the agent, who in his congratulatory email had written, "I think you and that place are a good match."

All these years, I had been looking for a match, and a commitment, with a man. I was about to make it – and most happily – with an acre of rock and oak and pine.

———

THE MOSQUITOES ARE so bad by the time my salmon dinner is cooked I eat in the bunkie. Even then I have company. Before I can get the door shut, millions of the buggers sneak in behind me. A mass murder is committed before bedtime.

———

IT WAS A DAMP grey cool morning in "mud month," ten days after I had become a land baroness. I was on the winding county road that led to the ranger's cabin, on the way to pick up an order of maple syrup from my woodman and his wife. I passed the field where Murray's trailer was parked and slowed down. The Oldsmobile was there, though not tarped. No sign of Murray. The last time I'd seen him, outside the general store in the village, he'd rolled the window down a crack, and I'd seen a dozen balled-up tissues on the seat beside him. He had a terrible cold, he said, and didn't want me to catch it. Under my sympathy and concern was a shameful pinprick of relief that I wouldn't have to gear up for a morning visit for a little awhile.

It had been a few weeks now. I should, I thought as I cruised past the field, drop in on my way home.

The couple hadn't seen him all week. My woodman relayed this as his wife handed me a carton of mason jars filled with dark syrup. "Usually we see him every day."

I didn't feel it was my place to ask if they shouldn't check on him.

Back in the car, I hesitated at the bottom of their drive. Was I up for a visit? I made my decision – an honest if not a generous one – and turned the car in the other direction, past the turn-off up to the ranger's cabin, to take the long way home.

Over the phone line the next day, Asante's concern for Murray spurred me to call his neighbours.

"Yes, we're worried too," said the woodman's wife. "We went over this morning but there was no answer. The door was locked. We've called the police."

"I'm on my way."

They stood in the driveway, arms crossed against the April chill, faces sober. When the cruiser finally arrived, a large-bellied plainclothes detective heaved himself out of the passenger side. He walked past us without a word and stopped at the shelter where the fire for the vat of maple sap still smouldered. "Someone's been here recently," he observed.

"Of course someone's been here," snapped the woodman's wife. "That's our operation. This is our house. Murray lives up the road."

We showed the uniformed driver the way.

The snow was gone from the field. Around the trailer and the uncovered Oldsmobile, the long wet straw-coloured grass was still pressed down from the weight of the winter's snow.

The woodman pounded on the trailer door and called out. No answer.

The uniformed officer stepped forward and broke down the door. He came back out almost immediately, hand over nose, and spoke to the detective, who in turn climbed the two steps, handkerchief to his face.

He returned, expressionless. "Not sure how long he's been there. Corpse is stiff. He fell back on the bed, his hands raised above him.

There's a bucket between his legs. Some clear liquid in it. We'll need your statements."

None of us said a word. He had died, alone in his trailer, in discomfort, in pain.

On the short drive back to the farmhouse, self-accusations whirled around my brain. *Why didn't you check on him more often? If you'd knocked on his door yesterday, you might have been in time to help him.*

The woodman's wife called a few days later to report that relatives had arrived to clear out Murray's trailer. "They found dozens of empty gin bottles under his bed."

Her words filled me with horror. And resurrected guilt. The image of Murray turning to alcohol after so many years sober, to try to "make the day go away," wouldn't leave my head.

She called again to share the results of the autopsy. "He had a stomach aneurism. No alcohol in his system. Those gin bottles must have been there for at least a decade."

Relief washed through me. He hadn't started to drink again. And even if I had knocked on the door that day, there would likely have been no answer, and I would have gone away thinking he just didn't want company. The day I'd seen him at the general store, he'd had a simple head cold. There was no reason I should have been concerned that he was seriously ill.

It didn't matter what I told myself. Guilt prevailed. Guilt *and* remorse.

THE HEADLAMP ATTRACTS the mosquitoes. When I can't stand them around my face any longer, I shut off the light and burrow into the suffocating heat of the sleeping bag. My pre-sleep thoughts drift inevitably to the agent.

When I attended weekly meditations at The Redeemer and listened to the short recorded talks of the Benedictine monk John Main, he spoke of the "chattering monkeys" in your head (an image I now know he borrowed from Buddhist principles). Don't try to shut them up, he'd say, but don't follow their chatter either. Just let them be. They will lose their power.

This is what Steve Hagen has been trying to tell me: don't try to stop the mind, just be aware of what it's doing.

What I see is that the agent is a loud, lovable, cheeky monkey in my head. I won't fight it – or dwell on it either. Why not be at peace with his continuing presence, even if it's pretty much now only in my nighttime dreams and daytime imagination? It will, if Steve H. is right, lose its power. As for the agent's real presence in my life, I haven't seen him since my house-warming party two months ago.

⸻

I HOSTED IT ON A sunny, warmish afternoon in late April, a month after I took possession and several weeks after Murray's sparsely attended funeral. The agent arrived with a six-pack and a smile. His wife was also in high spirits and even taller in platform sandals. She gave me a hug and enthusiastic congratulations on the house. I was grateful for her warmth. I was thinking of offering to babysit so they could get out more.

The agent retrieved my cedar canvas canoe for me from under the neighbour's deck and carried it down to the dock. I asked if he would help load the summer tires into the car – I had an appointment coming up to get the snows off.

He watched me unload things from the back to make room. "Do you have a family living in your car? You seem to have a whole other life in there."

I reached for the nylon sack holding my old four-person Diamond Brand tent and held it in my arms like a big overgrown baby. It had been part of a purge of clothes and other things, but when I arrived at the local donation centre I couldn't part with it. Partly from sentimental attachment but mostly because I didn't think anyone would be able to figure out how to set it up. Now, on impulse, I held it out to the agent. "Would you like a tent? There's nothing wrong with it except it weighs five-hundred pounds and smells a bit musty. It's the perfect size for your family. And it's free."

It was a spur of the moment offer, and I was delighted when he reached for it. "That would be great. We don't have one big enough for all of us."

I released Brenda's Palace into his arms. "Do you want me to show you how to set it up?"

"I'm sure I can figure it out. If I can't, I'll call you."

I teased him for being the typical guy unwilling to ask for directions. Then, together, we lifted the tires into the car and went back in the house to rejoin the other guests.

———————

I WAKE UP TO RAIN on the window and telltale abdominal cramps. Outside, in a lull in the rain, the little stove sputters and I barely get one espresso out of it. When I try to unclog the fuel nipple, the cleaning pin breaks. Reluctantly I gather sticks to make a fire for a second coffee and a pan of French toast, which I eat inside the bunkie to escape the returned drizzle and the bugs. Through the big window, I watch overlapping rings of raindrops appear and just as quickly disappear on the surface of the green-grey water. Between cramps and bugs, my enthusiasm to be here has seriously waned.

———————

L AST WEEK ASANTE gave me a searching look from the other side of the kitchen island, where we were chopping salad makings. "I've been hesitating to tell you, but I've been seeing that pioneer woman in your eyes again. The one living such a solitary, hard, embittered life."

Her words startled me. I hadn't thought about that pioneer woman since Asante had first "seen" her after my breakup with the ranger. Yet here she was again, nearly three years later, and I wasn't, really, surprised.

"I thought I had resolved it," I said at last. "But since I bought the house I do feel like I've resigned myself to life as a hermit." It was a relief to speak it. "But I don't want to go there."

"And you don't have to."

"It's not just about the house. It's everything. I keep hearing this question in my head – some vestige of my church-going days: 'What will be required of me?' What will be required of me, still, it seems, is to give up men and live this bush nun's life where I concentrate on my writing and on becoming a more compassionate, giving person."

"It's so interesting you feel you have to choose." She spoke with curiosity and sympathy. "I wonder where you got that from?"

My answer was unhesitating. "The Christian mystics. I studied them at university. They gave up all their worldly possessions and relationships, and went to live in the desert – well," I laughed, "the Desert Fathers did. Somehow it got drilled into me that that kind of renunciation is the only way to truly love and serve God. But I have this yearning for the other kind of love."

Asante smiled. "There is no 'other' kind of love. It's all love. It's all from God. It *is* God, in fact. Our human relationships are where we experience Love. Renouncing isn't about depriving yourself. It's about dropping the illusion that your happiness comes from something outside you. I think that's what you're really working on – and have been all these years. With every relationship that hasn't worked out, you've divested yourself a little more of the fairy-tale illusion. And I think that's where your current inner conflict and confusion are coming from. You're beginning to experience in a real way that your fulfillment doesn't come from an external relationship, so you think you're being asked to live without one. I don't think you are. I think it's just your focus that needs to change. And I think it *is* changing. I think your special agent, especially, has been pointing the way for you because you can't be together in the usual way. You really don't have to *choose* between God or man – any more than you have to choose between having a relationship and owning your own home."

Her words brought vast relief. Here was one more infinitesimal change of course by the unwieldy ocean liner that was my mind. I just needed to be willing to see the "new view," the true middle way I had been trying to reach with the agent that had nothing specifically to do with him. I wiped a stray tear. "It sounds so silly – the choice – when you put it like that."

"Besides," she added, "I happen to know there's room in your house for two."

THE DRIZZLE STOPS. The sun peeks through, and I brave the bugs to do a morning paddle. Along the shoreline, the damp birch and maple leaves shimmer, and at the end of each pine needle glistens a tiny droplet of water. Dead limbs sprawl across green branches. Tiny cedar trees are sprouting from the horizontal lengths of their fallen mothers. I find myself struck again by how serene the trees and bushes seem in their dense tangled dwelling. They aren't resisting each other. They just live beside and, in some cases, wound around each other in surprising harmony, even protectiveness. I think back to the snapper on the highway and Turtle's message of the protection the Earth will give us as long as we honour our connections to each other. The trees in their tangle show me how to do that. They show me that love – Love – just *is*, no matter what the surface conditions, no matter how much we fail to live up to our expectations of each other, or of ourselves. We do the best we can. The trees urge me to purge every negative, resistant, reproachful bone from my body and become as supple as a pine branch swaying in the breeze.

INTO MY HALF-AWAKE state in the middle of a chilly April night Murray came. Just his face, larger than life. Flashing a huge smile. That was all. No words. Just a beaming smile as I had never seen on his face when he was alive. The dream, visitation more than dream, woke me completely. I lay in the dark, awash in gratitude. He had come, I felt sure, to show me he was fine. To urge me not to feel bad for having let him down. Not to feel I had let him down at all. He was free from all his pain and sorrows, at last. He was more than fine. He was *happy*.

BACK AT THE DOCK, I put in a good hour of revisions on the novel. But physically and mentally I'm done. Time to pack up and head home.

It takes several trips to carry the knapsacks and bags and cooler from the bunkie down to the dock and heave them into the boat. Once loaded, they completely fill the *Empress*'s solid rounded shell.

The move to my new home didn't take a fraction of this effort. I already live there.

Paddling the *Empress* in the marsh near my new home, 2005 (Photo: Max Finkelstein)

7

A GRAND LEAP INTO THE VOID

Grand Lake: September 9–13, 2003
And, in recollection, Rain Lake Loop: August 5–12, 2003

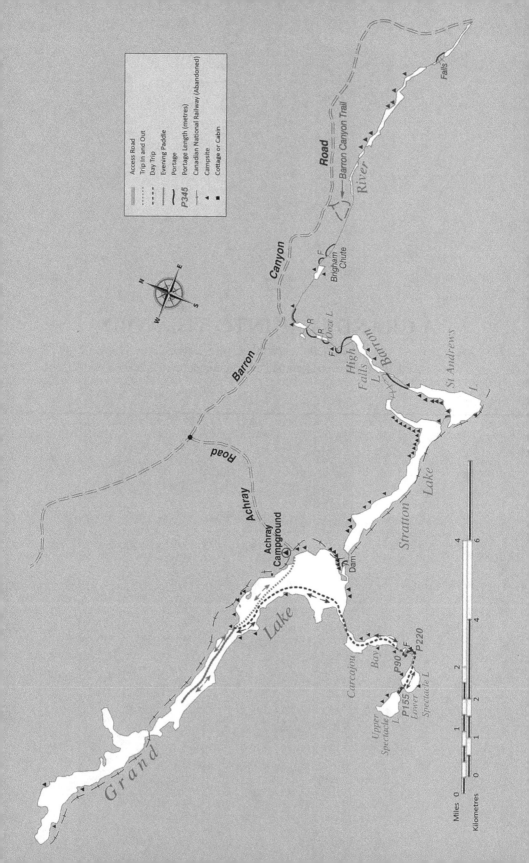

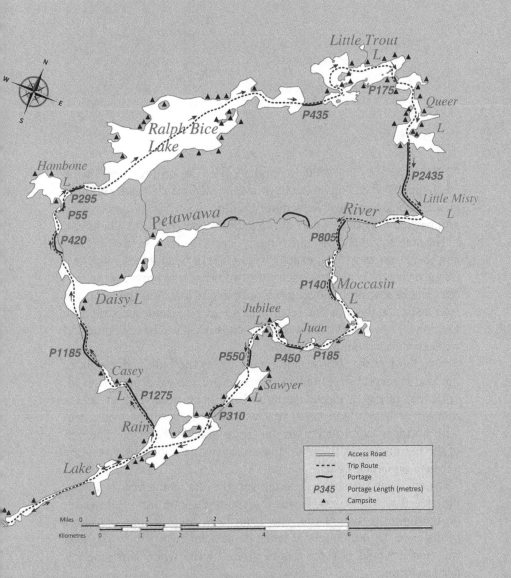

Little Trout
L

P175

Queer

P435

L

P2435

Hambone
L

P295

Little Misty
L

P55

Petawawa

River

P420

P805

P140

Moccasin
L

Daisy L

Jubilee
L

Juan
L

P1185

P550   P450   P185

Casey

Sawyer
L

L   P1275

P310

Rain

Lake

	Access Road
	Trip Route
	Portage
P345	Portage Length (metres)
▲	Campsite

Miles 0   1   2   4

Kilometres 0   1   2   4   6

THE SUN HAS BLINDED me and set the lake on fire. That's what happens when you set out in your canoe to find a lakeside campsite at six o'clock on a clear September evening. It's taken all day to shop and pack and drive to a part of the park I've never explored before.

The map shows there's a site directly across the lake. In this blinding sun there's no way to tell exactly where it is or what it looks like or if it's even vacant. I can't risk the time it would take to cross over to find out. The headwind is slowing my progress as it is, and the light will fade fast once the sun has set. I need to get to a campsite soon. I'm looking for one with lots of writerly rock, since it's to be my home and work space for the next four days.

It's a hard push. Slowing me even more is the bulk and weight of my load: a second sleeping bag, a second inflatable thermal mattress, an actual pillow, a big fat paperback for nighttime reading, and a number of heavy food items that would never be invited on a trip with portages. Not to mention the entire draft of the novel. The heft of the manuscript is the main reason for my decision to stay on one site here on Grand Lake.

I tried the writing trip last month, the one conceived of in my Pinetree Paradise Prison. It was a seven-night loop from Rain Lake, on the opposite side of the park from here, long in time but short in distance, with a couple of lakes booked for two nights. The idea was that it would give me lots of time to write while satisfying my need to move.

I SET OUT ON Ralph Bice on a coolish August morning in the wake of a thunderstorm. Now that it had stopped raining, the large, usually big-waved lake was as still as it had been in 2001. A relief. I hadn't been on a real canoe trip since then, and work had been so relentless these past few months I'd barely got outside. I wasn't as fit as usual.

At the far east end, near the portage into Little Trout, I had my pick of campsites. By six-thirty I was bathed and dined and ready for bed, exhausted from hours of unaccustomed canoe travel the past two days, including yesterday's kilometre-long portages in and out of Casey Lake. Tomorrow would make up for those long days. I was going only as far as next-door Little Trout, and would have two luxurious (and I hoped productive) days there.

Down at the water's edge, I leaned back in my camping chair and posed the eternal canoe-trip question in my journal: *Why do I make these trips? To some people they're a ridiculous endeavour, all the portaging and paddling, the setting up and taking down, ending up exactly where you started, just more exhausted. Hardly a "holiday."*

I looked out at the slate water and revelled in the stillness and the solitude. And had my answer, at least in part. Though unsure why I needed to come out here for solitude. It wasn't as if I didn't have enough at home. Was I becoming the dreaded bush hermit after all?

The sky was still grey, but friendly grey. It seemed to be a slow-moving system that was sitting over the mirror water. The stillness of the air seeped, ever more, into my bones. *Be still*, recited my bones, *and know that I am God.*

I STICK CLOSE TO Grand's north shore in the blinding evening light. From somewhere in the trees comes a familiar rattle, followed by abrupt silence. I scan the shoreline greenery. All last week, whenever I sat on the dock, a belted kingfisher serenaded my work. I would look up to see the long-beaked bird fly from one tree to another around the bay. Yesterday one landed on the dock ladder, giving me a rare close-up view of its shaggy steel-blue crest and shiny round black eye.

I drank in the sight for two gifted seconds before it chattered into flight. Moments later it flew back out over the water and plunged in, head first. Surfaced almost immediately, dinner in beak.

The rattle comes again. The kingfisher swoops out from the trees just ahead and rattles its way up the shore. Abrupt silence again when it lands in another tree. Each time the canoe comes close, the kingfisher is startled into noisy flight on to a new silent perch. Until, finally, it crosses the lake.

Kingfisher, according to *Animal-Speak*, signifies that abundance – prosperity and love – is about to come into your life. "Often it requires that you dive headlong into some activity, but it usually proves to be very beneficial."

It's nearly seven by the time I arrive at the end of the wider part of Grand. There are four sites to choose from, none with rock. Disappointed, I nose onto a tiny strip of beach in an otherwise weedy shoreline. The campsite interior is almost completely hidden by shrubs, except for a small opening like the entrance to a cave. Just inside the "front door" sits a huge boulder, much taller than I. At least I have my Shield presence, even if it's too statuesque to sit on. A Shield sentinel perhaps. Though its broad wall-like shape might lend itself more to bouncer.

I eat a quick cold snack of a dinner and search for a pack-hanging branch before I lose the light. My arrival is so late because I didn't know when I got up this morning that I was coming in today. I had to get the final chapter onto the computer and print out the draft – a full draft at last. I had to refresh my memory of key parts of Louise's journals, review my notes from the trial, and compile a list of revisions for each chapter. This was all done sooner than expected and here I am, a day early, about to make a kingfisher-dive into my final revisions.

Food pack aloft, I erect the tent and toss in the sleeping bags and self-inflating mattresses – bedding enough for two. I pile one air mattress on top of the other and zip one sleeping bag inside the other – cozy bedding for one. I sit back on my heels to arrange the rest of my home away from home, my mind on Louise and the edits I have to make.

It's such a relief when this happens, when my thoughts drift to my characters even when I'm not writing. When I'm living and breathing the novel and not just thinking about getting to the writing, or avoiding it altogether, nothing else matters. My mind is too occupied – not just filled but *fulfilled* – to think or stew about anything or anyone else. There's no space in my head to moderate the continuing interior debates and conflicts about whether I'm being called to give up my yearning for a still-elusive relationship and dedicate my life to God as a kind of bush nun scribe. This month I just am that bush nun scribe.

In the dark, I crouch down at the water's edge to wash my face. I'm about to head for the tent when pale light suddenly illuminates patches of ground. I turn back to the beach. Climbing up the sky at the far end of the lake is the moon, almost full, and, beside it, a large pinpoint of planetary light I know from recent news reports is Mars. For the past month it's been hanging out closer to Earth than it has in sixty thousand years.

The moon paints a blue wash over beach, boulder, and tent, though it does nothing to lessen the September night chill. In the tent, I wrap myself in the plush warmth of two sleeping bags on the cushioning of two thermal mattresses and close my eyes.

A horrific screech jolts me awake. I sit up, heart thudding. *Listening.* The silence is as abrupt as the screech. It sounded like an animal on the warpath. I strain my ears and pray I'm not on the path. Moments later, the sound of gentle hooting fills the air. I relax. I've just been unceremoniously introduced to a barred owl.

I lie back down, only to sit bolt upright again at a raucous yowling, followed by a loud squawking. My brain searches for safe identifiers. A heron? Some other bird? *Not* a cougar or bobcat.

This interrupted sleep is a sharp contrast to last month's trip, when I slept straight through all seven nights, and many of the afternoons (when I was supposed to be writing...). It was incredible to sleep so soundly – and so often! – on a canoe trip. Though maybe not so incredible, given how hard I'd been working and how unaccustomed I was to paddling and portaging. It seemed I was nothing more than *tired* – far too tired to lie awake worrying about bears.

Sounds of sloshing wake me yet again. Beavers, I tell myself. I seem to have unwittingly set up camp in the middle of an after-hours club. Tomorrow I'll move house. I rearrange the tangle of sleeping bags, snuggle back in, and try to recreate the interior state that brought on such sound sleep last month. It wasn't just from physical fatigue but from the stillness of the air, which lasted nearly the whole week, even during rain showers. The winds seemed to have been banished from the park. Now, in the noisy night, I make a half-hearted attempt to repeat last month's mantra: *Be still, and know that I am God. Be still...*

Asante might add, "And know that you are God too."

I WAS BACK HOME after my few days in the Smoke Lake bunkie. Asante was in the shower and I on the little couch in the front room for my morning meditation, legs crossed, hands palm up on knees. With each inhalation, my breathing slowed more. My heart rate slowed too, which relaxed my body. My mind became a little quieter for a little longer than usual between my wandering thoughts. Twenty minutes later, I opened my eyes in a state of supreme wellbeing.

I joined Asante in the kitchen. She looked up from the stove with a smile.

"I think something just ca-chinked into place about breathing being the way to experience bliss. Though I'm not sure why." I looked at her inquiringly. "Why?"

She placed an egg in a pot of boiling water and considered her answer. "The *Upanishads* – those are the Hindu scriptures – say we don't live by the breath that flows in and out, but by him who *causes* the breath to flow in and out. So when you become aware of your breath you're becoming aware of the source of your being. And when you slow your breath down..." She paused. "I'd say that makes you *experience* who you really are."

"And who am I?" It was a joking question.

She looked straight at me and said, as if it were the most obvious thing in the world, "You are God."

I blinked, unsure how to react to this blasphemous bomb. "I am?"

"Exactly. 'I am.' That's what God said when Moses asked his name, "'I AM WHO I AM.'" Jesus said it, too: 'Before Abraham was, I am.'"

I could hardly take in what she was saying. "But that's God and Jesus. And anyway, you don't believe in Jesus, do you?"

She poured water from the kettle into a mug of chai tea. "'Believe' is probably not the right word. Not the way I think you mean, not as a Christian. But yes, if you mean do I think he is Divine. I've experienced his presence."

There seemed no end to the shocking statements this morning. I couldn't remember Asante ever telling me about a personal experience of Jesus. I remembered only her sympathy for my own doubts. I made coffee and we carried our hot drinks to the couch.

"You remember I went to boarding school when I was seventeen."

I nodded. She had been sent to a school run by Seventh-day Adventists to be cured of what her mother called her "juvenile delinquency," for sneaking out to do all the things her mother forbade: attend dances, dress like the other kids, drive to the lake where her friends hung out.

"It was my first night. I was totally miserable. I couldn't get to sleep. I lay in bed, upset that I had been coerced into going there. I was in a strange building, with strange people, far away from home. The room was dark. I heard and sensed the door to my room open and close. It freaked me out. Then I noticed a light coming toward the bed – maybe the size of a beach ball. I was sure it must be something evil. I was terrified. But when the light got close to me, it emanated a love so pure and so gentle I relaxed a bit. The light came right beside me and became the form of Jesus. He put his hand on my shoulder and said, 'I'll stay with you until you fall asleep.' And he did."

I listened in astonishment.

"I never really thought anything of it. I had no doubt it was Jesus. It wasn't just the appearance of him but also the incredible love that emanated from him."

Her story suddenly brought back all the angst I had felt as a teenager at Pioneer when the counsellors and other campers gave "testimony" of their experience of Jesus – experience that eluded me.

Asante seemed to read my thoughts. "His coming to me. It didn't have anything to do with my being special. He comes to those in need. I was in need."

I struggled to absorb this. If she had experienced Jesus, why wasn't she a Christian?

"I think Jesus is the master," she said. "He realized his own divinity and points the way for all of us to realize our divinity too. Because we're all part of God. The *Upanishads* say, 'You are that.' You are God."

She went back to the kitchen to check on her eggs, leaving me to try to take in these revelations. She had experienced Jesus and considered him the master. She believed in his divinity, even though she wasn't a Christian. Most shocking of all, she had just told me we are *all* God, all divine.

I perched on the stool at the kitchen counter and tried for a light tone. "It's ironic you believe in Jesus when you're not a Christian. And I'm Christian but don't believe in Jesus."

She turned, and her voice was sharp. "You're not a Christian."

Her uncharacteristic sternness, almost rebuke, took me aback. "I don't believe a lot of the Christian beliefs but I'm still Christian."

"No," she said, a hint of laughter in her firm tone, "you're not. A Christian is someone who believes in the dogmas of the Church. You don't believe in the Jesus of the Church. You don't go to church. You left all that behind. You're not a Christian."

Her words brought me up short. We ate breakfast, and I took my journal out to the Muskoka chair on the point, hoping the bugs would stay away long enough for me to figure why her words distressed me so much. She was right; I hadn't had Christian beliefs in years. But it wasn't, I realized, about beliefs. It wasn't even about church. It was about my identity – my "cultural" identity, for want of a better word. It had been more than fifteen years since I'd left the Church. Still, I thought of myself as a small "c" christian. Or as "Christian" without the indefinite article. "Christian" without the article aligned me with the values of Western society. That was my thinking. The truth was I had no new label for myself, so I was hiding away in the safely familiar. With four short words Asante had pulled the safety net away. It was time to say it – and say it without fear or ambivalence: I'm not a Christian.

I wrote the words with trepidation. Giving up the Christian label seemed tantamount to losing my very identity. If I wasn't a Christian, who was I? The answer Asante had offered was just too wild. Too big a leap for my limited mind.

A WISPY MIST SLIDES across the morning lake and is swept away by the sunlight. It's a warm morning for September. Wading into the sandy-bottomed shallows out my front door, I scatter a dozen minnow-sized fish while several tiny frogs eye me from their half-submerged perches. The gradual sandy slope does make it easier to get in the water than if I had to jump in from a rock. But the water is *cold*. I decide it's fine to have morning dip only up to my knees.

Breakfast doesn't take as long now that I've given up coffee. The several weeks of caffeine-withdrawal headaches were worth it. Now I wake up *awake* and am much less fidgety in my sedentary occupation.

A light tail breeze hustles me into the day. In my day pack are manuscript, cheese and crackers, and an apple that would never be allowed on a regular canoe trip.

I peer at the map draped over the yoke. Grand Lake, here on the park's east side, resembles a cobra, the wider part its head and expanded hood. The other two-thirds are a long snake body of a waterway that begins, or rather ends, at the narrows next to my site. One day this week, I'll explore that long narrow waterway. This morning's destination is two little lakes to the south called Lower Spectacle and Upper Spectacle, which on the map do look like a pair of blue-lens glasses.

I cross the lake and follow the shore until I spot an orange tent sign on a large pine high on a hump of wonderful, craggy Canadian Shield. Here is the campsite that was invisible to me last evening, and it *is* vacant. I paddle past, eyeing the different angles of rock, searching automatically for that perfect writer's seat. If the site is still free when I paddle by again this afternoon, I'll move house. On a weekday in September, there's every chance it will be. There's only one canoe in the distance and it's headed toward the Barron River Canyon, the area's main attraction.

I've never been through the Barron. That's about to change. Max – the friend who taught me how to solo a boat a dozen years ago – called yesterday to regale me with stories from a recent family canoeing expedition, then announced they're off again this weekend, down the Barron River with friends. The place and timing of their departure –

from the very lake where I'm camping, on the very day I'm to come out – is so impeccable I invited myself along. Reward for a productive few days of work.

Beyond the campsite, the shore traces a wide convex curve down into Carcajou Bay. At the south end, the opposite shores close in and all but meet, which has the effect of squeezing the water through a short set of rapids. A yellow sign beside them marks a 90-metre carry-over.

I jump out, pull the *Empress* half out of the water, and brace the rounded hull against my thighs. I reach a hand across to the opposite gunwale – no problem on this narrower boat – and push off with one knee to give it a hoist into the air and over onto my shoulders. All in one smooth, satisfying motion.

I first performed this classic canoe flip on last month's not-so-productive writing trip – my first real trip with the Prospector. The dozen portages gave me lots of practice, and now it feels like second nature.

I climb the path. No worry about bears on such a short trail.

I SHRUGGED THE heavy food pack onto my back and noted the time. This was the longest portage of the trip, the 2,435-metre (times three) flat walk from Queer Lake into Little Misty – it would be about twenty minutes to the halfway point. With my newfound skill, I swung the canoe up onto my shoulders and settled into a semi-comfortable groove of pain. I didn't sing for the bears. I didn't even think about bears. I descended into a place of silence. A deep, rhythmical silence measured out in the steady pace of hiking boots on hard-packed dirt and steady breaths pulled from diaphragm. I immersed myself in the silence – and endured the pressure even carbon fibre couldn't spare my shoulders – for twenty-five minutes before I set the boat and food pack down in a tangle of tall grass beside the path.

I had just turned to head back when sudden movement on the trail caught my eye. At the top of an incline was a black face. A large, cute, *furry* face. I barely had time to register who owned the cute furry face when it saw *me*, and the furry black body attached to the face turned and *fled*.

Immediately I called out and clapped my hands. I even jumped up and down. Then I kept walking. In the direction of the bear. There was no choice: that way lay the rest of my gear. I did dispense with the silence. The woods resounded with hymns belted out in time to clapping hands. Amazingly, no fear accompanied this compulsion to make noise. A heightened awareness, yes, and a slightly elevated heart rate, as anyone walking at a slightly faster pace would have. But I was confident the bear wouldn't be coming back any time soon.

On the second relay, with the bulky gear pack, I switched over to my secular repertoire: "You Are My Sunshine," "Oh My Darling, Clementine," "Home on the Range," "The Quartermaster's Store," "There's a Hole in the Bottom of the Sea." Rousing renditions guaranteed to keep bears away. It was, I mused, good to meet that bear and find out first-hand that the theory works – normal bears run when they see humans. And that the other theory works too – humans, even small female ones, can call out loudly and make a lot of noise and maybe even look big.

———

I CROSS A SMALL pond, portage around a waterfall, put into a creek, and hang a right into a narrow channel, where I dip my paddle slowly to take in the serenity of the cool moss-green rock walls. All too soon the channel opens into a lake – Lower Spectacle.

I follow the shore. Not far from a clump of tall reeds, a grasshopper struggles in the water, trying, without success, to lift off. I bring the boat alongside and extend my paddle onto the water's surface next to the tiny straw-like creature. To my delight, it comes readily onto the blade. And there it sits.

Some rescue! With my little charge on the blade, I can't put paddle in water to get it safely to shore. We'll just have to wait for the wind to come and rescue us both.

I keep the paddle level, out of the water, and grasshopper and I wait together for a breeze to push us close to the reeds.

The breeze obliges. When it has nudged us close enough, I extend the paddle, high and level, into the air, and grasshopper performs a tremendous leap. Its trajectory seems destined to take it straight back into the drink, except mid-jump it executes an impressive ninety-degree turn and lands (I check to make sure) on a reed.

I carry on, blessing, Grasshopper, totem of "uncanny leaps forward" – and apparently sideways too. And wonder, where will sideways take me?

The two Spectacles, separated by a short portage, are no spectacle at all. Their shorelines are lined with scrubby bush, with few tall pines and no writing rocks. I do an about-face, back to the waterfall for lunch and Carcajou Bay. The winds in that bay are so fierce I have to fight to keep close to shore without hitting the half-submerged rocks. At last I reach the still-vacant campsite.

Canoe pulled onto a wide slant of rock, I climb up to the large open space next to the fire pit and look around. The pines are sparsely spaced, wood chips are scattered everywhere, and with little ground cover the wind blows right through. Below the site, the craggy humps of rock – perfect writerly seats with level ledges and walls to lean back on – make up for everything.

From the rocky water's edge, I survey the wind-whipped water. No point crossing in the gale. It's only three o'clock. Plenty of time to wait it out. I pull out chapter and notes and pen.

I rub cramped fingers and glance at my watch. Five o'clock. An excellent afternoon's work. The pages are scribbled over so completely with edits it will be a happy challenge to decrypt them all when I get home. Across the lake, sunlight glints off the chrome of tiny cars in the campground parking lot. No one seems to be on their way here. And the waves seem smaller. Time to paddle home, pack everything up and transport it over.

It's a hard push. The wind hasn't died as much as I thought. By the time I drag the canoe up onto the little beach it's nearly six o'clock and I'm done in.

I step through my open front door, past the Shield bouncer (who last night shirked on the job), and am struck by how cozy and secluded the site feels. A welcome contrast to the too-wide-openness of the campsite across the street. That decides it. I'm not moving anywhere. I can always paddle to a writing rock tomorrow.

Soon I have a bubbling pot of rehydrated chili, to which I add a fried-up chopped onion – another weighty item that would never make the cut on a portaging trip. I carry steaming bowl through the woods to find a waterside seat to dine and watch the sun set. On my Little Trout campsite last month I bushwhacked through the woods on a similar mission.

THE EVENING SUN had burned a small hole in the cloud that had been sitting over my head (and occasionally springing leaks) for four days now. I navigated through the underbrush and ducked under branches in search of a sun-facing waterside seat to bask in its warmth before we both went to bed. Though how I could even think about bed I wasn't sure, when I'd conked out in the tent much of the afternoon.

Just before I crashed through the brush to the shore, I came to a massive pine. Lying across one of its thick exposed roots was a huge slab of rock – table-top-flat and at least a metre long. The pine seemed to have sprouted right out of the rock and taken the top with it as it grew. Ice can move rocks and so, apparently, can trees.

And so, even more improbably, can lichens. This I learned from Annie Dillard. In *For the Time Being*, she claims more sand is created from lichens (working in tandem with ice and salt crystals) than from ocean waves. "Lichens secrete acids, which break minerals. Lichens widen rocks' cracks, growing salt crystals split them further, and freezing water shatters them."

I wondered if lichens had a hand in breaking down this rock so the pine could push through and break it in two. Astonishing that anything – a tiny lichen, a supple pine, an ice crystal – could split something that seems so indisputably solid, immovable. Immutable.

I ducked under the pine, patted the apparently not so solid rock table balanced on its root, and found a rock cousin at shore under the pine's long branches. The sun felt good on my sleepy face. I closed my eyes and into my mind came the mantra, along with Dom John Main's voice from one of the recorded talks we listened to at The Redeemer before our meditations:

... Jesus was saying: "The Kingdom of Heaven is upon you, is within you." But you must realize this. You must let your consciousness expand and your awareness develop... We must realize the persons we already are. This is the purpose of our meditation – to lead us to a full awareness of who we are, where we are... We must touch down in the concrete reality of the present moment where our divine splendour is revealed. We must become still.

I became still for a full hour, an astonishing feat. Then I bushwhacked my way to bed.

MY SUPPER AND I pop out at the serene shore. Here, tall grasses and bulrushes extend into a small marsh, dotted with a few good-sized boulders. I hop from boulder to boulder over to a flat rock, and sit down cross-legged. Dwarfed and hidden by the surrounding reeds, I feel like Baby Moses in the rushes.

The sun slips serenely behind the hills as I savour the last bite of chili (made quite decadent by the added onion).

Be still, and know that you are God, whisper my cheeky bones.

In one of my old journals, I recently found a verse I transcribed from one of John Main's recorded talks. He, in turn, was quoting someone he referred to only as the "Sufi poet":

I saw my Lord with my heart's eye and said, "Who art Thou Lord?"
"Thyself," he replied.

This, I realize, is exactly what Asante was trying to tell me last summer. It seems antithetical to anything Christianity taught me, even mystics like John Main. This is more than the merging between the Self and God I always understood him to mean, or even God "in our centre." This is the Self *as* God. No separation. Exactly as Asante said. Was this what Main was hinting at when he spoke of the need to become aware of who we *already* are? I'm not sure what spurred me to quote the Sufi verse in my journal all those years ago. I'm not sure I grasped its radical implications – or do even now. Sitting on my sunset rock, not quite connected to the shore, I feel like a grasshopper struggling to lift off the water's surface.

In the open water just beyond the marsh, movement catches my eye. A sleek brown head glides by, trailing a distinctive V-shaped wake. The brown head enters a small channel between the rushes, pauses, and puts something into its mouth with tiny human-like hands. Unaware of me in my natural blind, it swims to a boulder not three metres from mine, and climbs on to give fuller attention to the shoots it's eating. It's so close I can see the course slickness of its fur, dark and glistening. I stay utterly still except for the smile that spreads over my face.

Dinner finished, the beaver slides back into the water. Not quite the same kind of splash I heard last night, though no question my dinner companion was among the rowdy nightclubbers.

It's the first time I've shared a campsite with a beaver. Beavers, says Ted Andrews, are the builders of dreams. Builders for obvious, industrious, engineering reasons, and dreams because the beaver's main domain, water, has close associations with emotions and dreams. One of our most common dreams, says Andrews, is to have a home and family.

My own dream, since I was ten, has been to have a family of published novels. More than a dream, it's been my Life's Purpose. Despite the strength of this dream, I've spent years battling procrastination. Two unfinished "children" languish in a box in my office. Then Louise went missing, and an old school friend appeared in a dream to tell me to write it in a book. The dream spurred me to make a commitment to tell Louise's story, though I had no idea how hard it would be to get into her head and heart. Here, this evening, my industrious campsite mate seems a perfect reflection and acknowledgement of all the work I've done these past eight years, and especially this summer, to fulfill that commitment.

I look over to the flat rock the beaver has just vacated, and it comes to me that I'm not done dreaming yet. The novel will soon need a publishing home, something I've hardly dared think about. Beaver reminds me that it's time to build on my dreams, to polish the manuscript and dare to envision it in published form. Not just for me but equally for Louise. Dreams have to be dreamed before they are fulfilled. It's good to be reminded. Thank you, Beaver.

I stand on the little beach to wait for the moon. I wait. And wait. At last the eastern horizon takes on a pale glow. Slowly, over the hills, it comes, full and large and luminous. A white light to rival (almost) the one revealed to me in the red rose visualization Asante's friend led us through two decades ago. I stand in awe of its silent, slow-rising splendour. And then I go to bed.

THE BANK OF cooling cloud inched its way over Jubilee Lake, gradually obscuring what had been a rare blue-sky day (a rare productive day too, my second last). It was the same weather system, I was positive, circling around up there, in a lazy way, day after day – a pot on simmer given the occasional stir. The continuum of stillness had been having a decided effect on me all week, sending me to the tent every afternoon for a nap and, this evening, to find a place on the slant of shoreline rock for another rare canoe-trip meditation.

I looked out over Jubilee's inky waters. A few metres from shore, the dark silhouette of a thickish stick poked out of the water at a forty-five-degree angle. It was gliding at an angle unnaturally upright for a stick and with a steady progress no stick could make without a current. I smiled and kept watch in the fading light. The stick veered in close to shore, and I crouched down at the water's edge to greet my evening guest.

Sure enough, visible just under the surface, attached to the thick stick head, was the unmistakable curve of shell.

The turtle, a large snapper, made a quarter turn to its left and began to half paddle, half pad its way along the submerged slope of rock of my shoreline. On the same slope, above the waterline, I strolled beside it, so close I had a clear view of the thick spiny legs and long-clawed feet that propelled it forward in graceful slow motion.

Deliberately, it seemed, it turned to face the shore, where it paused, head still under water, before continuing its shoreline patrol. I paused with it, strolled on with it.

The next time it turned toward the shore, I crouched down just back from the waterline. This time the snapper raised its grizzled head out of the water. Dark, ancient, wise eyes met mine, and it came to me with certainty that this creature was the embodiment of my beloved Earth Mother.

Her dark, primitive, prominent eyes met mine for one long, awe-inducing moment. Then she lowered her head and resumed her underwater stroll, and I continued mine above water.

Again she turned to face the shore, and I crouched down at a respectful distance (she was a snapper after all). She raised her head out of the water, and our eyes met again.

Then... she blinked. A closing of her eyelids so slow and deliberate it felt like acknowledgement of my awareness of her identity.

In the deepening twilight, not a metre apart, we kept up our parallel evening stroll, mine on dry land, hers just under water, until we came to the sand where the slope of rock ended. There, the snapper turned around to lead me sedately the way we had come.

Back at the far end of the shore rock, she did another about-face, and we retraced our path. A second time we reached the bit of beach, and she disappeared, ghostlike, into the night depths.

DOWN THE DUSTY gravel road I cruise, as saturated with satisfaction as a bush nun scribe could possibly be. This morning I made excellent progress on the chapter revisions at the campsite across the lake and am now free to carry out the second phase of the day's itinerary. Though it's decidedly odd to be in the car in the middle of a canoe trip.

I pull into an empty lot marked Barron Canyon Trail. At the far end a large wooden board displays a map of a triangular-shaped trail, marked 1.5 kilometres long. That distance might be substantial on a portage, but on a regular gearless hike it's piddling. And only one of the three sides follows the rim of the star attraction. Still, it's a hike. I pick up a trail guide from the shelf below the map and set out through a forest of mixed hardwoods and conifers. Soon brighter daylight peeks through the trees up ahead. Then, straight ahead, the world drops off.

I approach the edge of the world with caution. And stop short: I'm looking across a wide, deep cavern to a high cliff with rich-coloured evergreens that curl right out of the vertical rock. A careful step brings me closer to the rim, and I look down to blue water far below. The vast open space before me feels tangible. As if it would catch me if I fell into it. I don't test this theory.

Ten thousand years ago, the booklet informs me, the river was the main outlet for glacial meltwater, which carved this hundred-metre-deep canyon between two jagged walls of rock. It extends as far as I can see in either direction, though the walls taper off in gradient and height.

From this point, the trail follows the rim of the cliff. There are no barriers or fences. Every few metres, I place my feet on solid-looking patches of well-worn pale dirt and peer up and down the canyon. Uppermost in my mind is the story I read in the local paper about a woman who fell to her death this summer from this very path. Each time I find a new careful stance along the path to take in another spectacular view I shudder. My eyes want to see farther than my feet can accommodate, and I'm afraid my feet are going to try to follow my eyes. I have a fear of heights, but along with the fear of falling is an even more potent fear of leaping. Did the woman feel this same irresistible pull? Did her eyes draw her, literally, into the view? The article reported she was hiking with her husband. He would have seen her go, or seen where she no longer was. How did he force his feet to stay glued to the path and not jump to the rescue? I envision him running up and down the path, calling her name, fooling himself that she's just gone ahead out of sight. I watch him flatten his body to the ground to peer over the edge, certain she's going to climb back up. Or maybe he freezes in shock. I can hear the wail he lets out, hear it hit the wall on the other side, echo back in his face. I can't begin to imagine how he must have felt. So much easier to identify with the one who has fallen.

Too soon, I come to the end of the canyon-side path, and the trail turns again to the right, to trace the third side of the triangle, back through the woods to the parking lot. I arrive at the car with the heart-racing relief of one who has just performed a death-defying feat. The short trail has, after all, provided the aerobic benefits of one ten times its length.

Behind the wheel again, I'm still thinking about the woman. The article ended with a quote from park officials that in spite of her death they would not erect a view-destroying fence. The decision relieved me. Maybe though, I muse on the drive back to Grand, there could be handholds for people at risk of being bidden by their mesmerized brains to hurl themselves into that stunning chiselled-out space.

**Alluring view of the Barron River Canyon
from hiking trail**

Windless waters make for an easy paddle back to the campsite. The sun is warm. I wonder what the agent is up to these days and am surprised to find him in my thoughts. Sometimes, I think, as I pull paddle through water, absence makes the heart grow *healed*.

Halfway to my site, I come to a small jut of rock beside a dock platform. Through the trees at the top of the slope, a white clapboard cottage is just visible, windows boarded up for winter. With little risk of intruding on someone's privacy, I tie the canoe at the dock, peel down to tank top and underwear, and jump off the rock. One quick dunk is enough: the intersection of September-cold water and July-warm air is both shocking and invigorating.

"THIS IS AS CLOSE to heaven as I'll ever get." So proclaimed Eve as she emerged naked from Jubilee's refreshing, sun-sparkled waters. It was the last morning of my (non-)writing trip. After the previous evening's stroll with my venerated guest, I'd slept yet another nine uninterrupted hours, and I was refreshed and energized for the paddle out.

Towelling myself dry, I glanced at the big white pine before me on the slope of rock. Nestled among the roots lay two mottled-brown snakes.

The Genesis story has given the snake a bad name. Other cultures have given it a much better one. Both *Animal-Speak* and *Medicine Cards* refer to the snake as a symbol of transformation or transmutation for North American Indigenous Peoples, and describe initiations that involved learning to transmute the snake's poison after being bitten. A person who survived had the ability to transmute all poisons, whether physical, mental, or emotional.

"Hello, Transmuter of Poisons!" I called out, cheerily.

It wasn't like me to be sanguine in the presence of snakes, but these two seemed harmless, not to mention oblivious of me. One slithered into a hole under the pine's exposed roots. The other glided over the thick curved roots – themselves fat indolent snakes – and disappeared. The first popped its head back out of the hole and seemed to bask in the sunshine.

I covered my nakedness with a sarong (because of the coolish breeze, not from Eve-like shame) and watched the snake slide, elegantly, all the way out of the hole. It was two-thirds of a metre long, maybe a water snake.

Another head appeared in the entrance. This snake crept out to lie beside the first. It rested its head on the back of the other, just behind its head, then inched across its back so that for a brief moment the two slim bodies formed an X, symbol for a kiss. Slowly, the second snake slithered itself around the first one's neck in what looked like an affectionate chokehold. It was the first time I'd ever seen snakes interact. It was all so sweet, either parent with offspring or sibling with sibling, or mate with mate. Nothing like my imaginings about scary snakes.

Under the serene sun, I combed out my hair and back to memory came a recent dream in which I was standing in front of the bathroom mirror: carefully, with both hands, I peeled a layer of skin off my face and then another off my chest. The layers came off easily, in large sheets, leaving me shiny and clean.

Before the snake begins to shed its skin, its eyes will begin to cloud over... As the skin begins to shed, the eyes begin to clear as if they will see the world anew.

—●—

THROUGH THE MESH screen of the tent, I have an unimpeded view of the rising moon, now with a sliver shaved off its right side. Waking at intervals through the surprisingly quiet night, I watch the big orb rise higher, brighter in the sky.

This more usual canoe-trip dozing and waking pattern makes me realize again just how exhausted I must have been last month, to have slept so soundly through the nights and so many afternoons too. The exhaustion not only of an editor at the end of a work marathon but of a creature at the end of a life cycle, a creature shedding the skin of an outmoded identity.

I've always thought of my spiritual journey as a journey to *reach* somewhere, to seek something out, take on something – enlightenment, wisdom. Jubilee's sweet snakes showed me otherwise. Enlightenment isn't something we "achieve"; it's a *divesting*. A peeling away of the thick layers of judgment, criticism, blame, rejection – whatever negative attitudes we bear toward ourselves or others. It's a dissolving of the seemingly rock-solid ego and its "longing and loathing" that keep us from experiencing what Buddhists like Steve Hagen call "the Whole," what the *Upanishads* describe as the Divine nature that is the core of our being – and what Jesus calls the Kingdom of Heaven within us.

It's still such a raw and unfamiliar idea – that Wholeness, or Divinity, or God, is within me – *is* me. And yet it became a little more familiar last month here in the park, with its almost motionless weather system and myriad blessings of fauna and flora. Not just the cooperative bear, sacred turtle, and rock-splitting pine, but several playful otters and cleansing frogs, a joyful hummingbird, and a self-reflective heron too. The trip was effectively a Cosmic Time Out (a Cosmic Nap maybe) that forced me to slow down and *see*. See that everything (and everyone) "out there" is also inside me: protective male, nurturing female, innocent child, joyful, immortal, healing, compassionate Divinity. Wholeness. Unity. The Kingdom of Heaven. I just (just!) need to let such awareness seep into my bones. Surrounding my holy bones with a new skin.

I turn over and there is the moon again, shining through the other mesh screen entrance as it makes its descent down the other side of the tent. I doze and wake, doze and wake. Each time I wake, the moon is a little larger, a little more coppery, a little closer to the horizon.

A blue-sky gale whooshes up the lake and straight through my front door. It's quite unexpected when the campsite faces south and is so cocooned by bush and boulder and tree. But this wind is *from* the south. If my resolve to stay put to work were in any danger of weakening, the wind has arrived to firm it up.

I take refuge behind the Sentinel. The boulder – so much taller and wider than I am – is a mighty fortress. Even the manuscript pages I spread around me are in no danger of blowing away.

For a break and a change of view, lunch is served on a wind-protected perch on one of the flat rocks among the rushes where Beaver and I broke bread last night. I take a bite of cheese, cuke, and avocado wrap, and open my journal.

You peel off the layers of old attitudes and identities and then… what? I've had ideas – scary, daunting ideas – about what will be "required" of me. That I give up men and join a convent, or sell all my worldly goods and devote my life to the poor, or whatever Christian notions I've retained about what it means to let go of one's ego and live a selfless life. Once my inner lichens have completed their dissolving work, what will be left?

In my mind's eye, I see the globe of the Earth. It's surrounded by a veil of continuous energy – Divine energy. Love. At intervals within the veil, I see little balls of solid energy that look like Tinkertoy disks. I know they're the individual selves of all the Earth's people, kept separate and distinct by the ego and personality we've each taken on as humans. The disks, I see, are connected to each other by bonds that take the form of Tinkertoy rods, millions and millions of them. Joined together, the disks and rods form a globe-shaped grid that overlays and completely obscures the veil of continuous Divine energy. Even though it's hidden, I see we are an integral part of that big round mass of Loving Energy. It permeates us and connects us each to the other, and I know that if all our little disks of individuality were to dissolve into that veil of continuous Energy, we would all *be* that sphere of perfect Love. We *are* that sphere of Love.

This vision – the first ever given to me – came on a hot evening last summer, a few weeks after my four-day retreat in Brenda's Bunkie. Asante had been offered another interview with the charitable organization in Montana, this time in person, and was to leave the next day. As a thank you for the nine weeks she had stayed in my home, she offered me a special healing. "It works through the energetic systems in and around your body – your aura around your body and the chakras within," she explained. "It will align you with your Higher Self – the part of you that carries the Christ consciousness – the awareness of your oneness with God."

It was an evening of unsettled weather. I lay down on the couch cushions we had placed on the floor and looked up with a nervous smile. "Is there anything you should tell me about what to expect? Anything I need to do?"

Her smile back was reassuring. "There's nothing for you to do but close your eyes. This healing will relax you and take you into slower brainwave patterns, which will take you into deeper places and into expansion. The more you relax into it, the deeper your experience can be."

I closed my eyes and worried my mind was too limited to have any kind of deep experience. I watched the thoughts that marched through my head with the attention of a wary guard. Then a crash of thunder sounded in the distance. Rain began to drum on the metal roof. My body relaxed, and then my mind, and I felt myself expand beyond my limbs into the space of the room. My expanded self touched Asante's space – a gentle, healing space. For an instant it felt like we might merge. We were no longer "individuals," the boundaries were dissolving, they were an illusion. For one brief moment, all that existed was the unity that had formerly been "Brenda," "Asante" and "the storm."

Into the miraculously relaxed open space of my mind the vision came.

TONIGHT'S DINNER is a bowl of rehydrated cheddar cheese and broccoli rice. I eat quickly. With the sudden calming of wind and re-emergence of sun, it's imperative I climb in the canoe for a final (and first) paddle of the day – westward, up Grand's long snake body.

It's a luminescent evening. The small bushes and maples that line the shore are beginning to turn cranberry and grape – a harvest of colour against the lush green of the pines. Everything aglow in the intensifying sunlight.

I'm not sure how far I'll get before I lose the light. Certainly not as far as the sole campsite the map shows at the far end: it must be a good ten kilometres away. I set my sights on a much closer point of pines alluringly shrouded in a feathery mist.

This is the last night on my own. Tomorrow I'm to meet up with Max and his family and friends at the car campground on Grand's northeast shore. I'm ready to be with people again, and tickled to get to do that without even leaving the park.

Beyond the shoreline bushes is a long, narrow stretch of clearing, which the map at my knees tells me is the abandoned CNR railway bed. I could have paddled up from my site any time and hopped on the line for as long a hike as I cared to take.

A figure on the railway bed catches my attention. A moment later I've caught her attention too. She leaps away in graceful long-legged bounds and flash of white deer tail, leaving medicine of gentleness and loving kindness in her wake.

On I paddle, chasing a kingfisher chattering of prosperity and abundance from tree to tree. A beaver splashes warning of my arrival too close to the lodge of her dreams. I have my own lodge. For the first time, I see the novel in published form – an actual book with printed pages and a cover with my name on it.

———————

I OPENED MY EYES. The thunder had stopped and Asante was smiling down at me. "Your third-eye chakra was just filled with Grace – very similar to Mary's loving, nurturing energy."

"Mary? You mean Catholic Mary?"

She chuckled. "She doesn't just belong to the Catholics you know, or even the Christians. She's the Divine Mother to everyone. She's available to all of us. Like Jesus is."

Mary's energy? Inside *me*? I sat up, stunned, humbled, honoured. I had never in my life paid attention to Mary. Yet here she was, the Divine Mother, bestowing her Grace on me. "Which is my third-eye chakra again?"

Asante pressed a finger to her forehead between her eyes. "It's associated with your vision and intuition and your creative insights."

I told her then about the vision.

———————

I REACH THE MISTY point and spot another farther on, equally veiled in soft mist. When I reach that one, another entices me, and on I go, lured to point after mist-shrouded point.

The map shows that the railway line crosses over the water at the narrowest section of the snake body, about halfway to the top of the lake. I decide to make the iron bridge my turnaround place. It will probably take another half-hour to get there, but it doesn't matter if I come back in the dark. How lost can a paddler become on such a straight and narrow lake? I'm familiar now with my own shoreline. I've even come to love that weedy sandy shore for all the life it holds (even the rowdy nightlife). Situated where the narrows open up, the campsite should be easy to find in the dark. Besides, there may well be a moon to light the way home.

The thought of the bright moon reminds me again of the red rose visualization. The meditation host had said I received my gift before arriving at the gates of heaven. I always assumed he meant the White Light. It strikes me now the gift wasn't (or wasn't only) the Light itself. The real gift was the *yearning* – the overwhelming yearning – the Light engendered in me. All these years I've reproached myself for being too preoccupied with yearnings for a human male. I look over at the soft mist embracing the little curves of shoreline, and breathe in. And out. I *have* yearned for God. I *do* yearn for God – for the Light, the Divine. Love.

I think back to what it felt like last summer when the boundaries between Asante and me began to dissolve during her healing treatment. It was my most profound experience of the permeability of our seemingly solid, separate selves. But not my first. That came a decade before, in a Toronto long-term care facility.

ITIPTOED PAST THE sleeping form in the first bed, and poked my head around the curtain to see the tiny gently breathing figure in the second bed that was my ninety-three-year-old grandma.

From the chair on the far side of the bed, my mother smiled hello and packed up her knitting. My father folded his newspaper. Mom looked worn out, and no wonder. She'd been here every day for the past several weeks, ever since Grandma had been transferred from the retirement home with undiagnosed back pain that made her screech in heartbreaking agony. Thankfully the pain seemed to have abated. The nurse said it wouldn't be long now.

"I'll be back in a few hours," said Mom. "Did you bring some lunch with you?"

"Yes, I have a sandwich."

Dad gestured to his newspaper. "Have you got something to read?"

I nodded, though I had no intention of reading. I had come to visit.

I sat down in the chair my mother had vacated and looked at the tiny form under the blankets. She didn't look like Grandma without her glasses or dentures. Her high cheekbones were even more pronounced, her eye sockets hollow. Through the slits of her eyelids, her normally twinkly shoe-button eyes were so piercingly bright, so filled with light, the dark irises were barely discernible. The light seemed to be consuming her wasted flesh.

I took her delicate-boned hand in mine. "Hi, Grandma."

She didn't turn to look at me but I thought I saw a glint of recognition in the half-open eyes. She opened and closed her mouth. No sound came out.

She let me hold her hand for a few moments, then pulled away, agitated. She hit my hand, the way I'd seen her hit the nurses who picked her up to change her – light hits that seemed to contain almost affection for her caregivers, even as they inadvertently bruised tender bones. I held my hand up to hers so we were clapping.

"Do you remember all the good times we had, Grandma?" I knew I should speak up so she could hear but didn't want to disturb her roommate.

At my words, she stopped hitting my hand, held her palm to mine.

I told her how much I had enjoyed the drives we'd taken during my Sunday visits to the retirement home. How I loved to see her enjoyment of the trees out the car window. "You would say, 'Oh, the trees! It's so nice to see the trees!' Do you remember?" I paused, and she clapped her hand against mine, as if to urge me on.

The moment it came to my mind what to tell her next, her hand became still against mine, as if she'd heard what I was thinking. There was no need to speak out loud.

Holding my palm to hers, I silently reminded her of all the times I had taken the bus to her Hamilton apartment for a weekend visit when I was at university. I reminded her of her scrumptious lemon loaf and the way she set the egg timer when I took too long to put a word on the Scrabble board. I told her how much her unfailing support had meant during the tumultuous years with my not-yet-divorced fiancé. When I paused, she resumed her agitated claps.

I searched my memory farther back in time, back to her duplex on Stinson Street, where my sisters and I came, two at a time, for week-long summer visits when we were kids. Silently I reminded her how we would climb the narrow staircase to the warm airless attic to bring down the boxes of toys she'd kept from her kindergarten-teaching days, and the perpetual mess we made playing house in the living room, and the novelty of not having to clean it up all week. How we crawled into her bed each morning to play I Spy With My Little Eye and breathed in her wonderful Grandma-Nivea-Creme scent.

In my mind, I recited all the Grandma phrases I could remember: "I'll wallop you all over the kerflummakerflop." "Be good now." "Go travelling *now* while you can, because there will come a time when you won't want to go." "Old age is *hell*." "You people are so good to me." "I love your phone calls."

Her hand clapped against mine. I tried to think of a hymn. Silently, I started in on "O God Our Help in Ages Past," and her hand stilled. When I stopped after the first verse because I didn't know the rest, her hand told me she wanted more. In my mind, I recited the Lord's Prayer and sang what I could remember of the *Jubilate Deo* – my favourite of the psalms set to music in the Morning Prayer service, with its exhortation to "be joyful in the Lord" and to "serve the Lord with gladness and come before his presence with a song." Each time I stopped, her hand clapped against mine. Each time I spoke in my mind, it came to rest.

And so we visited, palm to palm, mind to mind, until Mom returned. Then I kissed her translucent cheek goodbye.

I PULL THE PADDLE through the still, black water, remembering. The space between my grandmother and me, the space between Asante and me (the space that wasn't "between" us, that wasn't even "space"), was a "place" of infinite peace. I close my eyes. Letting go of one's ego is not a scary thing. Not a loss of identity. Not a loss at all. Rather, an *expansion*, to a place beyond identity, where we *are* all One. That's what I yearn for – not for an external "God" to worship or live through me, but for the individual "Tinkertoy" disk of my personality and ego to dissolve into an experiential awareness of Oneness with everyone and everything – every living creature on the Earth and the Earth itself.

It may take another twenty years before I have any real experience of what it means to shed my ego, before I truly accept that I am, that we all are, Divine. That's okay. I am a grasshopper in mid-air, about to execute an impressive sideways leap into a new paradigm.

There's no way I'll reach the dark railway bridge. I've been paddling for an hour and the dark brooding structure is still a good distance away. I pivot the boat. Up ahead in the eastern sky shines a familiar bright point of light. Mars, leading me home as if I were a wise king from the Orient.

The navy blue of twilight gradually overtakes the sky and deepens. The moon, I realize, won't be up for a while. The shorelines on either side of me are even blacker than the water. Within several paddle strokes, the shoreline darkness suddenly recedes: I've come out to the wider lake. Somewhere directly to my left is the campsite. I keep my pupil-widened eyes peeled for the bit of beach. I didn't think to bring a flashlight. I have to rely on memory and instinct. "Feel." I aim the boat toward shore and pray that infinitesimally brighter patch straight ahead is my beach.

Bow digging into sand announces home. I climb out of the boat, turn it over, stow paddle and life jacket underneath, and feel my way, with the confidence of a woman in her own home in a power outage, past the boulder sentinel to the tent. My pupils are as open as they can be, and all that pours in is the black warmth of the Void.

I curl up in my two cozy sleeping bags out of the night's damp chill. In the morning I'll pack up and canoe back to the parking lot, where I'll repack with a lighter tripping load and search out Max and his family and friends in the nearby campground. I've had my bird's eye view of the canyon and explored its surroundings: it's time to go through.

Going through the Barron River Canyon, 2003 (Photo: Max Finkelstein)

8

PADDLING WITH JOY

Rock Lake Loop: July 6–13, 2005

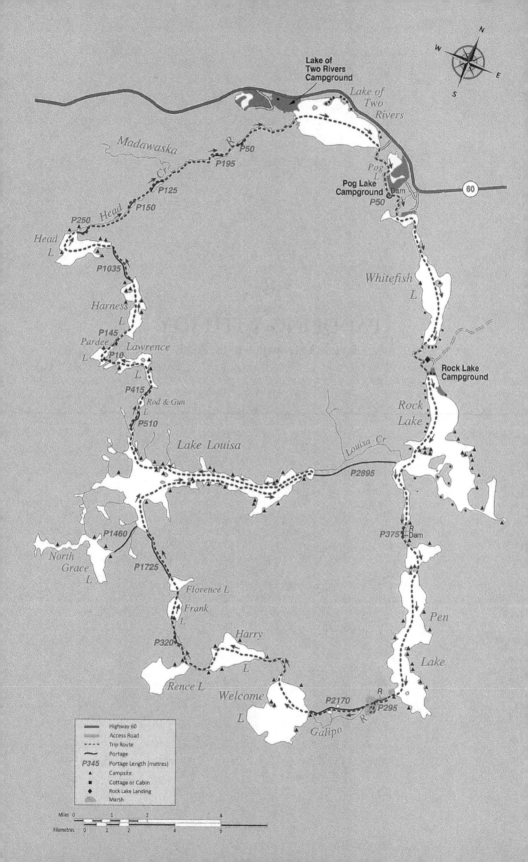

O N PEN LAKE I take out my pen. I arrived on this appropriately named long, narrow lake so early this afternoon I've already finished all camp-setting-up chores (including one unexpected one) and am lazing on the rock that towers over the shore. There was only one lake and portage to travel today. In a departure from solo trip protocol, I spent last night – my first – with friends who happened to be booked all week at a paddle-in site on Rock, the head lake I was launching from. This morning I left them with their noses in books in their strung-up hammocks to embark on my biggest, longest solo trip yet – an eight-day loop covering fifteen lakes, sixteen portages, and at least ten kilometres of creek and river. I paddled away from good conversation and company into familiar solo mode and the silence of solitude.

Though no longer certain about my solitary state. From somewhere behind me in the campsite comes the faint jingle of a bell. I remain unperturbed. It's not a bear about to rip into the food pack. Nor the pack on a romp through the woods. This jingling emanates from Joy.

Can a canoe trip be considered solo when you're paddling with an incomparable canine companion? Ever since this sweet little black dog came hurtling into my life, the word "solo" seems no longer to apply to my life in any capacity.

W E NEVER HAD a dog when I was growing up. During my decade in Chelsea, I looked after a neighbour's golden retriever, who became the model for the vision of what my own dog would be like: sweet natured and intuitive, affectionate and willing to go anywhere and do anything with me, a dog who would hang out on the doorstep without being tied up, a dog who would run a more or less parallel route to mine on a walk or ski. Not a puppy – I had no desire to do house training. Above all, she would be entirely comfortable, and calm, in a canoe.

This vision sat in my imagination, and I was happy for it to stay there. If I came across a dog that needed a home, or one found me, I would take it in, but I wasn't going to go looking, even at a shelter. A dog might seem ideal companionship for a single person, but what about when that single person had to go to Ottawa to see clients or to Toronto to visit family? Who would care for it then?

My younger sister answered that question during a phone call this past Christmas. We had both just read a *Globe and Mail* review of a book by a woman with autism about her relationship with her dog. One of her more unusual observations, one that struck us both, was that dark-haired or dark-skinned dogs are more intelligent than fairer-haired/skinned dogs. "There you go," said Lynne. "You need a little black dog."

"And what will I do with it when I have to go away? Mom and Dad won't have a dog in their house."

"We'd have a dog in the house," came my sister's astonishing response. "We love dogs."

That ten-second exchange evaporated my ambivalence. Toronto travel had been solved. Ottawa would be similarly solved. Not that I immediately set out to find a little black dog. I was still of a mind that one would find me if it needed me. The difference was that the mental blocks had been cleared: the way was free and open.

Not two weeks later I was on the highway on the way home from a food shop in town. I had just begun the descent into the second valley, in the frigid February twilight, when I spotted something trotting on the shoulder on the other side of the highway. In my half-dozen years in the area, I'd never seen a dog on this stretch of densely wooded highway. There are no houses nearby, and it's an unlikely place for a canine stroll. All of which prompted me to perform a U-turn on the empty road. The car crunched onto the packed-down snow on the shoulder, and I got out. Up ahead the dog started into the woods, seemingly unaware of me. Without thinking, I whistled.

Through the sparse winter vegetation I saw it come to a halt, prick ears, and turn. The next instant it was at my feet, looking up. No collar, no tags. Just a ball of mostly black fur.

I opened the car door. It wouldn't jump in but allowed me to lift it onto the back seat.

I got into the driver's seat. The little dog stood on the back seat, front legs perched on the console. I tucked my arm around it so I could still reach the shifter and whispered reassuring endearments. We started down the highway, as snuggled as driver and canine passenger could be without compromising road safety. We hadn't even climbed out of the valley when a zinging realization made me speak out loud: "Brenda, if you don't find this little dog's home you've just committed yourself to it for the rest of its life."

It was quite a commitment to make, when I didn't have the faintest idea who I had just let into the car, what kind or nature of dog. There are, however, some moments when the Universe presents you with an opportunity, or an obligation, and there is some part of you that simply takes over and does what is required in the moment. I wasn't thinking when I pulled the car over and whistled. It was more that I was responding – perhaps to Something whistling to *me*.

I did have to wonder whether I had just picked up a little black dog because I wanted one. I stopped at the next gas station. Charlie the proprietor didn't recognize her but directed me to check at various houses down various dirt roads I had never driven down before. No one recognized her except one woman who had a dog almost exactly like her – a medium-sized long-haired black dog with the same white and brown accents, part border collie or Australian shepherd. "We've been getting calls about that dog all winter. Everyone thinks it's ours."

Those words told me she must be a stray. Nevertheless, I put up posters and placed an ad in the local paper. After the two-week period recommended by the local vet (who also didn't recognize her), I took the posters down. I really didn't need any time at all to tell me she was mine: we'd bonded in that first ten seconds in the car.

F ROM THE LOUD CHIRPS and squeaks I hear in counterpoint to the jingling bell, it's clear Joy is giving the squirrels and chippies a run for their money. I'm of two minds about her freedom. At home, she has a habit of taking to the woods for a little independent exploring, and when her nose is on the job her ears shut down. She does, however, know where home is, and has always come back, since the very first day. It's a different case out here in the near wilderness, where "home" will change each night. I'm not so sanguine about her running free.

Bonded for life (Photo: Doug De La Matter)

The bell around her neck puts me more at ease. I attached it to her collar on this morning's portage to alert the bears but realized after we got here that as long as she's moving about it also alerts *me*. It's when the jingling stops – as it has now – that I worry: is she lying somewhere innocently nearby or gone on a wander in the woods?

I listen to the worrisome silence. No jingle. I whistle. No response. I scout around the campsite and call out. Still no response. Concerned, I head for one of the trails into the woods, and that's where I find her, at the edge of the site. Not facing in, as one might expect, but out, to the woods. She looks around, as if to say, "I'm right here."

I put mock-exasperated hands on hips. "You could at least raise your hand when I call your name." I'm amused, relieved, and touched, all at the same time. Clearly she knows where the campsite boundaries are. And just as clearly she's on guard duty. I leave her to it and go to check on the water in the cook pot.

This was the unexpected chore I had to do when we arrived: boil water. The water filter, which worked perfectly well when I tested it at home, refused to cooperate after we left my friends this morning. I'll have to boil water to drink.

The water is cool enough to pour into the water bottle. It's a blue-lidded Nalgene bottle, a replacement for my old one, the plastic still clear and scratch-free. Out of habit I grasp it by the lid, which is attached to the bottle by a ring around the neck. As I pour the water into the bottle, the ring suddenly slips off the neck, the bottle tips and a litre of newly drinkable water seeps into the ground. The lid is still in my hand. I stare at it in disbelief. I always held the ring on the old bottle and it never came off. It was obviously fastened more tightly around the neck. I laugh in amused frustration. Is *everything* going to go wrong this week?

No. If there's a lesson here, it's to be more deliberate and aware. There's nothing I can do about the water pump, it still has to go to the bottom of the pack. As for water, I'll boil a bottle full each night and when that runs out resort to drinking out of the lake.

I wake up giggling. Two white-tipped paws are pressed on my head and a wet tongue is licking my lips. It's not a new or unexpected morning ritual – just a little more thorough now that we're down on the same level. At home she has to repeat this ritual several times to coax me to get up and let her out the door. Here in the tent it's easy to reach over and unzip the entrance.

She slips out. In hazy half sleep, I worry she'll take off after some late-to-bed nocturnal creature. I drift in and out of morning doze. Each time I wake I sense her presence on the other side of the mesh entrance, face to the woods. My little sentry. I stretch in my sleeping bag and smile. I have named her so well.

⎯⎯⎯◆⎯⎯⎯

ONE HALF-AWAKE morning (several months before Joy came into my life), I woke up with a deep well of joy in my heart. It was such a serene sense of wellbeing and happiness I searched my sleepy morning memory for the trigger. Did something good happen yesterday? Did I have a particularly significant dream? There was nothing I could point to. It bothered me the source eluded me. The joy, so lovely, so pervasive, had to come from *some*where. I wanted to know what caused it so I could get it back. I called the only person in my life who might know.

Asante didn't hesitate. What I had experienced, she was sure, was a wellspring of joy inside me. "Joy is your birthright," came her voice through the phone. "It's your natural state of being – a state beyond human emotion. It exists in each one of us, but tends to get veiled by the plethora of human experiences and the emotions they spawn – so many of them joy*less*. With practice, you can create and recreate this state any time you want."

It was a novel idea: Joy not as an emotion but as a state *beyond* emotion, a state that doesn't come from any outside stimulus, a state I could cultivate by simple *recall*.

I began to try to practise cultivating joy, though the greater challenge was to *remember* to do it. And then I brought the little dog home. That first night I made a bed for her beside mine and reassured her the few times she whined and pushed her nose at my hand in the dark. In the morning my immediate waking thought was: "Her name is Joy."

It was the perfect choice, and not just because of the joy she had already brought me (and would continue to bring if her owners weren't to be found). It was a tangible, little, black, soulful-eyed reminder of the joy always available to me, no matter what my circumstances.

And she definitely does remind me, though there's something not quite right about hollering her name in a loud, annoyed voice into the woods she has no intention of emerging from until it suits her. However, impatiently yelling "Joy" eventually makes me laugh at the irony. And so, mission accomplished.

THE CANOE IS loaded and ready to go. Joy is nowhere to be seen. I call out (with not too much impatience). After a few moments she comes charging down, hops in the boat in her elegant way, and lies down in the middle, behind the big blue gear pack.

It took her no time to become relaxed in the canoe this spring; on our first time out on the river she lay as calmly as she is now. She's so small (though finally up to a healthy thirty-eight pounds after a winter of half-starvation) that when she lies in the bottom she can't see over the gunwales. She's never had to share the space with the packs before. I wonder how long it will take her to figure out she can have pride of place, and a clear view, on *top* of the gear bag.

I steer the boat into the channel that will take us through the marsh to the day's first portage. I worry I'm not in the right frame of mind for a contemplative canoeing experience. Prayer has been absent from my life the past few months. I've started wondering who I'm praying *to*. The more layers I peel away about the myths about God, the less I'm able to envision anything. Any *thing*. Even the Universe feels empty. Prayer seems futile if there's no God "out there." If God is within, is there a need for conversation? Frankly, my conversation these past five months has been with Joy.

I'm about to execute a sharp turn in the channel when my passenger gets suddenly to her feet. Before I can ask her to sit, she places both front paws on the pack. Deliberately, she hoists herself up onto the flat top and lies down.

I give her a pleased grin. "A much better view from up there, eh?"

Joy favours me with a look that seems to say she was just waiting for the right moment to ascend her throne.

Joy on her royal blue throne, July 2005

The channel ends at a tumble of rocks under the portage sign (295 metres into the Galipo River). Just as the bow bumps a boulder, Joy hops out. I mildly curse myself for not getting her on leash, and brace for a battle with the saddlebags.

I found them in Ottawa this spring, two red and black nylon-canvas compartments that drape over a furry body with a clip-on harness. If Joy is to be my new paddling partner without actually paddling, she is at least going to portage her own food and gear. This spring we did several practice runs on a spit of land downriver from my house, me with canoe, Joy with the empty bags. I put her on a leash I could fasten around my waist to leave both hands free. The first time we set out, I felt something bump against my leg. I looked down to see Joy walking with an exaggerated waddle, banging the saddlebags into me. *See? I can't walk with these things on.* I shook my head at her. "Nice try." Our next time out, she leaped out of the boat as soon as we neared the beach, and wouldn't come out of the woods. The solution was to get her on leash before we landed so I could get the saddlebags on her – something I've forgotten to do today.

I lug the packs out of the boat and hold out the loaded-up saddlebags to Joy. After a few minutes of coaxing, she lets me approach, and I slip them over her head and buckle them up. We head down the short trail together. Thanks to all our practice portages this spring, it now feels like second nature. Joy walks sedately beside me, straining on the leash only when she spies a squirrel that must be pursued. When we head back for the boat I let her off leash, and to my relief she stays close. At home her idea of going for a walk is to disappear into the woods and trace a more or less parallel route to mine on the path. I know this only because when I call out "Show me your face!" she invariably (if not immediately) pops out of the woods just up ahead.

Boat, paddle, packs, and saddlebags all relayed to the other end, we put in to a marshy section of the Galipo River. Deerflies buzz around, more than I've ever seen, mostly around Joy, who waits, alert, until one hovers right in front of her nose, then snaps her jaws around it. And eats it. I have to laugh at her expression as she chows down – lips pulled back, nose wrinkled, like a kid eating detested peas. She doesn't spit it out though. She waits for her next victim and repeats the show.

I glance up from the entertainment to see the channel widen to the left. I steer left. Soon the river narrows and winds through the marshlands. In the distance, a line of pines marks solid land. I scan the trees in vain for the yellow of the portage sign. Not that this means anything. The sign often remains hidden behind a branch or bush until you're almost upon your portage.

A maze of crisscrossing logs forces us to make myriad sharp turns. Once through the obstacle course, we come to a small beaver dam. I pause again. Are we really on the right route? We seem to be more than halfway now to the pines. I don't want to trek all the way back to the wider marsh only to find out we were on the right route after all. We press on.

And man do we press! Around waterlogged logs and over beaver dams, and around turns so sharp they require a several-point turn. Joy consents to jumping out onto slippery woven-stick beaver dam walls so I can heave the boat over them. The creek (a small creek now) turns sharply, only to be blocked by more logs.

"Out you get, sweetie," I coax again. Without her weight in the bow, I'm able to slide over the logs without getting out myself.

The creek becomes so mired in weeds I give up paddling altogether – and get over my squeamishness about mucky marsh bottoms. I'm out of the boat, up to my knees in the muck, pushing and pulling the canoe.

One more beaver dam, and we're in a serene pond that is clearly the result of all the beaver-engineered dams. The pine trees seem as far away as ever, and there's still no glint of portage-sign yellow. I glance back the way we've come and realize that although I (thankfully) know where we came into the pond, it wouldn't be at all obvious to someone coming from the other direction, and that would be highly unusual on an Algonquin Park route. That settles it: we're definitely on the wrong course.

About-face.

Look-out girl scouts the way back on course in
the Galipo River, July 2005

The trip back is a lot faster. I slosh through the water beside the boat, sometimes up to my thighs, half leaning on the gunwales as I push so I don't sink too far into the muck. Joy gets right into the spirit. She's in and out of the boat in response to captain's orders, jumping out onto a beaver dam, then back in to *stand* on the blue pack, or even the front seat, keeping watch ahead. Every so often she turns to grin at the captain, revelling in her new role as look-out girl.

At last we're back in the wider river. Where the way – the oh so obvious way – is straight ahead. The portage sign is even visible in the not-far distance. My carabiner watch says it's nearly one o'clock. We've just lost an hour and a half out of the day.

My frustration at the wasted time and effort dissipates almost as soon as it arrives. The detour has been worth it for our energetic team effort alone. If there were any lingering barriers to Joy getting her sea legs, they fell away on this little expedition.

The portage sign reads "Galipo R. to Welcome, 2,170 metres." Joy and I repeat the previous portage ritual. By the time I've made all the relays with gear pack and canoe plus food pack – an endeavour of more than two hours – I'm drenched in sweat and poor Joy is panting in her saddlebags.

Joy pants in her loaded-up saddlebags, July 2005

We met no one on the trail and no one is out on the lake. I'm about to strip down to plunge in Welcome's waters when Joy starts up a frenetic barking. I grab her collar. A blue canoe emerges from the woods. With a cheerful hello, the canoe-carrier splashes into the sandy shallows in his hiking boots, and tips the boat off his head and into the water.

Joy begins to bark again and two more young men emerge, each with a pack and several paddles. (So many paddles!) One stops to pat Joy. Then they, too, walk right into the water in their boots and dump the gear into the boat. The three take their places and paddle away.

"That," I say to my pup, "is called how to portage efficiently. As you've no doubt figured by now, we don't do it that way."

I watch the trio shrink in the distance, thank Joy for her timely warnings, peel down and plunge in. Even Joy, not a water lover, wades in to cool off and have a long drink.

My own water supply has run out. Once out on the lake, I grasp the empty Nalgene bottle by the lid (again from automatic habit) and lower it from the side of the still gliding boat. It fills rapidly, even eagerly. I lift it and there's a sudden, unnatural lightness. I stare down in time to see Welcome welcome my water bottle into its depths. Left in my hand is the lid and the attached ring – the ring I've forgotten is loose enough to come off the bottle neck...

I paddle on, taking stock of my water situation. First no pump to pump water into the bottle, and now no bottle not to pump water into. I do a mental inventory of gear to think of something to use as a container. The only thing with a lid is a half-litre Nalgene jar, currently holding leftover chili. Not nearly big enough, but it will have to do.

Clouds have quilted the sky by the time we arrive on Harry Lake. It seems to take forever to get camp set up; seven and a half kilometres of unaccustomed walking under heavy loads, not to mention all the hours of paddling, has exhausted me. Joy too. She barely makes any forays into the woods. I check on her between all my campsite tasks, and find her, variously, down by the water, up by the tent, near the fire pit. I can't help smiling. She looks so at home, as if she's always hung out on this campsite. My insides feel expanded with love – and joy – that she's here in the park with me, here in my life.

I leave her sprawled on the expanse of rock and make a fire for my new evening water-boiling ritual. A sudden growl from Joy brings me to the shore at a run. She wouldn't growl at a small animal, and no one else is camped on the lake. She's standing alert at the water's edge, eyes trained on the woods across the small bay. I scan the shore, see nothing but tree and bush. Beside me, Joy relaxes and I relax too. Whatever it was is gone.

I wash the chili container, fill it with boiled water, and drink it down, although warm water that tastes faintly of chili is not, I discover, very thirst quenching. I pour the rest of the boiled water into the container and put another pot of lake water on the fire for tomorrow.

I do a location check on my little companion. Even just two days in, it's clear all my focus is on her. The plus side is my mind is so occupied I barely give a passing thought to bears. The downside, not that there could ever be one, is that she *is* another being on the trip, and her very presence seems to prevent me from descending into that serene solitary state that so naturally brings on the silent running dialogue with the wind, the trees, the water, the sun. It's not a bad thing, I muse, to have a running dialogue with Joy. But it may well be why I took the wrong turn in the river. I need to make sure I'm aware of what's going on around me as well as with the pup travelling with me.

I look out at the peaceful grey-green lake. I like that we have Harry to ourselves. I always like it when I find space in the (near) wilderness to be alone. It's when I'm alone (even with a dog) that I truly realize – experience – that I'm *not* alone out here. Whether God is out there (somewhere) or inside me, there's no doubt inside me that God *is*. Whatever *It* is. But just Who is watching over me I'm not sure anymore. The possibilities are widening.

———

L AST SUMMER'S SOLO trip wasn't in a canoe. I drove across the continent to Montana to attend Asante's wedding to her long-time beau. I took my road bike along. One of her work colleagues is a cyclist too, and one afternoon he took me on a ride that looped us around paved backroads in a mountain-surrounded valley. At the end of the ride, he commented that I must have good dog karma because there were several dogs that usually chased and nipped at him along the route. I was glad he hadn't told me this before we set out.

The next day he wasn't available so I set out to retrace the route on my own, hoping my good dog karma would hold.

Halfway around the loop, on a section of the road dotted with ranch-style houses, I was dismayed to spot two large black dogs up ahead. One lay in a driveway, the other sat right out at the edge of the road.

I stopped pedalling. Coasting closer, I found myself addressing them in my head: *Now just stay there. Don't chase me.*

At my cautious approach they both got to their feet. My heart began to beat even faster than it was from the exercise.

The dogs, already standing, suddenly came to attention. Their backs straightened, their ears pricked up, their eyes became trained on the same object. That object wasn't me. They were looking past me. I rode right by them, and they never moved, not even to follow me with their eyes. I might have been invisible. Their gaze never wavered from whatever had their attention behind me.

Once safely past, I couldn't help looking back. I fully expected to see a car, driven by their master, approaching the driveway.

There was no one else on the road. No car. No person. Nothing. The dogs had resumed their relaxed positions.

I picked up speed, marvelling at what had just happened, and mystified. Around the next bend, it hit me: someone *had* been on the road. Someone who had commanded their attention. Someone who had elicited not fear or suspicion but respect, obedience. I had a sudden image of an angel, or, heck, maybe Jesus himself, standing on the road behind me, eyes locked in love on the dogs. The visible had become invisible, the Invisible visible.

Asante didn't hesitate when I told her my tale. "That just plays up the difference between you and so many other people, who fear the worst and then experience it. You have a mindset that allows the Universe to do whatever is necessary in the moment to keep you safe."

I liked the way she put that. It wasn't that I had some special powers over dogs, or some great faith in Jesus, or, thankfully, a delusional mind. It was a mindset. I don't know where mine came from. The fundamentals have always been there – by Grace, I'll say – though they've definitely been honed by experiences like that one, and so many here in the park.

FROM OUT IN THE little bay comes a soft coo. Three loons, all adults, are gliding around. I keep an eye on them, wanting them to put on a performance. Am I ever going to have more wildlife experiences? It seems impossible to top the ones I've already had. How do you top seven loons performing a synchronized swimming routine in front of your campsite, or seven ravens flying in a near-perfect V-formation out from their hiding place in the woods past you on a cliff-top? How do you top a family of moose sounding their joy in a small marsh, or a stroll with a snapping turtle along your shoreline? I worry I'm not in an open enough frame of mind, and too distracted by my travelling companion, to invite any similar kind of experience.

The unseen sun sets, leaving a wispy pink swath just above the horizon in the otherwise overcast sky. From above I hear a distant but all-too-familiar whine. I get to my feet. "Come on, Sweetie. The mozzies are coming. Time for bed."

In the tent I read for a few minutes, then click off the head lamp and let sleep come. The great bonus of having Joy along is I let her do the listening in the night. Though I'm not sure it's necessary anymore. The bears and I have signed a peace treaty.

WATERTON LAKES National Park was not a planned stop on the drive back to Ontario from Asante's wedding last summer. The sign for it on the highway that leads up from the US border lured me in.

It was early evening by the time I got the tent erected and supper into me. I had been in the car all day and needed a good leg-stretching walk. On the advice of the park attendant, I drove to the parking lot for the Blakiston Falls trail. A large sign was posted at the trailhead: WARNING: BLACK BEAR IN AREA!

I had to laugh. In an area known for the much more dangerous grizzly, the posted warning was for my nemesis. Well, if hymns worked in Algonquin, they would darn well work in Waterton Lakes too. No one else was around. I set off down the wide spruce-lined trail and, in my best church choir voice, started in on my all-time favourite, "How Great Thou Art."

At the sound of rushing water, I stopped singing. Up ahead the falls cascaded into a deep canyon beside the trail. A long flight of wooden steps took me down to a look-out platform. I absorbed the splendour of the falling water and the green forest and the dramatic treeless mountain peaks rising above it all, and just kept singing the oh so appropriate lyrics about brook and forest glades and lofty mountain grandeur.

I started back up the stairs, glanced up, and stopped short. Not far from the stairs, right on the trail, sat a black furry figure. It had its back to me, and looked to be snacking on berries on bushes beside the path. To my vast relief, it was totally unaware of me. The relief was short-lived: to get back to the car, I was going to have to let my big black nemesis know I was there.

I reached the top of the stairs, heart triple-knocking in my chest. The bear was about ten metres along the trail, still engrossed in its snack, still unaware of me. Girding my loins, I clapped and whistled – and prayed it would bolt rather than charge.

The bear turned its head, as if at some distant distracting sound, gave me a bored glance and returned to its dinner.

Emboldened by its indifference, I clapped again and launched into the hymn's chorus.

At all the ruckus, the bear deigned to stand up. It lumbered a little farther along the trail and sat down at a new, delectable bush.

More adrenalin-enhanced clapping and singing. More reluctant moving forward by the bear, followed by another snack break.

I was now singing "how great thou art" to the *bear*.

The homage failed to impress. The bear moved along only another few metres.

At my next adrenalin-enhanced surge of encouragement, it disappeared around a curve in the trail.

No! I couldn't lose sight of him. Now I was all but *running* after the bear. Still belting out how great it was.

Around the bend, I slammed on the brakes. The bear had sat down yet again, maybe five metres up ahead. He must have been on dessert by this time, and it must have been delicious, because he cared not a jot about me. Which was both a blessing (considering the not so pleasant alternatives) and a nerve-wracking frustration (considering my continuing dilemma).

Many times in my life I have experienced the voice that speaks through me in fraught or painful situations – the voice that knows the right thing to say when my conscious self gets tongue-tied. It was that voice that released the park ranger from his vows in the Smoke Lake bunkie and the same one, months later, that asked him over the phone to release *me*. That voice called out to the angels to hold onto me as my car sped toward a ditch, and asked two large dogs on a Montana road to stay put and not chase me. It's a voice that speaks from some part of myself that is much wiser and more knowing (and in most cases much calmer) than my conscious mind. It's a voice that speaks without thinking. Not because it's being heedless but because my conscious mind has no thought or say in what comes out. Nevertheless, what comes out is the right thing. This was the voice that now spoke, without any input or permission from me, to the bear that had plunked itself down yet again on the path before me.

"Please," it (I) said out loud, "could I ask you to get off the path? Just for a few minutes. I don't want to bother you. I just need to get by."

A considered moment later, the bear got to its feet and lumbered into the bush. It sat down no more than three metres from the trail and seemed to watch me from the gloom.

I stared, almost unbelieving. My first thought was: *That's not far enough!* Then my conscious mind and I registered that the bear had just complied with my request to leave the path. I needed to take advantage of its cooperation and get myself past without delay.

Not running, but not dawdling either, I made my way along the vacated path, head swivelled to keep a wary eye on the dark shape of benevolence in the woods. All the while, that same voice, *my* voice, was calling out, in somewhat breathless, heart-palpitating gratitude, "Thank you! Thank you! Thank you!"

———●———

THE MORNING SKY is still overcast as we set sail but it's neither hot nor cool. Room temperature. To get to the creek that snakes into the next lake, we skirt the shoreline on the other side of the small bay. From the woods beside the canoe comes a drawn-out growl from something with a big voice box. I pause in mid-stroke and do a quick mental review of Algonquin residents with large voice boxes. I dismiss wolves (too low for a wolf) and moose (I don't think they growl). There's only one Algonquin creature that has such a deep voice.

It doesn't, to my surprise, unnerve me. It didn't sound threatening. It sounded more like, "I'm here and just want you to know it." This must be what Joy growled at last night. She must have seen it (could she have smelled it from that distance?) across the bay. It's been a very considerate bear that kept its distance through the night so we could camp in its territory. I call out my thanks to the woods, and we paddle on to the creek.

This spontaneous expression of gratitude to the unseen bear in the woods brings to memory the Waterton Lakes bear. Our exchange that summer evening – song of praise, supplication, granting of request – still fills me with awe. And it turns out that requesting permission to pass through an animal's territory is the appropriate thing to do from the perspective of different First Nations. Asante told me this when I called her the next day from a payphone in the village of Waterton. "Some part of you clearly knew," she added. "Some part of you and some part of the bear were clearly connected by that knowing."

It was humbling, and overwhelming, to hear.

Loaded up to leave Harry Lake, July 2005

I'm manoeuvring the canoe into the creek when the answer comes to the question I posed last night, of how you top the experience of seven loons and seven ravens (or a bear encounter of surreal proportions). You don't. You get different ones, unimaginably different ones. You don't go looking for them. You just go about your business. What you need will find you.

The clouds blow out, leaving behind a beautiful blue-sky morning. In the long arm of the bay at the southwest end of Lake Louisa, we're greeted by a hot bull-headed wind that seems to gather force as it rushes down the arm. I fight my way to the top of the bay, wishing not for the first time that Joy could pull her weight in the bow – though I appreciate that she is weight in the bow. If she can't help propel the canoe, she at least helps keep it on course.

A shelf of shoreline rock at the point indicates a promising campsite. And it's vacant. I manage to pull up beside the rock, and Joy hops out to check it out. I don't need to check it out; the huge main part of the lake is frothy with whitecaps and we are not doing another paddle stroke, no matter what the site looks like.

Or how big it is. The campsite turns out to be on the side of a high, many-tiered slope.

I pull canoe up onto the rock (tier one) and make my way up the pine-needle-carpeted slope, past a level area (tier two) that would do for pitching a tent or four if the day weren't so windy. Tier three produces an optimum food-pack-hanging tree. On tier four I find the campfire pit, with a flat spot a short distance away for the tent. From the top tier, where a path leads into the woods, I survey the grounds. They're far more than one person and her dog need, but the wind is far bigger than any guilt that might prick at me for hogging such a vast site. And besides, it will give Joy ample room to run without any need to venture into the woods.

Camp set up, I cool off in turbulent but refreshing waters, dress in my campsite finery – navy tank top and hip-wrapped sarong – and treat myself to a rare hour of reading by the water. It's totally unalloyed pleasure; there's no manuscript with me that I *should* be working on. The novel is finished at last and out looking for a publisher.

Up at the fire pit I rummage in the food pack for dinner. From far below comes a clanking sound. *Clanking?* I stop and strain my ears. Nothing but the relentless wind.

I set up the stove. There it is again. A metallic clanging. What the heck? The only metal thing down by the shore is my tin mug. Could a critter, or the wind, possibly be tossing it around on the rock? It sounds way too loud for that, but there aren't any credible alternatives.

Joy leads the jingling charge down the hill. A canoe has stopped at my shore. Its single paddler, back to me, is holding onto the rock. "Hello," I say to its back.

The paddler turns, and I see a bearded young man, hair turbaned under a T-shirt. The reason he has had to stop (if the gale-force wind weren't enough) becomes obvious when he shows me his unusual paddle – fourteen inches in diameter and made of Teflon.

"You're paddling with a *frying pan?*"

"Yeah, lost the first one. It was smaller. And lighter. And easier to paddle with. I hope you don't mind if I take a break here. The wind was swinging my canoe completely around each time I took a stroke. It's taken me an hour to get up here from the portage."

I shake my head in amazement and sympathy too. Even my own battle up the arm took only twenty minutes. "You're welcome to stop here awhile. In fact, I'm just about to make supper, if you'd like to join us." I figure his tale will be worth the price of a freeze-dried dinner.

Between bites of tomato fusilli, he tells me his story. He's twenty-three years old and just quit a gross-sounding job at a tannery near Barrie ("I don't want to work ten hours a day just to make money to pay rent"), broke up with his girlfriend who wants to settle down ("I'm not into that, I want to travel around"), and is hitchhiking to Montreal to visit a friend (female, I gather). When he reached the park, two days ago, he decided to travel this part of the province by canoe. "I rented a boat at Canoe Lake. I'm going as far as Whitney." I try to think where the outfitter would be for dropping off a rental from Canoe Lake. When I ask, he shrugs. "I'll find it."

To my astonishment he has no map. He tells me he memorized the route from the map on display at the park office and has a good sense of direction, as well as a good sense of where the portages are likely to be located near the creeks that empty out of the lakes.

And then there's his unique paddle. He assures me he did start out with the usual kind. And managed to keep hold of it until yesterday, when he arrived at the end of a portage into what he thinks, when we consult my map, might have been Lemon Lake. "When I put in, the water was serious muck. And it went on and on. I couldn't paddle it. I had to get out and push the boat through. (I'm familiar with this kind of muck.) It swallowed both my shoes, though I managed to retrieve them. (His shoes are, indeed, covered in dry mud.) I was swarmed with more deerflies than I've ever seen in my life. (We know about these swarms.) When I finally got through the muck and into paddleable water and climbed in my canoe, I discovered I'd left my paddle at the portage." He shakes his head. "There was no way I was going back for it. Not back into all that muck and swarming deer flies."

He found a more or less paddle-shaped piece of driftwood that worked until it snapped in two, and after that he made fairly good progress with the smaller frying pan. But he lost his grip on it, and it sank like a stone. "Amazing how fast a frying pan will sink." (Tell me about it.)

"That left me with the big frying pan." Which, he adds needlessly, is heavy and awkward and none too efficient in a headwind.

I peer through the trees down to the water. The whitecaps are as big as ever. "That wind doesn't look like it's dropping. You're welcome to stay here tonight if you don't want to keep going. As you can see," I add, with a sweep of my arm, "there's plenty of room."

He accepts the offer with obvious relief.

Back down at the boat he unloads a ratty backpack and filthy tarp. The sight of his gear on shore gives me pause. I've just invited a total stranger – and a male one at that – to camp on my site. The question runs through my head: *Will he steal from me?* The answer comes immediately. *No.*

If I'm concerned about other risks, Joy alleviates them. As soon as he lifts his pack, she barks and nips his heels. As if to say a visit is fine but you're not staying! In response our guest bends down, scoops her up into his arms, and says, "I'm bigger than you."

Joy is surprised into silence. And secretly, I can tell, pleased to be held in strong male arms. As soon as he puts her down, she's wagging her tail, looking up at him for more affection. Her capitulation is quite embarrassing.

The Frying Pan Paddler – FPP for short – turns the rental canoe over for the night. It's a white fibreglass boat, a couple of feet shorter than mine, with way more scratches. Seeing my eyes on the hull, he explains, "The yoke isn't positioned well for carrying it. The balance is off. So I've been dragging it across the portages." As I absorb this shocking revelation (and wonder what the rental company is going to say, though maybe they're used to people battering their equipment), he gestures to the filthy tarp. "And all my gear too. I just wrap it all in the tarp and drag it across the portages. Much easier than carrying it."

I make no comment on this portaging approach, which seems so disrespectful to his equipment. I show him where he can set up his tent on the second tier and leave him to it.

The campfire is a much bigger blaze than I would ever make myself, thanks to my enthusiastic fire-making guest. We sit and talk across flames that considerably brighten the darkness beyond us. It's not entirely easy conversation. He feels "strange," not so much in the sense of not knowing him as in his methods of travel, his work ethic (though I sympathize with leaving a gross-sounding job at a tannery), his methods of hygiene. The T-shirt, when it comes off his head, reveals dreadlocks of dirty-blond hair. It feels like more than age separates us (there are equally wide age gaps between me and many of my friends). It feels like a cultural gap, a difference in approaches to life. At the same time, there's an odd feeling of connection, perhaps between one in need of a haven and one providing it. Not to mention our mutual love of canoeing. He says he wishes *all* the highways were waterways.

The conversation is reassuring in one way; there's no innuendo, no suggestiveness, no threat of going somewhere I don't want to go. My person is as safe as my belongings.

Faithful protector, Louisa Lake, July 2005

I'm taking down the tent in the cool early morning air when Joy sets up a sudden furious barking. I turn to see FPP has come up to the fire pit. Joy keeps him well back from the tent, and it's gratifying to see he didn't charm her out of her guard duties.

Conversation seems, for whatever reason, easier this morning. He makes a fire and I bake an extra large breakfast bannock. "You're helping me lighten my load for portaging," I tease.

His own diet – pasta twice a day – sounds pretty bland. "I supplement it with wild mushrooms," he adds. At my dubious look he assures me he knows which kinds are edible.

Louisa is remarkably calm this morning. In my canoe I lean back against the bow seat, facing the stern, where the Frying Pan Paddler, now just a Regular Paddler, is doing all the work (with a real paddle – mine). Between us, Joy lies on her royal blue throne, and following behind the canoe like a leashed puppy is FPP's empty boat. At my suggestion, he's paddling us down to the east end of the lake to his portage over to Rock Lake. Even though my route is in the opposite direction, I offered to help him help himself this way, happy to explore the lake first. He figures once he gets to Rock he can knock on a cottage door to ask for a paddle.

A tailwind helps us along. Halfway down the lake a blue canoe overtakes us, and I recognize the three young men from the portage into Welcome. We exchange hellos.

It takes over an hour to paddle to the 2,895-metre portage I went five lakes out of my way to avoid. When we land the boat, the last of the three young men is just gathering up three paddles to head down the trail. Oh yes, all those paddles! Boldly, I explain FPP's predicament. The portager confirms the paddles are all his and offers to leave one at the other end. Before we part, I give FPP my address so he can send me a postcard from Montreal. I add my phone number. "For emergencies."

"You've been very nice to me. I owe you."

I brush this off. "I like to think if I were in trouble someone would help me."

A hug for me, a pat for Joy, and he's on his way, dragging the tarp behind him.

I begin the return trip along Louisa's north shore with a renewed headwind on the lake and a renewed sense of wellbeing in my heart. It feels good to help where help is needed. It's a bit of a surprise to be again lending assistance here in the park, where my preoccupation has mostly been to keep my*self* safe. A perception feels like it's shifting, a realization that I'm not out here by the skin of my teeth. I'm walking at ease in my skin. And if I don't quite feel FPP and I are kindred spirits I have no doubt we were meant to meet. It's not just what you need that finds you, but what needs *you*.

Our Lawrence Lake campsite is a disappointment. The water at its shore is mucky and weedy and punctuated with deadheads, not swimmable at all. A steep, soft-dirt slope leads up into the campsite, whose focal point, once an impressive tall pine, is now its uprooted roots. Next to the fire pit are the blackened upended roots of another fallen tree, a hemlock, which someone has tried to involve in an overkill campfire. Branches and wood chips are scattered around. I find myself wishing we had stayed on our beautiful Louisa palace grounds another night.

I pull the tent out of its sack. The faint jingle of bell tells me Joy has gone into the woods. I can't blame her. With the huge uprooted trees, there's barely any room on the site. There don't seem to be any squirrels for her to chase either. It's altogether too silent: no chattering of small critters, no bird song. With the loss of the biggest trees, and the prominence of the big ugly blackened roots, it seems *no* one wants to stay here. Least of all me.

I drag myself around, setting up camp and cleaning up scattered branches and bits of garbage. I'm done in. Almost wishing the trip were over.

Evening comes, and I realize it's still extremely warm. Without a thermometer, it's hard to gauge the temperature; you just take what the day brings without modifying your activities. Maybe the sheer heat has knocked the enthusiasm out of me. The day's exertions have left me feeling grimy, though not enough to get in the weedy water down below. Besides, on this east-facing site, we've already lost the sun behind the trees.

I make dinner, then scout for Joy, who has become ominously silent. I smile in relief at the sight of her lying on the trail to the biffy, face to the woods, as usual.

Pot of rehydrated Thai ginger noodles in hand, I make my way through the underbrush to a high point that faces out over the water and plunk down on a tiny granite platform. (If there's even a lip of rock, I'll find it.) I look out to a sprawling island of low-lying rock aglow in sunlight a couple of hundred metres offshore and wish that sun were shining on me.

In the distance, the gentle jingles resume. At the sound of such sweetness roaming the woods, the thought comes to me: Stop thinking about what you want from a campsite, Brenda. This campsite needs healing and love. It's lost its anchoring trees. It's been mistreated by humans. It needs Joy jingling around in the woods to rejuvenate it and bring back the small creatures. It needs you to tidy it up and appreciate it. It needs your love.

Chastened, I close my eyes and send healing love to the site around me. All regret that we're here is gone. There are blessings. One of them glows in the evening sun a short paddle away.

The waters off the island are clean and clear and warm, and grime-rinsingly refreshing in the last rays of sun.

Back on the dear little campsite that an hour ago was a supreme disappointment, I'm reminded of a scientific study university researchers conducted on happiness that I read about in my alumni magazine. Sounding very Buddhist, they concluded that happiness is about "mindfulness," about changing our attitude to our circumstances. They also found that we each have a "baseline" of happiness, and that while we experience an increase of happiness in, say, the first five years of marriage, we ultimately revert to our usual level. After I finished the article, I checked in with my own happiness metre about the lack of companionship in my life and found the metre registering "content." I even made myself take an unwavering look at the possibility that my future might continue without a partner (assuring myself this was not about capitulating to such a vision). And the future looked pretty much like the present, with no change in my happiness baseline. Possibly I lowered that baseline by thinking I would be happier if only I had a relationship. I could blame pop culture or societal expectations for making me chase after illusions. Or I could be grateful for finally seeing them for what they are.

Into the evening's silence comes the pan-flute song of a thrush and a squeak of squirrel. The creatures have come back.

Head Lake is *hot*. I'm relieved to have arrived here at my site before noon on a short travel day, and to have the afternoon to *not move*.

The afternoon's not moving activities are: write, swim, nap, swim, snack, swim, read, swim. The swims are just cooling dips. I do a lazy breast stroke and take the water straight into my mouth to keep hydrated.

Gulls chuck at me from lazy circles overhead. A band of ravens holds an animated assembly in a tree across the lake. A woodpecker taps pileated Morse code onto a tree trunk. A mother merganser quacks around my point ahead of three babies that look like they've been splashed with dots of white paint. In the early evening, the loons yodel to each other, a thrush practises haunting scales in the woods, and a choir of bullfrogs sings vespers in amphibious Gregorian chant.

All the campsites within view are empty. It's just me and Joy and the ravens, loons, ducks, gulls, woodpeckers, thrushes, and bullfrogs. And the heat.

That last companion has me a little worried about tomorrow. From the map it looks like I will cover a full third of my entire loop in one day. There was no way around this in the planning. Between here and the next lake for canoe-camping are miles of snaking creek and river and two lakes that host car campgrounds near Highway 60. A half-litre container of water isn't going to get me very far down the creek and river and their five portages (all, thankfully, short carry-overs). I boil extra water. The portages are so short I will carry the cook pot full of water over the trails in a plastic shopping bag.

Knocked out by the heat, I'm in bed by eight-thirty and wake up, rested, at 5:00 a.m. The lazy sun rises after me, so orange it looks already sunburnt from its own heat.

We're on the water by the record getaway time of quarter to seven, in the somewhat cooler part of the day.

The creek is wide and deep. No bogs or mud to worry about. Just a zillion deer flies. I've never experienced them this bad. Joy hones her already excellent fly-catching skills.

It's also dragonfly day. The beautiful big guys with their finger-length bodies. All morning they zoom around the boat, landing on the gunwales and once or twice on my arms. Dragonflies have an incredible amount of peripheral vision – a nearly 360-degree field of view. Their visionary powers are awe-inspiring. They see so much *more*, and more perceptively, than humans. In some First Nations' teachings, Dragonfly is the totem of seeing beyond illusion. It helps us to see what *is* so we can come to a new perspective or embrace change and transformation.

The portages are so short and the air so hot I don't make Joy wear the saddlebags. I stuff them into the top of my pack and let her off the leash. Halfway down our third carry-over, something in the woods catches her nose's attention. A sharp "No!" stops her from taking flight.

On the trek back for the canoe, she pauses again at that particular spot.

Loading up the canoe at the put-in, I'm startled by the piercing cry of a hawk right overhead. That instant, Joy takes off back up the trail.

I shout and race after her. I know where she's headed but I need to see exactly where she goes in, horrified I'll lose her in the woods. I round a bend in time to see her fluffy black tail disappear into the trees. Winded, I arrive at the spot, and call and whistle. No response. No surprise. I make my way in through the tangle of bushes, still calling. Many metres in, I stop. This is foolish. Without a trail or compass, I'm the one likely to become lost, not Joy.

I force myself back to the boat, where I sit on a rock and utter a prayer to the hawk who gave warning of her imminent rebellion: *Please watch over her and bring her back safely.*

I wait, worried and pissed off. There's no question this little black dog, whom I love unconditionally, has tried my patience in a way it hasn't been tested in years. What is there to test it when I live alone in an idyllic cottage with no button-pushing spouse or children? The funny thing about the untried temper is you can delude yourself you don't have one.

An eternity passes (or maybe just ten minutes). I'm only just keeping the panic at bay and my bum glued to the rock. At last she arrives sedately from the trail. Worry evaporates into relief, which gives anger full reign. I order her into the canoe.

Joy disregards the order. Even more pissed off, I manhandle her none too gently into the boat and give her a shake, even as I sympathize with her reluctance – the bugs are relentless and it's stinking hot, with absolutely no relief from the sun in the wide-open creek. But the boat is going on, and she's going with it.

I push through the weeds, glaring at Joy on top of the pack. She looks back, not cowed, not even reproachful. Her gaze is steady and sure, as if to suggest I might try a different response.

Glaring into those calm brown eyes, it strikes me how ridiculous it is to be angry on this (albeit fly-infested) beautiful creek in the middle of the near wilderness, doing what I love most in the world. I can't change *her* unwanted behaviour. I can only change my own.

To decide not to be angry – and to stop – is a wonderful thing. You don't deny what you feel. You face it and see who your anger is really directed at. It's not Joy's fault she takes off into the woods, where she probably survived for months before I found her. Not her fault she gets into a cupboard I've left open and eats a bag of treats or climbs on the couch I've forgotten to put a chair on for the night. Or gets into my unfenced compost heap, when such scraps likely kept her alive. It's myself I'm angry with for failing to have perfect control, for failing to *be* perfect. And I can decide not to be angry about that. Maybe even forgive myself for it.

So now I sigh at Joy. "I'm sorry, Sweetie. I know it's hot and buggy, and this is the last place you want to be, but we have no choice. And you gave me a heckuva scare. I don't want to lose you. Please don't run off like that again."

In response, Joy gets back to fly-catching business with renewed fervour.

The creek soon opens up, and we come to the T-junction with the wider Madawaska River. We hang a right (I doublecheck the direction on the map), and carry on.

Four hours, five short carry-overs, and all my boiled water gets us to Lake of Two Rivers. We emerge from the river into a crowd of people and boats near the car campground at the west end of the lake. The signs of civilization don't even bother me. The heat seems to have slowed all activity, muted all sound. And deflated the big lake to a dead calm. I clip my bug jacket to the gunwales to rig a sunshade for Joy but can't persuade her to lie under it. As soon as we reach the middle of the lake, I scoop up water to quench my thirst.

It takes six hundred tries and four different trees – not to mention a break to eat and swim – before I manage to get the food-pack rope slung over a branch at our Whitefish Lake island campsite. The branch that finally accepts the rope is *not* regulation height. I can only hope the night-roving critters are too heat-dazed to mount a raid.

My poor dog lies panting in the shade. I can't coax her into the water and have to hand-feed her to get her to eat.

The evening drags. I realize I'm waiting for the sun to drop so I can go to bed, and it's only seven o'clock. I dangle my legs in the water and listen. For a cottage and motorboat lake, it's remarkably quiet. Even the birds are silent. It's just too hot for anyone to make any effort.

Still, I listen. As I've found myself listening all week.

Who hears prayers? I do. The Earth does. The animals do. Jesus does. Other people do. How else do I explain two Montana dogs who stand to attention and allow me to ride by as if they haven't seen me? Or a Waterton Lakes bear that moves off the path after I (politely) ask it to? How do I explain the set of circumstances that put my niece and me on a lake in time to rescue a hypothermic couple? Or a First Nations Elder arriving all the way from Alberta to help me let go of a dead relationship? If the Divine is within us, then prayer I think must be a communication between the Divine in each of us and the Divine in the people and animals and environment around us, a *knowing* between us, as Asante put it. And protection comes, I think, from walking in alignment with the elements and the environment, with other people and creatures. You make your plans, and then you stay vigilant to determine whether they are in harmony with the conditions of your environment or with someone who may need you more than you need to carry out your plans. It's not about imposing your will at all costs (or, the other extreme, always denying it); it's about walking in mindfulness and openness – surrender – so you become aligned with the Oneness of Everything.

It's still a theory in my brain, this idea that we are all God. It's a theory I'm willing to continue to test with my heart. To *be* the test.

At last the sun slips behind the hills, as burnt-orange as when it rose. I have one last cooling dip, and Joy and I make our panting way to the tent.

We're up, rested, at five, and on the still mirror water by eight. It's already very warm, and also unexpectedly lovely because, at this hour, this cottage and motorboat lake is cottager- and motor-less, and I'm left to carry the illusion of solitude to the take-out.

The dragonflies accompany us on our way. The big guys again, with their aviator eyes and their impressive peripheral vision. They hover around the boat, a miniature (and silent!) helicopter escort out of the park.

One lands on my shoulder. (I see it, even with my limited peripheral vision.) I stop in mid-stroke and angle my head to have a better look.

It faces me, brilliant fluorescent green eyes fastened on me. We look at each other for some thirty seconds or more, months or years in an insect's lifetime. And then I make an involuntary movement and it's gone.

Seconds later, a dragonfly lands on my other shoulder. The same one, I'm positive. Again, it faces toward me. Again I stop paddling. Again we gaze into each other's eyes, its opaque penetrating green ones into my awestruck grateful blue ones, for another long stretch of seconds, or eons. Then it lifts off and swings away into a non-existent breeze.

Its position on my shoulders, first the left, then the right, seems significant for how close it was to my ears – both ears – as if to make sure I hear its message. What that message is, beyond the general medicine of dragonfly – what its particular significance is at this juncture of my life – I couldn't say. The only thing that registers on this hour-long paddle to the take-out is the heat. Nevertheless, I feel certain that silent subliminal wisdom has been whispered in my ears for future consumption.

"Rock painting," Pen Lake, July 2005

9

BREATHING LESSON

Smoke Lake to Rock Lake: August 7–10, 2005

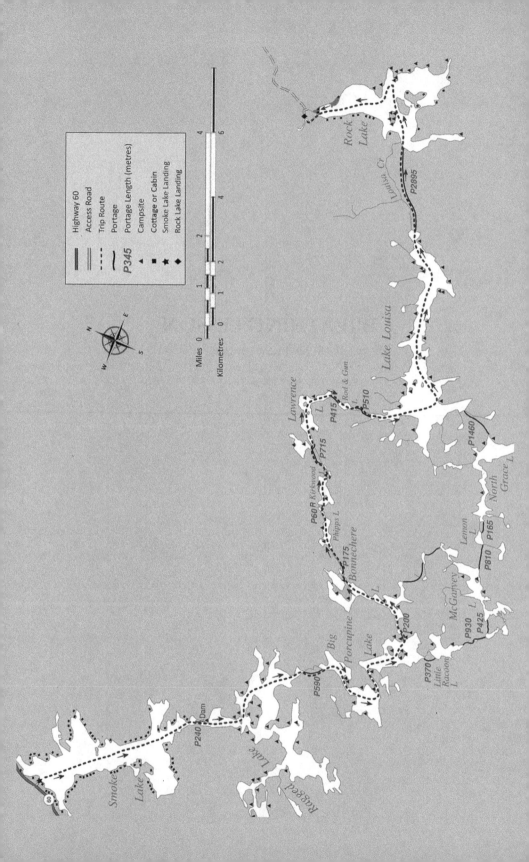

THE AIR IS SOFT and warm for an August evening, the lake calm at last. I tidy up around the fire pit to eliminate all bear-enticing dinner remnants. Down in the twilight water, a thick stick floats by close to shore. I do a double take. It's moving in a decidedly un-stick-like way, one end right out of the water. I rush down to the water's edge to meet my guest, a big beautiful snapper who is apparently on an evening stroll in the shallows.

I crouch down on the rock, honoured and amazed by this visitation. It seems an answer to a prayer I uttered on my paddle here this very afternoon.

My journey started at Cathy's cottage on Smoke Lake on this last day of our annual summer visit. My *paddle*, however, didn't begin until just before the first portage, into Ragged Lake. That's because, after we shuttled my car over to Rock Lake, where this little canoe trip is to end, it was well into the afternoon, and Cathy insisted on giving the *Empress* and Joy and me a motorboat shuttle to the south end of Smoke.

Starting out in Smoke Lake's calm south bay, August 2005 (Photo: Cathy McLeod)

Although it seemed like cheating, I was grateful, given the fierce headwinds that had come up out of the south. Headwinds also seemed an appropriate metaphor for the usual bustle in my brain, and as I battled the external winds, I tried to quell the internal ones with meditation. It was on the upper part of Big Porcupine that I paused in the mantra for prayer – a prayer of intention for this three-night trek from Smoke to Rock. My usual prayer on my solo trips is to become regrounded, to be freed from the mind's preoccupations, to be in the moment – and of course kept safe from harm. This afternoon a new prayer flowed out of me, a prayer addressed to the Earth: Show me how to honour you while I travel your waterways in this beautiful near wilderness. Show me how to assist you and love you.

The prayer was, in part, an expression of my longing for a return to the awareness and mindfulness that were largely absent (thanks to Joy's presence) on last month's loop, a return to my internal dialogue with the Earth and the elements. In uttering this prayer to the Earth, I wasn't thinking about turtles or totems. Yet here she is, just out from the shore of my campsite on Big Porcupine, a beautiful snapper, sacred symbol of our Earth Mother.

She pauses on her prowl of the shallows and turns to face the shore, in uncanny imitation of the turtle on my Jubilee campsite two years ago. This one too raises her head out of the water, not a metre away from the human creature crouched before her.

Her eyes meet mine, and then… she takes a breath. A slow audible intake through her nostrils. I've never heard a turtle (or any other wild creature) breathe. It's a startling, humbling sound.

She lowers herself back under the water and continues her unhurried travels along the shoreline. Leaving me in a state of awe and gratitude for the Earth's capacity to respond. Even if my dialogue on this trip is, of cheerful necessity, with Joy, the important thing, Turtle seems to say, is to breathe with her, deeply, mindfully, every step of the way.

The sound of agitated barking from the woods brings me out of my thoughts. I give a sharp whistle. My little dog is immediately at my side, with nothing, thankfully, in hot pursuit. And then, as if nothing were the matter, she pads her elegant way down to the rock below me and stations herself beside the water. Whatever made her bark hasn't spooked me. Nevertheless, in this sweet little dog, there's no question I have a protector. It's ironic to have one now that I'm no longer looking for one. The need to attract protectiveness as an outward demonstration of internal caring feels gone. (Though the agent, who responded to that need, lingers as a sporadic friend and intermittent fantasy.) The need is gone, I believe, because it fulfilled its purpose, which was to show me I *am* worthy of being cared for. It's hard now even to remember that little girl who didn't feel she deserved love. Looking back over the last six years, I realize the ocean liner that is my mind has completed an almost 180-degree turn. It happened one slow beloved degree by slow beloved degree.

Darkness swallows the lake and its living, breathing shore prowlers, and Joy and I head for bed.

I pack my way out of the tent – pummel sleeping bag into sack, roll air out of thermal mattress, compress clothes into compression bag (my own now), slide book and head lamp into zip-lock bags – all before I've emerged for my morning pee. It's a ritual of new efficiency I instituted on last month's trip that is supposed to get me on the water before the winds come up. We have many lakes and portages to cover before tonight's destination on Louisa. The portages, though, shouldn't take half as long as usual. If my spiritual intention for this trip is to demonstrate my love for the Earth, my earthly intention is to push the portaging envelope: I plan to carry everything in one relay.

I've never been able to consider this possibility before, since I've always brought two packs. For this short little trip, I dispensed with the food pack. My food is stashed either in a small bag inside my big canoe pack or (unbeknownst to her) into my canine partner's saddlebags with hers. And I've been ruthless in my allotment of clothes and gear, including no plate or bowl (I'm eating straight out of the pot), which has made the big gear pack a little lighter.

Most of the portages on this trip are less than a kilometre, and I've traversed most of them before. The only new territory will be the three-kilometre trek from Louisa to Rock – the portage where I dropped off the Frying Pan Paddler last month. At the time I was happy for *him* to walk it. This morning, contemplating that portage, my longest ever, I'm almost (almost) looking forward to it. The ox in me is keen for the challenge. But that's not for two days. The ox has more immediate tasks at hand.

I arrive at the second portage of the day, a 175-metre carry-over from Bonnechere into Phipps. Joy consents to the saddlebags with no hesitation, and I lash the paddle to the boat. Cathy was appalled when I told her my ambition to carry everything overland in one go. "Why would you do that to yourself?"

I had to laugh. In just about every way we're opposites. She's feisty, outspoken, and practical-minded, has been married to her university sweetheart for two decades, and is a dedicated mother of three children. All my other early friendships have faded because the point of connection faded. The truth is, beneath the surface differences, Cathy and I still engage each other's minds and hearts. Like the agent, she doesn't pay much attention to any worlds beyond this one but has a gratifying openness to hearing about, and debating, spiritual matters. We listen to each other's counsel. And we've always made each other laugh. We just spent three days talking and laughing, non-stop.

A trio of friends on Cathy's dock, Smoke Lake, August 2005

In my love of canoeing I'm now much more like her father, a cheerful bowlegged Scot, who motored over from his cottage to sup with us the other day. When Cathy told him my plan to do the portages in one relay, he got it. "You'll shorten your travel time considerably." He also offered a practical solution to the question of how to get the canoe on my shoulders when I've already got the big bulky pack there: lean the canoe up against the fork in a tree, and walk under it with the pack already on my back.

Now, on the portage, I swing the pack onto my shoulders and look around for a forked tree. They've been notably absent on previous portages, and my ambition has so far been unfulfilled.

To my delight, I find an obliging white pine and within minutes have the canoe balanced on my shoulders over the pack. With the paddle attached, the boat weighs at least a hundred more pounds than usual. But, hey, everything is on our backs. *Everything.* So buoyed, I follow saddlebagged Joy down the trail.

After being an ox all day, Brenda likes to become a gazelle. Such transformation involves peeling off all sweaty portaging clothes, plunging into a refreshing lake bath, combing tangles out of now-squeaky-clean hair, and dressing in a tank top and sarong.

Joy has no similar need to transform herself. She is simply her wonderful doggy self, pleased as punch (judging by the erratic jingles that echo around the upper tiers) to be back on our palatial site on Louisa, where she can resume squirrel-herding duties. By the time we leave, two days from now, she'll have them all in order.

I relax in the camping chair to bask in the day's accomplishments: six lakes and five portages crossed in eight hours, three of those portages in a single trip, including, the crowning achievement, the 510-metre trail from Rod and Gun Lake here into Louisa. Not to mention tailwinds and a happy cooperative unleashed dog the whole way. It has been a strenuously serene day.

There's no guilt for taking this palatial site again, even for two nights; there are no canoes going by or large groups in need of a large site and, besides, we didn't get a chance to enjoy it on our own last time. Which seems unjust, given what I now know about our campsite guest.

A master meditator sits in unmoving
concentration under a treed
squirrel, 2005

H E CALLED, a week after my return from the park.
I was on the dock, with a plate of barbecued steak and salad. On the arm of my Muskoka chair, the portable phone began its high-pitched ring. I had brought it down even though its battery had given warning beeps of impending death on a previous call.

I hadn't expected him to actually call and wasn't too happy about it. I didn't want him to show up on my doorstep. It was a relief to hear he was, if not in Montreal, then in Ottawa, two hours away.

"I'm in a phone booth. You mentioned you knew Ottawa, and I was wondering if you knew how to get to Elgin Street."

I asked him where he was and gave him directions. Then, because Elgin is a popular street for restaurants, I added, "Are you looking for a place to eat?"

Master Frying Pan sounded slightly abashed. "No, I'm looking for the probation office."

While the phone paced out beeps that echoed my growing wariness, he told me why.

He had been, as he put it, "a bit bad." The canoe he had dragged across all the portages had not been rented. He had helped himself to it, and the paddle he lost, from a cottage on Smoke Lake (thus explaining why he wasn't worried about how he was treating the boat or where precisely he was going to "return" it in Whitney). He had broken into a couple of cottages too, though he didn't elaborate on what he took. (A couple of frying pans?)

Mushrooms were his downfall; his knowledge of the edible kinds was evidently faulty. Sometime after we parted ways, he ate some that made him so ill that when he got to Whitney he went straight to the police station for help, where they just happened to have a description of a thief he matched.

Through the intermittent beeps, he continued his tale. He'd spent a couple of days in the local hospital, apparently near death, but recovered sufficiently to be taken first to the Ontario Provincial Police detachment for a night, and then on to the detention centre in Ottawa. He also had a court date in Pembroke, where he was put on probation for a year.

"The police confiscated all my belongings and made me sign a waiver I wouldn't come back to claim them."

Recalling the state of his gear, I could well imagine the OPP's reluctance to store it. Clearly he had kept my phone number and address. I was a little perturbed about that. But his plan, he said, was still to head to Montreal. "I only stopped in Ottawa 'cause I have to check in with the probation office once a week." He paused. "You're the only one – "

At that moment my phone beeped its last beep and the line went dead.

I was too far from the house to grab the other phone to rescue the call, and not willing to expend the energy to run up on the off-chance he might call back. I couldn't imagine he would: he would think I had hung up on him. While part of me felt bad about that, a much larger core was relieved. Although I don't like to be thought of as a rude sort of person who hangs up on people, I also don't need the acquaintance of someone with a propensity for theft or lies. I suddenly had a bad taste in my mouth, as if the steak had gone off. This phone call, with its fuller (and who knew if entirely full) disclosure, suddenly negated the good things about our encounter. I felt I'd been duped, felt he'd been a guest on my campsite under false pretenses, our experience together no longer valid.

Abandoning the steak, I went up to the house and retrieved the little journal from my last canoe trip. Rereading our campsite conversation and interaction brought some reassurance. He had told just the one overt lie – that he had rented the canoe. The rest had been lying by omission. Was that, in our brief acquaintance, so bad? From his point of view, it wasn't relevant, and I might not have given him dinner and shelter if he had arrived announcing, "Hi, I'm paddling a stolen canoe with a stolen frying pan because I lost the paddle I also pinched."

From his point of view the omission made perfect sense. And, if I put it in larger, more philosophical context, who reveals everything about themselves during the first encounter or even first few? We all have deeper layers and secrets; in some ways we're all "liars." What was really at issue was feeling I'd let myself down: why hadn't I caught on to him?

I closed the journal, noticed the portable phone, and put it back on the charger. If there was any consolation it was that justice had prevailed, right down to his mushroom-addled brain marching him to the police station door and my phone cutting off our conversation right after he conveyed the information I needed to complete our acquaintance and before he had the chance to ask anything else of me. I couldn't help wondering what he had started to say. I was the only one who what? Foolishly trusted him? Generously gave to him? Or was I the only one he'd told the truth?

MY STOMACH URGES me up to the kitchen tier. Tonight's meal is lentil dahl in a vacuum-sealed package. I brought two of these curries. They're weighty things compared with freeze-dried dinners, and I declare both must be eaten before Wednesday's three-kilometre overland expedition to Rock Lake.

I cook on the stove, too lazy to comb the woods for firewood. My little protector sprawls on the soft dirt nearby, ignoring her own meal in its collapsible nylon-canvas bowl.

I stir the bubbling dahl. What bothers me most, still, about the Frying Pan Paddler's visit is that I didn't cotton on to him. If I consider myself to be protected out here in the near wilderness, and I do, my personal warning system needs to alert me when danger is near.

Unless, I muse, blowing on the curry, I'm not in personal danger. I think about the little Q&A session that played out in my head when he unloaded his gear onto the shore. The question I would have asked if I had been thinking with my logical brain would have been, "Will I be safe?" The question that did run through my head – *Will he steal anything from me?* – indicated that at some subconscious level I knew about his thieving ways. More important was the answer – *No.*

The curry dahl is pretty good for a prepackaged meal. I sop up the remnants with a soft tortilla wrap and continue to muse on the guest I shared tomato fusilli with on this same site last month. Truly, it was the safety of my belongings (and my own safety) and not what Master Frying Pan had done in the past, or what he might do in the future, that was the only relevant thing under the circumstances, which were that I was offering food, shelter, and a more efficient means of propelling a canoe than a frying pan to a guy literally up the creek without a paddle. It wasn't my place to judge whether he deserved my assistance. My role was to provide it. Whatever else he might have done was his own affair.

As an extra precaution, I had Little Miss Fierce Protector, who wouldn't let him anywhere near me or my tent.

I glance around to smile at my little fierce protector. She raises her head and looks at me with narrowed eyes. I've seen this look once or twice before. It's not a squinting or a threatening look, just not her usual wide-open bright-eyed soulful doggy look. Her eyes are somehow more focused, as if she's trying to get right inside my mind. Or already there. I hold her gaze, unperturbed, and then, in curiosity and some amusement, ask, "Who *are* you?"

Whoever she is, I feel unending gratitude for her protective, caring, loyal companionship. Gratitude for this precious foundling, who lies, so sure of herself and her place in the world, on the ground close by. I've never experienced this level of loyalty and protection from another human being. The realization doesn't make me sad. Dogs are people too – especially, it seems, the one who holds my gaze in that penetrating, unnervingly human way across the fire pit. Hello, whoever you are. Thanks for being here. Would you like some curry in your kibble?

Twilight descends, and I hang the pack and get ready for bed. Squatted at the shore, cool wet cloth to my face, it comes to me that my intuition, which knew I would be safe from FPP's thieving ways – he *didn't* steal from me – is in fine working order. And... it always has been. My intuition, which told me all those years ago I had met the man I was going to marry, did not betray me. It was my attachment to the thought that screwed me up. I made it a fixed thought, an event chiselled in stone, a vow made before the vows were even spoken. Nothing is chiselled in stone. Things change. That's what intuition is for – to guide you through the maze of changing circumstances.

I SPOTTED HIM NEAR the end of the ski trail and waited until he caught up. Calm, even glad to see him. He wore the same dark wool cap I remembered from our very first ski, on Kioshkokwi Lake on Valentine's Day. Here we were, six years later, on skis again, at the other end of the park.

"I thought that was your car in the lot," said the ranger. "Have you been out awhile?"

"A couple of hours, including a break at the cabin. I did the Thistle trail. You?"

"Just Leaf Lake after I finished grooming."

"*Thank* you for grooming." Then, in a natural, relaxed, smiling way: "Rumour has it you're seeing someone." I had heard this only the previous evening, and my internal response to the news was one of genuine happiness for him, not one malevolent thought.

The ranger studied my face as if to gauge how I really felt. His "yes" sounded relieved it was out in the open. "What about you?"

I laughed. "Single. As ever. Do you mind if we keep moving? I'm soaked in sweat and getting cold."

We skied the final half-kilometre out to the parking lot, where he invited me to share a beer in his car.

It was a newer Toyota, and I climbed in, thankful for the vent blast of warm air. He held out the bottle and asked how I was enjoying life on the river. I told him I'd bought the cottage. "I've always wanted to tell you how grateful I am to you, for introducing me to this area, for helping me find my home. Did you feel it even as I was pissed off with you?"

"I felt something like that coming through." His tone equally dry.

I asked about his new girlfriend.

"She lives on the other side of the park. I like that. I like my independence and my solitude – I need that time on my own. Then I enjoy seeing her."

I told him how happy I was for him and knew he could tell I meant it. I knew my eyes were radiating everything I saw in his: recognition, familiarity, affection – and simple joy in reuniting, too. Most of all, no pain. It was our first conversation in years that wasn't layered with his guilt or my reproach and hurt. We talked and laughed as easily as in the early days.

I took a sip from the bottle and handed it back. "I learned a lot when I was with you, even though it was for such a short time." I rolled my eyes. "I *always* learn from my relationships, whether I plan to or not. But I feel like I'm ready to *be* myself in a relationship, rather than *grow* into myself in a relationship. Know what I mean?"

"*Yes.*"

It was one of the things I always liked about him, that we could talk on this level. Whether he ever acted on the things he understood so well was another matter and, I finally knew, not my business.

He passed the beer again. Now I was warm I wished it were colder.

I asked about his fellow rangers. He described a falling out he'd had with one of his coworkers. "She's had ample opportunity to apologize, but she hasn't."

I could have told him it's possible to forgive without waiting for the other person to apologize but I just listened, and we went on to other things. The parking lot emptied out.

I looked at the clock on the dashboard. We'd been talking for an hour. "I should get going. Thanks for sharing your beer. Take care of yourself." I reached for the door handle. Without his saying a word I suddenly knew he wanted to take me home.

"You're looking great."

I pulled the door shut again. "So not bad for forty-two?"

"Is that where you are now? I'm going to be forty-nine this year."

"The numbers feel irrelevant, don't they?"

"As long as we keep skiing," he agreed. "And other things." His tone spoke volumes.

Amused, I shook my head. "If you weren't attached elsewhere I'd be happy to have a fling, but I don't want to interfere. If you want to be platonic friends, I'm open to that."

"Platonic friends."

I laughed at him. "You say those words as if you have *no* idea what they mean."

I reached to hug him goodbye.

He held me tight. "Humour is good."

I pulled back. "I did like you, you know, before all the shit hit the fan."

THE SHIT HAS CLEARED now, and the ranger drops over now and then. We share a cup of tea and catch up on each other's lives. He's still with the same woman, and I'm still genuinely glad. The last time he came over, a few weeks ago, he told me they were talking about moving in together. "I'm just not sure. I like my independence."

"Compromise." The counsel came out of my mouth in the easy way I would advise any friend. There was no martyrdom feeling to it, no hidden agenda, no secret pain that he was considering a move with another woman he had denied me. My heart was on my sleeve. I wrapped those sleeves around him in a parting hug. And then smiled up at him, a joy-filled smile.

"What are you smiling at?"

I just shook my head. If I had said, "Because I love you," it might have freaked him out.

Now, as Louisa's waters lap at the rocks by my feet, I take in another peaceful, smiling breath. It fills me with joy to feel that love again. To simply want peace and happiness for him without it having anything to do with me.

I don't think the love ever actually ended. It just got tumbled into a pot of slow-simmering anger. Now that the anger has boiled dry and forgiveness arrived, the love has been distilled to its pure form, with no alloy of excitement (at the one extreme) or bitterness (at the other). No alloy of want or need or disappointment. Forgiveness for myself has come too, for loving wholly, unconditionally, for better or worse, in a one-sided vow.

It's possible that if I'd stayed connected to my interior knowing, not unattached but truly *detached*, I would have seen more clearly how things were changing, in spite of spoken intention. Maybe I would have accepted those changing circumstances and not hung on for quite so long.

Maybe. Except I think things unfolded the way they were supposed to. Thanks to the way things unfolded, I see clearly now that my contract in this life is not with a ranger or an agent or any man. My contract is with the Divine source of my being, in all its divine manifestations: God and Jesus and Mary, the Universe, the Earth and all her creatures, and my own Self.

Here, on the darkening shore, I make a vow that doesn't depend on anyone else's participation. I vow to listen to those little messages, the ones that arise not out of any logical or emotional thought process but come into my brain from out of the blue. The thoughts that come without conscious thinking. Those are the ones we often pay little or no attention to because they're so quiet and fleeting. I make a pledge to listen to what they are telling me but not *fixate* on them. Rather, to stay in a state of detached awareness of what each message of inner knowing is offering me, moment by changing moment.

It's a gift, intuition. A gift of our Divine nature. A gift that connects us *to* our Divine nature, and to the Divinity of every creature and creation. Like all gifts it needs to be appreciated, understood, heeded – and honed.

The navy blue of clear-sky darkness begins to overtake the twilight. I stand on the shore with my little companion and watch the deepening darkness bring into bright white relief a thin sliver of new moon. It has traced its usual path over our heads, unseen, through the day and now hangs suspended in the west. Not far (maybe a centimetre, give or take a light year or two) from the tips of the moon's crescent arms gleams a large star. They both shine, the star like a diamond in an invisible setting, the moon like the curve of a white-gold band. And in the darkness I suddenly hear Grandma: *She got her diamond.*

Lovely Lake Louisa at sunset, August 2005

I'm out of the tent, on my so-called rest day, at 6:00 a.m. From a front-row seat at the water's edge, I watch the sun rise as, last night, I watched it set. Rather, I watch – *try to see* – the Earth rotate. The sun, I tell myself, is not *rising*, just as it did not *go down* last night. The sun is moving not a jot. What is moving is me, all of us, on this incredible Earth sphere that's so big it sure looks flat to me. The illusions are so strong the mind boggles. For an instant, I get it. I see the lake, the hills, Joy, me, all rotating, subtly, toward the eastern sky – which has the same delicate rosy hue the sun left in its (I mean the Earth's) wake last night. Maybe part of what Dragonfly was trying to impart to me last month was this, the ability to see beyond the illusion.

I pore over the map to plan a little day trip while I munch, from the pot lid, granola sprinkled with wild blueberries that Cathy sent along in a tiny plastic container she insisted would *not* add weight or bulk to my pack.

Joy and I set off in a light breeze. In the absence of her royal blue throne, she lies in the bottom of the boat. We head into the bay at the west end of the lake. My early morning shadow is so long it stretches out in front of me and literally overshadows my little dog, covering her and encompassing her – the way my love does.

We approach the marsh at the back of the bay. While I scout automatically for moose, my thoughts turn, also automatically, as they do at some point on all my trips, to the question of why I come out here. The answer, as always, is to reconnect. But what *for*? To learn how to *be*, certainly. To be present, to be mindful, to detoxify, to re-energize. But, ultimately, why?

The translator of my edition of the *Tao Te Ching* helpfully comments that "the more truly solitary we are, the more compassionate we can be."

This is why I need to retreat and be alone, even at home. The Earth replenishes the wellspring of generosity and compassion within me. The more time I spend in solitude – the more I experience oneness with all of creation – the more I'm able to give of myself. I don't feel guilt anymore about Murray Prentice, though I still feel some remorse. Perhaps resolve is a better word. My gauge for spending time with older friends has always been how I *feel*: Am I up to it? Do I want to?

And it's a legitimate gauge when you're trying to give from your heart, not from obligation. But that doesn't take into account what the other person might need. My resolve is to listen not to my feelings but to that still, small voice within that knows what's appropriate both for me *and* for the other.

This morning, watching my shadow cover Joy, it strikes me that my ultimate purpose in coming out here is to be reconnected and refilled with the Earth's Love so I can carry it back with me into the world. I come out here, a vessel to be, by turns, emptied (of my preoccupations) and refilled (with Love), so I can share myself with others, no matter what my personal feelings may be.

A new prayer breathes out of my heart: Make me an instrument of your Love. Shape me with your wind, bake me with your sun, purge me with your waters, mould me with your rock. Purify me with your fire (which I have been too lazy to make on this trip). Send me back into the world kiln-dried into a vessel of Love and Compassion.

I'm in the tent. It's not even eight-thirty but with the hatches battened there's nothing else to do.

The hatches are battened – canoe tied at both ends to exposed pine roots, tent fly strung taut to nearby trees, Joy's saddlebags (containing *all* our food) hung in a tree under a water-resistant garbage bag, and all loose gear stowed in the pack or here in the tent – because I'm sure a storm is on the way. As soon as I pulled the canoe up on shore after our morning excursion, the winds gusted into the campsite and haven't let up since. They're the kind that discourage travels on big lakes like Louisa, and I didn't see a single canoe all afternoon. This evening they blew in suddenly cooler and damper, and the sky turned dark and rumbly. And no one could say I can't take a hint.

Now that I'm all cozy in the tent though, the twilight sky is no longer unnaturally black, and the wind sounds like it's abating. If the rain must come, my vision is that it will arrive tomorrow while I walk the three-kilometre portage under an umbrella of a boat.

The only thing not battened is Joy. She's still so full of beans after a relatively sedentary day I'm letting her roam awhile longer.

My reading is interrupted by a distant banging. I sit up, ears perked. It's an erratic, rhythmic, dull sort of banging, like that of plastic paddle against aluminum canoe. Many paddles. Possibly many canoes. Getting louder.

The banging is punctuated by sudden barking down at the shore. In an instant I've unzipped the tent, whistled for Joy, and zipped my surprisingly obedient dog inside. I'm groping for sandals to go investigate when a male voice calls out. "Could you please come here for a minute?"

I pick my way down the pine-needle-prickly hill in bare feet in the near-darkness – it must be nearly nine o'clock – and peer out onto the lake. Hovering just out from shore are four shadowy canoe shapes. It's immediately obvious that their occupants need a place to camp or they wouldn't be out on the lake at this time of night. I start to extend an invitation but the male voice speaks over mine, words coming out like a recitation made several times already: "We're behind schedule. We had to evacuate a girl with a broken leg. We booked two sites on this lake, but we've been to every campsite, they're all full. We asked – "

"You can camp here," I interrupt. "There's lots – "

The rest of my words are drowned out by a startling chorus: "Thaaaank youuuuu."

The timbre of the voices makes me realize the occupants of the canoes are girls – ten fifteen-year-olds, it turns out, accompanied by two counsellors, one of whom is the spokesman. He jumps out of his boat and extends a hand. "I'm Josh. I can't tell you how grateful we are. Can you show me where we can pitch our tents, and where the fire pit is? Would you mind if we used it? We haven't had supper yet."

They've battled the headwind for hours, he explains. I hide a smile when he admits the girl's injury might have only been a sprain; a broken leg would be an understandable exaggeration in a tale of desperation.

I show him all the flat tent sites on the second tier and gesture up the hill. "The campfire pit is at the top but I'm afraid there's no wood."

Behind us the shoreline has become a dark moving shadow of bodies, canoes, and packs serenaded by excited girl voices, thuds of aluminum boat on rock, and one shriek and splash from a camper who has tried to straddle her boat and the slippery shoreline rock.

The two leaders who took the injured girl back are to meet up with the group tomorrow at the portage into North Grace Lake, Josh tells me. They're headed over to Smoke, doing the reverse trip of mine except by a different route from here.

"We really appreciate your taking us in. We asked at a couple of other places but they said they didn't have room."

I gesture around the site and laugh. "There's no shortage of that here." But I know I couldn't have turned them away even if it had been the tiniest of sites. I ask if there's anything else they need, and when he says no, tell him I'll be in my tent if they do.

I last all of five minutes. Impossible to lie in my tent when there's a group of kids in need of food and shelter. I leash Joy, and we make our ginger way into the woods by headlamp to collect firewood – a task we're too lazy to do for ourselves by daylight but happy to do for others in pitch dark.

Josh and the other counsellor, a slim young woman, arrive to a big blaze of a fire. My thought was they would use it to cook, but Josh lights a Coleman stove and sets on it a large pot so brimming with water it will surely never boil.

One by one, the girls straggle up, full of tales of their gruelling day. "You're my *saviour*," one girl declares.

Joy is their real saviour. They pet and fawn over her, and she gazes back at them with her thoughtful brown eyes and receives all the attention as her due.

Josh puts a thick wad of spaghetti in the not-quite-boiling water. He's good-looking, in an appropriately rugged outdoorsman way, with a cotton headband wrapped around shaggy locks and an easy confidence. The young woman, long-haired and pretty, looks like she would be more at home painting toenails at a girls' slumber party. Beyond asking if each of her charges has enough layers on, she doesn't pitch in to help. Her flashlight emits only a faint beam and seems to be the only light they have.

But one flashlight among twelve is better than no cutlery at all. "The packers forgot to put any in," says Josh without a trace of frustration. "Last night, we made forks out of sticks, then" – he laughs and taps his head in a "stupid us" gesture – "we threw them in the fire."

No cutlery and possibly only half-cooked pasta with a colourless unidentifiable sauce don't dampen a dozen appetites when dinner is finally served up at eleven o'clock. They eat with their fingers or fold the pasta into tortilla wraps.

Bellies full at last, the girls become even more animated. They tell me their names, where they live, the pets they have at home, how many times they've been to camp. It seems slow to dawn on them that it's just Joy and me here, and when it does they're amazed: Am I really out here on my own? With just a dog? Awesome! Don't I get scared? How do I manage the canoe?

I answer all their questions, and then Josh and I discuss their planned route. He's determined to go through North Grace and McGarvey, despite the daunting portages that link them and the reports I relay (courtesy of the Frying Pan Paddler) of mud and bogs. The portages may be longer, says Josh, but there aren't as many as on the route I took to get here. Unconvinced, I make a mental note to check the map in the morning.

A few of the girls disappear into the dark to wash dishes down at the lake.

"You wouldn't happen to have a guitar?" inquires Josh in the flickering firelight.

"That would be the icing on the cake – to happen upon the campfire of a woman with a dog *and* a guitar." It would also wreak havoc with my portaging ambitions.

Cries from down below interrupt our laughter. "Come quick! Help us!"

I rush down the hill with the female counsellor and the other girls. Beside the shore, my headlamp illuminates a tall blond girl, dripping with water and tears. "She was washing dishes and the rock was slippery!" "She fell in the water and hit her head on the rock!"

I hang back to let the counsellor take charge, but when she offers only a hug, I step in to check the girl's head for lumps and abrasions. Thankfully there's no sign of injury. She is, however, shivering in a soaking-wet cotton hoody and sweatpants. I ask her friends to bring dry clothes.

There ensues much discussion about where they are. "It doesn't matter whose clothes!" I call out, laughing. "Just bring some! And a towel!"

Clothes and towels emerge out of the dark, and half a dozen of us circle the girl, some pulling off sodden clothes, others drying her off. This complex operation involves much giggling, including from the victim, which further reassures me she's fine.

Finally we're all settled in our tents. Rain teems down in the night.

The day dawns overcast and cool but calm and dry. The campers have their breakfast down on the lower tier and I'm not sorry: I'm used to my quiet, solitary mornings.

Remembering Josh's intention for their route, I head down the big hill to retrieve the map from under my boat, which has four aluminum canoes resting against it, like fallen dominoes. The girls' camping area is strewn with soggy green garbage bags full of clothes that were apparently left out in the rain. Most of the girls are standing around in bikinis (possibly their only dry clothes), despite the morning coolness. They greet me with enthusiasm. "Did you hear the storm?" "Our tent leaked. We slept in wet sleeping bags!" "We had terrible sleeps!"

Their cheerfulness amazes me. "At your age, a canoe trip was my worst nightmare. You guys are troopers."

Back up at the fire pit, I eat breakfast. Josh appears, a mug of tea for me in hand. The gesture touches me.

He stays to pack up the kitchen gear. I want to ask if he doesn't find all those nubile – in some cases, frankly gorgeous – bodies a distraction. Instead I say, "I can't imagine taking ten adolescent girls on a canoe trip."

He laughs. "There's lots of dramatics and tears – you heard some of that last night. And they complain a lot, but they seem to enjoy it. This is my seventh trip out this summer." He seems to view the girls as nothing but his charges. More astonishing to me is that there don't seem to be any crushes going the other way. I would be deep in crush, myself.

I load up the gear pack and carry it down to the shore, where my canoe is still buried under their boats. Good thing I'm not in a rush.

One canoe is in the water, and I realize this is a fifth; the other two counsellors have caught up with the group. I look around the chaotic milling group and spot them – a young woman with short-cropped hair maybe the same age as Josh, and a blond male with a ready grin. When I catch her eye, the young woman comes over and grips my hand. "Thank you so much for taking them in. I don't know what they would have done without you. We came back after dropping off the injured girl at the parking lot – she's all right – some people from the camp came to pick her up. A couple took us on their campsite last night."

When she tells me they're "trippers" – leaders of canoe trips – I realize she's the one to speak to about the canoe route. I show her on the map how much easier my route is.

"Oh, well," she says flatly, "that's the way we're going then."

When word gets out I've saved the girls from at least a kilometre of gruelling portages (and goodness knows how much boggy mud they don't even know about), their thanks become even more profuse.

One by one the camp boats are launched into the water, and then mine. I load it up and Joy jumps in and takes her place on the gear pack. I call out goodbye to the campers.

"Aren't you coming with us?" one girl asks.

"I'm going the way you just came, and you're going the way I just came." The symmetry of meeting at the halfway point appeals to me, though the girls look gratifyingly disappointed.

Josh crouches beside my boat. "Thank you again, for everything. You've become a hero for these girls. They'll probably be talking about you for the rest of their lives."

My busy Lake Louisa campsite, August 2005

A prayer for the continuing safety of the camp group repeats in my head as I make my calm way down the calm lake. It's ten o'clock (such a late start!). A closeness in the air tells me it's going to rain again. I have a sudden certainty that the timing of everything is within the Universe's benevolent plan. I'm permeated with that same sense of wellbeing I felt a month ago on this same lake after we dropped FPP off at the portage I'm on my way to walk now. There is great joy to be had in assisting where assistance is required. In assisting in ways you're qualified to assist. It's not about needing to be appreciated, or thought of as a hero. (Or a saviour!) The only way you can be truly effective in this world is to know who you are. And act accordingly.

And who am I?

I pull air deliberately in through my nose and down into my lungs. Breathing the paddle, as much as pulling it, through the water. Breathing in, as much as seeing, the rich green of the trees and the deep grey-green of the water around me. And the answer comes, the answer I received from Asante several years ago but wasn't ready for then. On this lake, in this moment, it permeates my being. As surely as breath.

To quote a reliable source from the Old Testament: *I AM.*

I am Creator and Created. I am Lover and Beloved. Divine and Human. Protector and Protected. Journey-maker and Chronicler. There's no separation between one and the other. It's the words that are inadequate, and our own human perception, which is one of separation and duality. There is no duality. It's an illusion. This, surely, is what Dragonfly was trying to whisper into my ears last month.

I did have a clear moment of *seeing* that stormy summer evening two years ago in Asante's healing presence in my living room. What I saw was an image of Love as a continuous veil of Energy that surrounds and permeates the Earth. In ignorance and blindness we've done our best to break it down. Like the ozone layer, we've ripped holes in it, torn its fabric through our neglect and our selfish uncaring of the planet and each other. What the Earth needs is to be built up again, both literally, as in the small way Joy and I built up that abused, neglected campsite on Lawrence last month, and in the way we extend love and caring to each other (like Tinkertoy rods), person to person, heart to heart, all around the world. *This* is what the Earth needs, and oh so much more of it. This is the way to love her and assist her. And one day, if my profound, if fleeting, experience of oneness with Asante that night is any indication, the "disks" of our individual egos and separateness, and the "rods" of our individual bonds and connections, will vanish, like dissolving stitches that have done their work, and we will be left with – we will *be* – what has always been and evermore shall be: Unity. Love.

The first drops of rain tap down as I lug the pack out onto the rock below the yellow portage sign and shrug it onto my shoulders. Boat converts to brolly, and I walk peaceably through a thunderstorm that, if we had left the campsite at our usual early hour, would have caught us out on the next lake, Rock. It's my last lake, where I'm to meet up with a couple of friends already camped there.

The trail, though long, is relatively flat, and my aching shoulders and I tramp along behind Joy, who waddles in the saddlebags that, nearly empty now of food, I have loaded up with other gear to lighten my own pack a little more.

We come to a large log that has fallen across the trail. Someone has cut a narrow section out of it for walking through. The gap isn't wide enough for a small dog burdened with bulging saddlebags. Said dog steps into the gap and becomes stuck.

I look around for a tree to lean the canoe on. There are none with the necessary fork to hold it up. I'll never be able to get the boat back on my head if I put it down, not with the big gear pack on. There's no help for it though: Joy is not going to get unstuck without assistance. I ease the boat off my shoulders and down onto the ground beside the trail.

Hiding unkind laughter at my pooch's predicament, I push her through. Then I grasp the canoe, brace it on my thighs, and flip it onto my pack-laden shoulders.

Holy moly, I can do it after all.

We reach the mirror-still waters of Rock Lake. The portage (which would be a nearly three-hour affair under ordinary doubling-back circumstances) has taken just over an hour and a half. I'm permeated with sweat and satisfaction. There's something truly gratifying about carrying all your belongings at once. Even if the pace is slow, even if there are, of necessity, a few relays with canoe and pack separately. I'm a plodding turtle, my house on my back.

And suddenly She's here. With me. Inside me. Her breath is my breath. Her lungs are my lungs. I fill them, slowly, deliberately, and expand them to their capacity, so I can, like Turtle, go back "under" and continue my unhurried travels along the shoreline. With Joy.

Paddling with Joy, Rock Lake, August 2005 (Photo: Darrell Neufeld)

Acknowledgements

If it takes a village to raise a child, it takes an oversized canoe propelled by many paddlers to bring a memoir to publication.

My thanks first to Darrell Neufeld, who gave me the germ of the idea and read early drafts with unmerited but gratifying enthusiasm. I also appreciate his professional input on the choice of photos.

Thanks also to Marguerite McDonald (now passed on), who after hearing the topic of my new opus, introduced me to Ottawa editor Kevin Burns. Kevin, bless him, told me I had a publishable book before the first draft was even complete. Once it *was* complete – and then rejected by a number of publishers, thank heaven – Kevin worked with me for several years. He helped transform *Tumblehome* from its rambling, journally-style roots to a tightly structured, forward-moving narrative. He pulled a deeper, more honest book out of me too. I am deeply indebted to him for his guidance.

What I owe my dear friend and spiritual mentor Asante Penny is barely contained in the preceding pages – my gratitude needs at least a full-length book, though I had no idea that by the time this one was published, it would be a tribute to her memory. It makes me all the more relieved to have captured at least some of her essence, and with her own input and blessing.

A work in progress needs readers (and their judicious comments), and I'm very thankful for mine. In addition to Darrell and Asante, they include Barbara Baxter, Andrea Beatty, Nancy Beverly, Connie Downes, Max Finkelstein, Maureen Kensit, Cathy McLeod (who in reading her portrayal never demurred, at least not out loud), Eleanor Orr, Nancy Peel, Krista Sims, Cori Slaughter, Brenda Stanghini, Domenic Stanghini, and Sandy Thomson. And I do hope I haven't forgotten anyone. Joseph Kertes rebooted my confidence that the memoir would be published.

Each person featured in *Tumblehome* has my profound gratitude for their presence at the various pivotal points of my life.

This book would not be in your hands if it weren't for Luciana Ricciutelli. Inanna's editor-in-chief (and copyeditor, production editor, designer, publicist, and more) really *was* Inanna. Her death in

December 2020 left a huge hole in the publishing world and my heart. I cannot thank her enough for her unwavering belief in and support for me as an author.

The Inanna team have my utmost admiration for the way they have managed the challenges, and sorrow, arising from Luciana's unexpected passing (to say nothing of a persistent pandemic). The editors assigned to me were a joy to work with. Mary Newberry competently stepped into Lu's copyediting shoes to hone and polish *Tumblehome* with thoroughness and sensitivity. Ashley Rayner capably steered the manuscript (and its author) through every step of the production process, while Leigh Kotsilidis demonstrated great skill – and patience – in simplifying the map scans kindly provided by The Friends of Algonquin Park for the beginning of each chapter and adding my routes. Leigh also did an amazing job laying out the text and positioning the images.

Meaghan Beverly – part of the Missen clan, not the Inanna team – lent her incomparable online sleuthing skills to ferret out original sources of quotations. She even braved a trip to the wilds of central Ontario to offer her eagle eyes on the proofs and, as always, made a slew of "good catches."

My sincere thanks to Wilno, Ontario, artist Linda Sorensen for allowing *Autumn Sojourn* – my favourite of all her canoe portraits – to grace the cover. Enhanced by Val Fullard's elegant design, the cover is even more beautiful than I envisioned. Toronto Image Works created gorgeous digital scans and crops from my film negatives for the images in each chapter.

Although not directly involved in *Tumblehome*'s creation and now passed on, my parents were important influences who sent me to summer camp to learn (however reluctantly) all the canoeing and camping skills I would later embrace, and they never stood in the way of my desire to go solo. (In his understated way, my father expressed his worry about my first solo canoe trip in six quietly uttered words: "It's not advisable to travel alone." My mother survived fifteen of my solo trips by pretending I was safe at home so she wouldn't have to lie awake worrying each night.) My dear sisters, Nancy, Kathryn (also now passed on), and Lynne, have always unfailingly supported both my canoeing and my writing, and in recent years Nancy and Lynne have capably served as the Keeper of my Canoe Route.

And with me every paddle and pen stroke of the past thirteen years was Maddy (worthy successor to Joy). Her quiet, unassuming but attentive presence in the boat, on the dock, or under the desk grounded my writing in a way I had never experienced before.

Gratitude spills out of me for *all* my paddling partners who have helped this work tumble home to its place in the world.

Permissions and Sources

Epigraph is from *The Dream of the Earth*, by Thomas Berry, Sierra Club Books, 1988.

Map illustrations at the beginning of each chapter are adapted from the *Official Canoe Routes Map of Algonquin Park* with permission of The Friends of Algonquin Park. The complete park map can be purchased at algonquinpark.on.ca/virtual/canoe_routes_map.

Excerpts on pp. xvii, 58, 59, 66, 70, 92, 195, and 234 and reproduction of the Bear card illustration on p. 91 are from *Medicine Cards: The Discovery of Power Through the Ways of Animals*, by Jamie Sams and David Carson. Illustrations by Angela Werneke. Text copyright © 1988, 1999 by Jamie Sams and David Carson. Illustrations copyright © 1988, 1999. Reprinted by permission of St. Martin's Press. All Rights Reserved.

Brief excerpts on p. 9 are from *No Man Is an Island*, by Thomas Merton, Harcourt Brace Jovanovich, New York, 1955.

Biblical quotations on pp. 14, 32, 73, 118, 178, and 220 are from *The Holy Bible: Revised Standard Version*, published by Wm. Collins Sons & Co. Ltd for the Canadian Bible Society, Toronto, 1952.

Brief excerpts on pp. 24, 71, 150, and 242 are from *Book of Common Prayer*, issued by the Authority of the General Synod of the Anglican Church of Canada, Oxford University Press, Toronto, 1959.

Brief excerpts on p. 30 are from *The Color Purple*, by Alice Walker, Houghton Mifflin Harcourt, New York, 1992.

Lyrics on p. 52 were adapted (liberally) from the traditional gospel hymn "Angels Watching Over Me."

Quotation from Pawnee tribe chief Letakots-Lesa on p. 59 (as reproduced in *Animal-Speak: The Spiritual & Magical Powers of Creatures Great and Small*, by Ted Andrews, © 1999) is from *The Indians' Book: An Offering by the American Indians of Indian Lore, Musical and Narrative, to Form a Record of the Songs and Legends of Their Race*, recorded and edited by Natalie Curtis, Harper and Brothers, New York and London, 1907. Note: Although I found the quote in Andrews, I've used the wording and spellings from the original source, including of "Letakots" and "Tirawa" ("Letakos" and "Tuawa" in Andrews).

Brief excerpts on pp. 65, 178, and 190 are from *Buddhism Plain and Simple*, by Steve Hagen, Broadway Books, New York, 1997. Used with permission.

Lyrics on p. 74 are from "What a Friend We Have in Jesus," by Joseph M. Scriven, 1855.

Excerpts on pp. 95, 129, 162, 163, 195, 218, 226, 229, and 235 from *Animal-Speak: The Spiritual & Magical Powers of Creatures Great and Small*, by Ted Andrews, © 1999, are used with the permission of Llewellyn Worldwide Ltd.

Brief excerpts on pp. 106, 194, and 295 are from p. viii and #s 8 and 13 in *Tao Te Ching by Lao Tzu, a New English Version, with Foreword and Notes by Stephen Mitchell*. Translation copyright © 1988 by Stephen Mitchell. Used by permission of HarperCollins Publishers.

Brief excerpts on pp. 118 and 227 are from *For the Time Being*, by Annie Dillard, Penguin Books Canada, Ltd., Toronto, 1999.

Brief excerpt on p. 118 (as quoted in *For the Time Being*, 1999) is from *Teilhard de Chardin: The Man and His Theories*, by Abbé Paul Grenet, translated by R.A. Rudorff, Ryerson Press, *circa* 1961, and is copied under licence from Access Copyright. Further reproduction, distribution or transmission is prohibited except as otherwise permitted by law.

Paraphrase on p. 220 and quotation on p. 222 are from *The Upanishads*, translated by Eknath Easwaran, Nilgiri Press, Tomales, CA, 1987.

Brief excerpt on p. 228 is from *Twelve Talks for Meditators*, by John Main, OSB, World Community for Christian Meditation.

Poetry verse on p. 228 (as quoted by John Main in *Twelve Talks for Meditators*) is by the ninth-century Sufi poet and mystic Mansur Al-Hallaj.

Additional Reading

Here are a select few online sources on Algonquin Park's history and land claim status:

Algonquin Provincial Park: Official Website of The Friends of Algonquin Park. "Natural and Cultural History." algonquinpark.on.ca.

"The Algonquins and Algonquin." A talk by Kirby Whiteduck (then-Chief of the Algonquins of Pikwàkanagàn First Nation) at TEDxAlgonquinPark, 2012. www.youtube.com.

Algonquins of Ontario. "Our Proud History," "Treaty Negotiations Update." tanakiwin.com.

Government of Ontario. "The Algonquin Land Claim." ontario.ca/page/algonquin-land-claim.

Over the years, I've come across only half a dozen solo paddling memoirs by women, most kayakers (which in no way takes away from their considerable accomplishments). Recently, however, I discovered two canoeing memoirs. *Bijaboji* is Betty Lowman Carey's memoir of rowing a dugout canoe up the Inside Passage in 1937, when she was twenty-three years old. In the same decade, at nearly the same age, Esther Keyser embarked on a dozen solo trips in Algonquin Park. Alas, these solo trips merit a scant few sentences in her memoir, *Paddling My Own Canoe*, which focuses on the trips she guided and those she later enjoyed with her husband and children. The memoir is a fascinating read for anyone interested in what it was like to canoe (solo or not) in Algonquin in the 1930s and ensuing decades. If you've read any solo paddling memoirs by women besides those listed below, I'd love to hear from you through my website: brendamissen.com

Bijaboji: North to Alaska by Oar, by Betty Lowman Carey, Harbour Publishing, 2004.

Deep Water Passage: A Spiritual Journey at Midlife, by Ann Linnea, Little, Brown and Company, 1997.

Tumblehome

Kabloona in the Yellow Kayak: One Woman's Journey through the Northwest Passage, by Victoria Jason, Turnstone Press, 1995.

Paddling My Own Canoe: The Story of Algonquin Park's First Female Guide, by Esther S. Keyser with John S. Keyser, The Friends of Algonquin Park, 2003.

Paddling North: A Solo Adventure Along the Inside Passage, by Audrey Sutherland, Patagonia, 2012.

Paddling with Spirits: A Solo Kayak Journey, by Irene Skyriver, Green Writers Press, 2017.

Photo: Nancy Beverly

Brenda Missen is a Canadian writer and editor, active outdoors person, and author of the literary thriller *Tell Anna She's Safe* (Inanna Publications, 2011). Her personal essays and short stories have appeared in newspapers, outdoor magazines, and anthologies. She lives in Ontario's Madawaska Highlands near her canoeing home, Algonquin Provincial Park, where she has been paddling for thirty-five years, two dozen of them solo. Visit her at brendamissen.com.